Making Laws
and
Making News

## About Brookings

The Brookings Institution is a private nonprofit organization devoted to research, education, and publication on important issues of domestic and foreign policy. Its principal purpose is to bring knowledge to bear on the current and emerging policy problems facing the American people.

A board of trustees is responsible for general supervision of the Institution and safeguarding of its independence. The president is the chief administrative officer and bears final responsibility for the decision to publish a manuscript as a Brookings book. In reaching this judgment, the president is advised by the director of the appropriate Brookings research program and a panel of expert readers who report in confidence on the quality of the work. Publication of a work signifies that it is deemed a competent treatment worthy of public consideration but does not imply endorsement of conclusions or recommendations. The Institution itself does not take positions on policy issues.

# Making Laws and Making News

## Media Strategies in the
## U. S. House of Representatives

TIMOTHY E. COOK

The Brookings Institution
Washington, D.C.

Library of Congress Cataloging-in-Publication Data
Cook, Timothy E., 1954–
  Making laws and making news : media strategies in the U.S. House
of Representatives / Timothy E. Cook.
    p.   cm.
  Includes bibliographical references.
  ISBN 0-8157-1558-7
  1. United States. Congress. House—Public relations.   2. United
States. Congress. House—Reporters and reporting.   3. Press and
politics—United States.   I. Title.
JK1447.C66   1989
328.73'0731—dc20                                        89-22271
                                                           CIP

9 8 7 6 5 4 3 2 1

The paper used in this publication meets the minimum requirements of the American
National Standard for Information Sciences—Permanence of Paper for Printed Library
Materials, ANSI Z39.48–1984

Set in Linotron Electra with Frutiger display
Composition by Graphic Composition, Inc.
  Athens, Georgia
Printed by R. R. Donnelley and Sons, Co.
  Harrisonburg, Virginia
Book design by Ken Sabol

*To my father and to Jack Yeager*

# Preface

THIS IS A BOOK about how members of the U.S. House of Representatives make (or try to make) news and how that activity affects their jobs and the way they go about them. Not long ago the news media seemed to be bit players on Capitol Hill, especially on the House side. Today they have become so ubiquitous that observers have expressed concern about the appeal of their spotlight—that it may affect the distribution of power and alter the way the chamber conducts its business.

Because speculation has been rife while inquiry and analysis have been surprisingly limited, this book examines the who, what, when, where, how, and why of House news coverage and of legislators' strategies for seeking it. Part of this study focuses on what the news looks like: who makes news, what is newsworthy, when does the legislative process get reported? The other part emphasizes the view from members' press offices; why do members seek publicity, how do they attempt to shape the news, are they successful?

In general the study elucidates a relationship of mutual benefit and limitation. Reporters need the news and the insights House members can provide; members need coverage to further legislative strategies. In effect, making news has become integral to making laws or, as one press secretary commented, "Press work is an extension of policy." But the relationship also limits the kinds of issues on which legislators focus and shapes the processes by which policies are drafted, debated, and enacted.

This study began with a conversation some years ago with Burdett Loomis. He, Stephen Hess, and Lyn Ragsdale have been invaluable sources of information and encouragement. Lee Sigelman and Steven Smith provided key suggestions at the earliest stages.

The research was mostly accomplished during a year in Washington provided through the aid of an American Political Science Association Congressional Fellowship and an Adsit Fellowship from Williams College. A grant from the Everett McKinley Dirksen Center for Congressional Leadership Research and Division II grants from Williams funded the collection and coding of data. The Brookings Institution provided a guest scholar position, and additional support was provided by the Cissy Patterson Trust Fund.

The Congressional Fellowship allowed me to gain experience as assistant press secretary for Representative Don Pease, whom I thank along with his staff, especially Steve Bailey, Sharon Gang, Bill Goold, and Peg O'Laughlin, for permitting me to take part in all aspects of the office's operations.

This study would have been impossible without the interest and cooperation of the House press secretaries who were interviewed or filled out questionnaires. I particularly thank Lynn Drake, then president of the Association of House Democratic Press Assistants, for collaborating on the survey and arranging for the distribution and collection of the questionnaires. I also thank the research assistants who worked on the data, including Betsy Andersen, Tim Murray, Carolyn O'Brien, Kurt Rumsfeld, and the seemingly indefatigable Francine Davis. Although I originally intended to avoid citing sources by name, the journalists with whom I spoke so favored on-the-record interviews that I have compromised, thanking them here even though they are not cited in the text: Ann Compton, John Dancy, Helen Dewar, Jonathan Fuerbringer, Phil Jones, Richard Meloy, Robert Mitchell, Irvin Molotsky, Susan Rasky, Cokie Roberts, Alan Schlein, Hedrick Smith, and Richard Wilde.

Robert L. Faherty, Thomas E. Mann, and Lyn Ragsdale gave incisive readings of the manuscript; whatever errors remain are due entirely to my stubbornness. James R. Schneider edited the manuscript, Linda Keefer verified its factual content, Susan Woollen prepared it for publication, and Margaret Lynch compiled the index.

I save my biggest thanks for last. My father has long been an unflagging source of support. And Jack Yeager, since the decade began, has provided the intellectual encouragement and irreplaceable companionship that were crucial to starting and completing this project.

TIMOTHY E. COOK

*Williamstown, Massachusetts*
*August 1989*

# Contents

Making Laws
and
Making News

# 1

# Making the Connections

MARCH 19, 1979, was like many other work days in the U.S. House of Representatives. Speaker Thomas P. (Tip) O'Neill, Jr., called the House to order at noon. After the chaplain's prayer and a smattering of one-minute speeches, a relatively minor bill, the Strategic and Critical Materials Stockpiling Act, was sent to the floor and introduced by Charles Bennett of Florida. The act passed with a minimum of debate and a voice vote. Several communications were reported to the Speaker, followed by debates on the international shipment of lottery materials and on establishing a new Select Committee on Committees. After three one-minute speeches and three short special orders, the House adjourned at 2:21 P.M. All in all, a quiet day.

In one important respect, however, the legislative day was unlike any previous one: for the first time, floor proceedings were televised and broadcast across the country through C-SPAN, the Cable Satellite Public Affairs Network, to 350 affiliated cable systems. A transformation begun in the early 1970s had finally been completed; in less than a decade the House had changed from an institution that virtually prevented television from covering any part of the legislative process to one that almost welcomed its presence.

The House of the late 1960s was what one scholar termed "a large, impersonal . . . machine for processing bills."[1] Its unspoken norms and folkways favored behind-the-scenes specialization and legislative labor, and the rules discouraging reporters' access to crucial behind-closed-doors decisions supported those norms. But by the end of the 1970s, at any of its legislative stages the House could bar scrutiny from reporters only with

1. Nelson W. Polsby, "Policy Analysis and Congress," *Public Policy*, vol. 18 (Fall 1969), p. 64.

difficulty, and both print and electronic journalism were paying closer attention to it. The legislative process since then has occurred not so much in the light of sunshine laws but under the media's spotlight. Switching on the television cameras on March 19, however, may have been a landmark not in what it did but what it symbolized, the advent of a media-conscious institution.

That consciousness was very much a product of the mid-1970s, which remain a watershed in recent American history for all political institutions. After the Watergate scandal, the forced resignation of President Nixon in the summer of 1974, and the Democratic landslide in that fall's elections, reform-minded politicians came to Washington to clean it up. In the process they may have created arrangements that made the policy process, never known for its coherence or completeness, even more dispersed and fluid.[2] As more groups took advantage of the new permeability of the political process and entered the fray, coalition building moved away from assured management toward artful construction, issue by issue. The process of governance became more cumbersome, volatile, and unpredictable. All these changes should have encouraged, or at least facilitated, a more media-conscious membership, and indeed, changes within the House itself increased the importance of the media.[3]

—The personal staffs of members expanded tremendously, and most legislators now employ full-time press secretaries, a post that was a rarity in 1970.

—The so-called Subcommittee Bill of Rights in 1973 mandated that committees set up subcommittees according to established jurisdictions, and the House Democratic Caucus in 1975 prevented members from chairing more than one subcommittee, effectively providing more bases for hearings and other events designed to win publicity.

—Junior members were no longer expected to serve an apprenticeship in which they might be seen but not heard. By the end of the decade virtually any member was expected to have a chance to sit on a desirable committee and to address his or her concerns.

—Sunshine reforms opened up committee and subcommittee hearings and deliberations to outside scrutiny. Closing committee meetings to keep out the press became the exception to the rule.

2. Thomas Byrne Edsall, *The New Politics of Inequality* (Norton, 1984), provides a succinct account of this sea change; see also the essays in John E. Chubb and Paul E. Peterson, eds., *The New Direction in American Politics* (Brookings, 1985).

3. For a good overview of these reforms, see Leroy N. Rieselbach, *Congressional Reform* (Washington: CQ Press, 1986).

—The number of reporters credentialed to cover Congress grew dramatically, providing legislators more potential points of access to print and electronic media.

—Television began to dominate many congressional campaigns. By the end of the 1970s, over half of House campaign budgets went for media and advertising. A new generation was elected that was, of necessity, comfortable with the new technology.

—Members of the House and reporters for national news outlets had begun to discover each other, especially because the extraordinarily positive coverage of the House Judiciary Committee hearings in 1974 on the impeachment of President Nixon showed representatives what could be done with media attention and showed reporters that the House could be newsworthy.

As a result of all this, one would expect changes in the House and how it deals with publicity—as Michael Robinson phrased his "First Law of Videopolitics": "Television alters the behavior of institutions in direct proportion to the amount of coverage provided or allowed; the greater the coverage, the more conspicuous the changes."[4] But has the ubiquity of the media really changed the most essential functions of the House? Has the new importance of making news transformed the process or the outcomes of making laws?

Many would reply that it has. Senators charged that the House's new visibility was enhancing the legislative power of the "other chamber" to their detriment. At least, that was the argument successfully advanced by senators who wished to follow the House's lead in televising floor proceedings. In 1985 Robert Byrd, then Senate minority leader, complained, "The Senate is fast becoming the invisible half of Congress. We cannot hold our own with the White House and the House of Representatives when it comes to news coverage of the important issues of the day."[5] Others alleged that the chamber had become a group of unruly individuals more concerned with self-publicizing than with legislative labor.

This interpretation was not only widely held but plausible, and it continues to have proponents. Nevertheless, I consider it mistaken. But neither do I find the counterargument—that the media's impact on legislating in the House has been vastly exaggerated because the news reflects rather

4. Michael J. Robinson, "A Twentieth-Century Medium in a Nineteenth-Century Legislature: The Effects of Television on the American Congress," in Norman J. Ornstein, ed., *Congress in Change: Evolution and Reform* (Praeger, 1975), p. 241.

5. Steve Blakely, "Prospects Seen Brightening for Senate TV," *Congressional Quarterly Weekly Report*, September 21, 1985, p. 1877.

than creates internal influence—fully satisfying. Newsmaking is neither incompatible with nor superfluous to the legislative process. Instead, perhaps making news has become a valuable component of making laws.

## Observation: Publicity Drives Out Legislating

The news media are accustomed to being blamed for (or credited with) many political developments. Television, especially, has been accused of contributing to the drop in the public's confidence in political institutions, the decline of political partisanship, the rise of image-oriented and candidate-centered campaigns, the drift toward a government more dominated by the president, and the general fragmentation of the American political system.[6] Critics have also contended that the media aided the dispersion of power within the House and made congressional leadership and collective decisionmaking even more awkward and difficult than it already was. Making laws and making news, they have argued, are not compatible tasks.

Claims of such a dichotomy are nothing new. They hearken back to the oft-cited distinction between industrious work horses and self-promoting show horses, the two hypothesized types of members of Congress. There was renewed concern, however, that show horses were becoming dominant. In an influential 1984 article in *Atlantic Monthly*, Gregg Easterbrook declared, "The yearning for a Washington badge of recognition and the additional perquisites that would make Capitol Hill life what [the new legislators] imagined it to be can set in almost immediately. . . . Fame may be an elusive goal, but publicity is not."[7] Publicity was said to undermine the coherence of the legislative process. Hedrick Smith argued, "Television helped break up the policy monopolies of established committees and throw open the power game. Overshadowing the grinding 'inside' spadework of bill drafting in committee, television offered shortcuts and a showcase . . . a marketplace for all 435 members of the House and one hundred senators to become policy entrepreneurs. That is one major reason why Congress seems so unruly today."[8] Or in the words of a political

6. See, for example, Austin Ranney, *Channels of Power: The Impact of Television on American Politics* (Basic Books, 1983).

7. Gregg Easterbrook, "What's Wrong with Congress?" *Atlantic Monthly*, December 1984, p. 59.

8. Hedrick Smith, *The Power Game: How Washington Works* (Random House, 1988), p. 39.

scientist who wrote on the nationalization of American politics, "The corrosive influence of television does not end when the elections are over. The Senate is now notorious for being less a legislative body than a publicity mill for many members, and the same trends are spreading, inexorably, to the House."[9]

The most sophisticated version of this observation has contended that the fragmentation of power within Congress is directly connected with the growth of the Washington media, the ascendancy of television as a major news source, and its gradual incursion into the workings of the institution.[10] The media have supposedly helped create an "open Congress," in which members need not play by inside rules to advance the issues that concern them or to advance their careers. Mavericks are no longer tacitly disciplined and team players are no longer quietly rewarded; mavericks receive welcome attention, while the others are lost in the shadows. Members who seek publicity also have available to them increased staff and technological support, and legislative coalition building has taken a back seat to public relations. The media have, it is said, contributed another centrifugal force, dispersing power and hindering leadership and collective decisionmaking.

There is certainly evidence favoring this point of view. Many members have achieved publicity without leadership or committee positions. Members have devoted more resources to publicizing themselves and have become more sophisticated in pursuit of the now-willing Washington reporters. Yet, while credible, this conventional wisdom from the early 1980s has not gone unchallenged.

## Response: Publicity Is Irrelevant to Legislating

In *The Ultimate Insiders* Stephen Hess began by attacking the Achilles' heel of the argument, showing that most members of Congress are invisible to the national press. Those covered most heavily are "the *Ultimate*

9. William M. Lunch, *The Nationalization of American Politics* (University of California Press, 1987), p. 22.

10. The two best statements in 1983 were Ranney, *Channels of Power*, pp. 142–47; and Norman J. Ornstein, "The Open Congress Meets the President," in Anthony King, ed., *Both Ends of the Avenue: The Presidency, the Executive Branch, and Congress in the 1980s* (Washington: American Enterprise Institute, 1983), pp. 185–211. See also Michael J. Robinson, "Three Faces of Congressional Media," in Thomas E. Mann and Norman J. Ornstein, eds., *The New Congress* (Washington: American Enterprise Institute, 1981).

*Insiders,* the ones who call the committee meetings or direct the floor action, or would do so if their party were in the majority."[11] Zealously seeking publicity pays little dividend if the publicity-seeker is not in a category that reporters find newsworthy—presidential candidate, party leader, committee chair, sponsor of a key proposal, and so forth. The show horse–work horse dichotomy makes no sense as long as those receiving most of the attention are also those contributing most to legislative labors. The power of the media has been exaggerated, Hess concluded; instead of determining power on Capitol Hill, the press reflects it. Making news is then superfluous, even irrelevant, to making laws.

This perspective has also had proponents beyond the ranks of political scientists. A 1987 article on power in Congress argued, "Reporters will want to talk to [a committee chair or party leader] regardless of how articulate he is or how well he looks before a camera. What he has to say is important because of who he is, not how he says it."[12] An op-ed piece in the *New York Times* during the 1988 campaign also considered that reporters reflect power, but interpreted the situation as being less benign: "[Journalists] have frequently ended up pulling their punches for fear of appearing biased. . . . Too often, the press has functioned as merely a stenographer to power."[13]

But the response was not without its own problems. Though a handful of senators are accorded the lion's share of national media attention, such dominance cannot suggest that other members have not altered their behavior. Hess granted this point, though he argued that it would be irrational for senators to pursue national publicity, given the media's lack of interest. Yet legislators could be more inclined to seek publicity diligently without succeeding every time. In fact, if backbench legislators are actively pursuing publicity, leaders might be maintaining their place in the spotlight only by aggressively wooing reporters, in which case the primacy of leaders in the news is even more to be expected.

More important, Hess argued that the Capitol Hill press corps is "almost totally reactive."[14] Yet in a collegial institution in which the chain of command is attenuated, knowing who or what to react to is far from obvious.

11. Stephen Hess, *The Ultimate Insiders: U.S. Senators in the National Media* (Brookings, 1986), p. 7.

12. Nadine Cohodas, "Press Coverage: It's What You Do That Counts," *Congressional Quarterly Weekly Report,* January 3, 1987, p. 29.

13. Mark Hertsgaard, "Electoral Journalism: Not Yellow, But Yellow-Bellied," *New York Times,* September 21, 1988, p. A23.

14. Hess, *Ultimate Insiders,* p. 110.

Because current journalistic practice requires stories featuring individual authorities, covering Congress has been called "the search for the ultimate spokesman."[15] Elsewhere in Washington, such a search is more straightforward. Throughout the executive branch, press officers are designated to speak for the agency, the department, or the president. Reporters' tasks are simplified: they need only turn to the appropriate spokesperson when a given topic becomes newsworthy.[16] With Congress, the solution is less simple. After all, neither chamber has anyone who can speak on behalf of all or even most of its members.

The national media do disproportionately favor leaders, committee chairs, and senior members as being in a position to know. But holding such a position is no guarantee of news coverage. After all, even if much of legislators' visibility can be explained by institutional power, there remains at least as much that is unexplained. Either additional reasons have yet to be discovered, or much of the coverage of members of Congress remains unpatterned and unpredictable.[17] Reporters, even when conscientiously attempting to depict congressional power accurately, inevitably exercise choice in deciding whom to cover in Congress. Merely reflecting congressional power without contributing to it may be the goal of reporters, but it is a well-nigh impossible task.

## A Third Possibility:
## Making News Leads to Making Laws

To comprehend the relationship of making news to making laws, one must understand that reporters and politicians are constantly negotiating and renegotiating the process by which news is made. Instead of a Congress that plays by reporters' rules or reporters that defer to Congress's decisions about what is important, the interactions between legislators and reporters are shifting and flexible. Making news can become a constructive component of the legislative process. By anticipating what a reporter will

15. Susan H. Miller, "News Coverage of Congress: The Search for the Ultimate Spokesman," *Journalism Quarterly*, vol. 54 (Autumn 1977), pp. 459–65.

16. See Michael Baruch Grossman and Martha Joynt Kumar, *Portraying the President: The White House and the News Media* (Johns Hopkins University Press, 1981); and Stephen Hess, *The Government/Press Connection: Press Officers and Their Offices* (Brookings, 1984).

17. See, for example, Timothy E. Cook, "House Members as Newsmakers: The Effects of Televising Congress," *Legislative Studies Quarterly*, vol. 11 (May 1986), pp. 203–26; and Peverill Squire, "Who Gets National News Coverage in the U.S. Senate?" *American Politics Quarterly*, vol. 16 (April 1988), pp. 139–56.

find newsworthy, House members can use the media to address an issue, move a proposal along, and enhance their career ambitions. Indeed, given the contemporary confusion in American politics, a media strategy may be a necessary part of many legislative strategies. Such a process is most accessible to those who wield the most power; but backbenchers, too, can become an authoritative source on a particular issue and thereby court publicity and accomplish legislative goals.

To understand how this process works, one must recognize that newsworthiness is inherently an elusive quality.[18] If reporters are asked for the difference between news and non-news, they are likely to provide anecdotes or examples, not a hard-and-fast dividing line. Yet the demand for fresh news is incessant. To standardize an inherently unpredictable process, reporters routinely turn to people in positions of authority within an institution, thus not only ensuring a steady flow of copy but also helping guard against charges of bias or incompleteness by covering politicians whom peers, superiors, and audiences generally agree upon as newsworthy.

Such connections work to officials' advantage. Their involvement makes something newsworthy enough to get in the paper or on the air and creates events that can serve as occasions to write stories. Because reporters must worry about alienating their main sources, they come to report the world in ways fundamentally similar to the perspectives of those they are covering: they become "unwitting adjuncts to City Hall."[19]

Yet the reporters do not merely reflect a reality constructed by others. News inevitably constructs and reconstructs a public reality from privately experienced events. And journalists' selections and emphases do diverge from those that their authoritative sources would make. American journalism is based on the tenet that news must be both important and interesting. Reporters' judgments on what is important and interesting must anticipate not merely the political sources but the judgment of the news organization for which they work. Collusion is unlikely because reporters and politicians do not share identical definitions of what news is and how it should

18. See Edward Jay Epstein, *News from Nowhere: Television and the News* (Random House, 1973); Leon V. Sigal, *Reporters and Officials: The Organization and Politics of Newsmaking* (Lexington, Mass.: D.C. Heath, 1973); Gaye Tuchman, *Making News: A Study in the Construction of Reality* (Free Press, 1978); Herbert J. Gans, *Deciding What's News: A Study of CBS Evening News, NBC Nightly News, Newsweek, and Time* (Pantheon Books, 1979); and Mark Fishman, *Manufacturing the News* (University of Texas Press, 1980).

19. Walter Gieber and Walter Johnson, "The City Hall 'Beat': A Study of Reporter and Source Roles," *Journalism Quarterly*, vol. 38 (Summer 1961), p. 289.

be covered. The media thus act as powerful gatekeepers to the political arena.

Instead of determining or reflecting power on Capitol Hill, reporters and sources *negotiate* power, constantly bargaining with each other over the rules of their interactions and the shape of the final product.[20] Each tries to manage the other—the sources to place the most favorable light on their activity and the journalists to extract the information they seek with minimal difficulty. Sometimes the relationship may be adversarial. More typically, however, politicians need publicity and journalists need copy, and the two sides can and do perform valuable services for each other.

Despite some disagreements with journalists, House members may, through effective media strategies, be able to manage the news from Capitol Hill. Journalists may go along to ensure the routine production of news. Frequent interaction leads to an unspoken set of ground rules. The forces encouraging collaboration instead of conflict tend to be greatest in dealing with those legislators who are important and hence regular, prized newsmakers. The adversarial model does not work most strongly at the highest levels of the political hierarchy, then; it may actually be most applicable toward those who *least* frequently make the news.

At the same time, there is enough flexibility in covering a collegial body that observations cannot stop there. As more members are perceived to be important newsmakers, they may be able to use media strategies to raise issues to prominence and advance their careers. Moreover, the ones reporters consider more interesting may be able to win coverage if leaders cannot provide news that conforms to the media's demands.

So concerns that backbenchers can grab headlines are not unfounded. This book will show that the media in general and the national media in particular have become more important for members of the House as the dispersion of power has made legislating more difficult. Legislators can use the media in various ways in addition to pursuing the publicity necessary for getting reelected. But this is not to say that the House is overrun by a new breed of legislators interested in publicity for its own sake. Making laws and making news are not contradictory. Nor are they synonymous. Instead, they are different but complementary parts of the same process.

The outside strategy allowed by media publicity offers the potential to

20. The best theoretical account of this relation is Jay G. Blumler and Michael Gurevitch, "Politicians and the Press: An Essay on Role Relationships," in Dan D. Nimmo and Keith R. Sanders, eds., *Handbook of Political Communication* (Beverly Hills: Sage Publications, 1981), pp. 467–93.

manage an increasingly unmanageable work load in a balkanized and balky political system. In the lingo of Washington the retail method of persuasion has been supplemented if not supplanted by the wholesale style. After all, the number of interest groups has dramatically increased, the legislative agenda is crowded, and the dispersion of power to more individuals makes one-on-one lobbying increasingly difficult. As presidents and interest groups find persuasion through media more useful to get things done in Washington, the same should be expected on Capitol Hill. After all, the media provide an important means to help set the Washington agenda, winnow down the alternative courses of action, keep pressure on politicians, and thus get something done in Congress.

## The Capitol Hill Perspective

This book focuses on media strategies in the House of Representatives from the perspective of the House offices themselves. The reasons for doing so are simple: while much is known about news organizations, Capitol Hill reporters, and the shape of congressional coverage, much less has been written from a perspective of House media operations.[21] Dorothy Cronheim's 1957 complaint still rings true: "Despite some pertinent comments in recent books and articles by and about congressmen, the first major work on their communication practices is yet to appear. Even in the cursory review of available sources that follows, this dearth of comprehensive studies is all too apparent."[22] In the decades since Cronheim wrote, the media in general and television in particular have become more important forces in American politics. It would seem logical that media strategies would be useful and perhaps necessary to members of the House. But

21. Virtually the only studies of House media operations have been dissertations. Dorothy Hartt Cronheim's sadly neglected "Congressmen and Their Communication Practices," Ph.D. dissertation, Ohio State University, 1957, deserves greater attention, especially as it sheds light on the prereform Senate and House. Susan Heilmann Miller, "Congress and the News Media: Coverage, Collaboration and Agenda-Setting," Ph.D. dissertation, Stanford University, 1976, provides a rich source of information from a nonrandom sample of members of Congress, congressional staffers, and congressional correspondents in 1973–75. This neglect is not confined to Congress. While much is known from within the media about how the news is selected, covered, produced, and distributed, empirical research has yet "to examine the journalistic enterprise from outside the news organizations, beginning with newsmakers but systematically covering all the other nonjournalistic participants as well." Herbert J. Gans, "News Media, News Policy, and Democracy: Research for the Future," *Journal of Communication*, vol. 33 (Summer 1983), p. 176.

22. Cronheim, "Congressmen and Their Communication Practices," p. 3.

little has been written about their press operations, what they seek and what they avoid, and their effects on policymaking and representation.

What research there is on House members' relationships with the media focuses almost entirely on how members use media in their districts to communicate with their constituents, project a positive image, discourage a strong challenger, and get reelected.[23] This work is informative, but House members have long had active and generally positive relations with their district media to the point that, if matters have changed with local newspapers or television, they are unlikely alone to have provoked major changes in the House.[24] One must pay attention to all the media, both local and national, from the Washington perspective where members and their press assistants labor.

What follows is an attempt to understand how and why members of the House seek publicity through the mass media, and what the effects of that publicity seeking have been upon the legislators and the institution. Many forms of communication that members use, particularly to reach their constituencies, will not be considered except in passing. Ways of gaining publicity are inherently different when individually communicated (such as solicited mail) or unmediated (such as trips home). Unlike person-to-person communication, where one can respond to and test the environment, the audience for mass-mediated communication is "completely at the mercy of the instrument of [their] perceptions."[25] The new role of mass-mediated communications from the House raises a number of questions about the possibility of manipulation, but one must also ask: who is manipulating whom? And finally, if publicity has indeed become a major

23. Richard F. Fenno, Jr., *Home Style: House Members in Their Districts* (Little, Brown, 1978); Peter Clarke and Susan H. Evans, *Covering Campaigns: Journalism in Congressional Elections* (Stanford University Press, 1983); Edie N. Goldenberg and Michael W. Traugott, *Campaigning for Congress* (Washington: CQ Press, 1984); and Jan Pons Vermeer, ed., *Campaigns in the News: Mass Media and Congressional Elections* (Westport, Conn.: Greenwood Press, 1987).

24. Some authors claim that the ability of House members to control the information about them in the district allows them to get reelected on their own and permits more independence from persuasion by party leaders, thus contributing to the dispersion of power. It is, however, doubtful if members are any more able to control their coverage than before. Moreover, in an odd way, earlier critiques of the seniority system noted that members' control over district media increases their ability to secure reelection. "This reenforces the development of the seniority system which, in turn, enhances the power, especially in the House, of committee chairmen." Robert O. Blanchard, *Congress and the News Media* (Hastings House, 1974), p. 93. Blanchard's point casts doubt on the media as key contributors to the dispersion of power if they had been earlier an aid to the concentration of power.

25. Kurt Lang and Gladys Engel Lang, "The Unique Perspective of Television and Its Effect: A Pilot Study," *American Sociological Review*, vol. 18 (February 1953), p. 11. As my usage suggests, all media provide greater bounds on perception than does immediate observation.

raison d'être for members of Congress, they may adjust their activities to win the attention they seek. Media effects on politics thereby occur by providing incentives to act in ways that were bypassed when reporters were not watching.[26]

To be sure, the media's influence can be channeled and controlled by politicians, enabling them to use publicity in seeking to accomplish legislative goals. But although politicians largely decide what is important, journalists define what is interesting. So while the House has regulated the media, directing reporters toward more favorable coverage in both formal and informal ways, journalists are far from powerless. Their selectivity is strongest in the choice of subject matter. Their differing emphases on issues and policies may have a far-reaching effect on Congress, since members must find issues that interest journalists in order to receive the publicity they seek.

In their pursuit of the press, House members have become ever more sophisticated with the assistance of the increasingly professional press secretaries. Recruiting ex-journalists to serve as press secretaries, though, is a double-edged sword. Members can better manage the news about themselves and their issues, but this encourages cooperation between two inherently distinct organizations. House offices thus anticipate news values when deciding what to do and how. And these strategies have become more closely linked to legislative strategies, since they help set the political agenda, frame the way in which issues are understood, maintain pressure on colleagues to do something about problems, and enhance the reputations of members as important players in Washington.

The media matter to members of the House of Representatives. Media strategies are important activities, not only to get reelected but increasingly to accomplish policy-related goals in Washington. And it matters that the media have been welcomed into the legislative process. How members of the House deliberate and decide, which issues they treat and which they ignore, and what the results are for democracy have been changed by the entry of the institution into the public spotlight.

26. The best statement of this media effect remains Todd Gitlin, *The Whole World Is Watching: Mass Media in the Making and Unmaking of the New Left* (Berkeley: University of California Press, 1980).

# 2

# Regulation and Accommodation

FROM THE MOMENT the House of Representatives was created, its members have been preoccupied with the press. Aware that their words reach not only their colleagues or the immediate spectators but a potentially much larger audience, they have consistently used perquisites of office to gain publicity and have restricted press access to their deliberations to achieve favorable coverage. The restrictions per se were not beyond their powers. The Constitution includes no presumption that legislative activities should be open to the press. The Constitutional Convention, which itself met in near-total secrecy, obliged each house of Congress to keep a journal and to publish it from time to time, but went no further, overruling the contention of delegate James Wilson that "it should not be in the option of the Legislature to conceal their proceedings."[1]

The ability of Congress to establish the rules by which journalists gain access to proceedings does not, however, mean that politicians have inevitably dominated interactions with the press. Reporters have resources with which they can respond. Most notably, if they are unwilling to consider something newsworthy enough to merit prominent coverage, members must accommodate themselves to journalistic definitions of news if they wish to be covered.

The rules by which Congress and the media operate in one another's presence today result from an evolving negotiation between two changing institutions over two centuries. The results of these negotiations are not politically neutral. Instead, deciding the rules of access has political ef-

1. Daniel N. Hoffman, *Governmental Secrecy and the Founding Fathers: A Study in Constitutional Controls* (Westport, Conn.: Greenwood Press, 1981), p. 28.

fects, and the practices and conventions of newsmaking contain political presumptions.

## Before the Reporter

The relationship of the press and the House of Representatives was a subject of debate as early as the First Congress. To be sure, what passed for the press in 1789 was very different from newspapers fifty years later.[2] In rural areas, where most Americans lived, newspapers were scarce. Those that did exist were one-person operations assembled by a printer; advertisements covered the outside of a folded sheet, and assorted bits of commercial and political transactions appeared on the inside. There were no paid reporters; printers depended on cribbing accounts from domestic or foreign newspapers or on letters from friends and cronies—literally correspondents.

Newspapers were not the full-fledged commercial enterprises they would later become. Typically partisan, they were sometimes financed by public officials who considered them extensions of themselves and who could protect them from the harassment and violence to which they were vulnerable. Circulation was small, mostly by annual subscription of like-minded, typically well-to-do people. Any notion of impartiality was not seriously considered until the 1830s, when the penny press aspired to capture a larger circulation and fit into the egalitarianism of the time.

When the First Congress convened, reporters followed debates from the floor of the House, most transcribing them for the numerous and usually short-lived privately printed precursors of the *Congressional Record*. Congress tolerated this recording with some suspicion because "political debate in each house was staged as an oral performance, not an exchange of texts."[3] House proceedings received more coverage than those in the Senate because they were more open and extended and because the popularly elected chamber was considered more newsworthy than the one that state legislatures selected. When Samuel Mitchill of New York moved from the

2. Michael Schudson, *Discovering the News: A Social History of American Newspapers* (Basic Books, 1978), and Thomas C. Leonard, *The Power of the Press: The Birth of American Political Reporting* (Oxford University Press, 1986), provide excellent histories of the transformations in American political journalism through the Progressive Era. Both shed revealing light on the contemporary media.

3. Leonard, *Power of the Press*, p. 72.

House to the Senate in 1804, he wrote to his wife, "Henceforward you will read little of me in the Gazettes."[4]

House members used direct methods to ensure that reporters would provide favorable accounts of their speeches. Shortly after the First Congress met, the reporters' apparent selectivity occasioned the wrath of Aedanus Burke of South Carolina, who introduced a resolution charging that they blatantly misrepresented debates and proposing that their access to the floor be denied: "being done within the House, at the very foot of the Speaker's chair, [access] gives a sanction and authenticity to those publications, that reflects upon the House a ridicule and absurdity highly injurious to its privileges and dignity."[5] Despite the dramatic difference between the press of the 1780s and that of the 1980s, the debate on Burke's resolution revealed tensions and exasperations still familiar today. Elbridge Gerry of Massachusetts complained that

[T]hese publications had a tendency to exalt some members and to depress others. Whence it arose that this was the case he did not pretend to say. He would exercise charity in this regard, and suppose it arose from inability or inadvertency in the reporters. But there was one thing very remarkable, that all the arguments on one side were fully stated, and generally took up some columns in the newspapers; while the arguments of the other side were partially stated, and condensed to a few solitary lines.[6]

Burke withdrew his resolution when he saw that the printer who prompted his complaint was not present, although he promised to reintroduce it should the man return. The absence was easily explained; the stenographers had already fled the floor for the public galleries where they remained for most of the rest of the session.[7]

In the House's first century its relationship with the press was commonly marked by tolerance if not indifference. But a reporter's privilege of attending the sessions—especially access to the floor rather than the acoustically inferior public gallery—could be and was withdrawn if his coverage

4. Quoted in Noble E. Cunningham, Jr., *The Process of Government under Jefferson* (Princeton University Press, 1978), pp. 259–60.

5. Quoted in Robert O. Blanchard, ed., *Congress and the News Media* (Hastings House, 1974), p. 9, where the full debate may be found.

6. Quoted in Blanchard, *Congress and the News Media*, p. 10.

7. Elizabeth Gregory McPherson, "Reporting the Debates of Congress," *Quarterly Journal of Speech*, vol. 28 (February 1942), pp. 141–48.

seemed derogatory, biased, or perhaps just insufficiently favorable. Even when sanctions were not carried through, the threat was always there. Little wonder that reporters routinely withheld publication of legislators' remarks until they could rewrite them in a way that flattered or until the members themselves could improve on them.[8]

So few reporters covered Congress, however, that when the government moved to the isolated new capital in the District of Columbia, congressional news threatened to disappear from the newspapers altogether. In 1800 when the House discussed the value of allowing reporters to sit at a desk inside the chamber's rail, one member scoffed at a colleague's concern that they would require more room: "at Philadelphia the number was small; seldom more than two, and often not more than one persevered during the session, though a greater number appeared on its earliest days."[9] The Jeffersonian era saw the first appearance of letters to newspapers by "our correspondent at Washington," but the letters were irregular and the correspondents' tenures short. Legislators themselves often acted as correspondents. Indeed, the first identifiable Washington correspondent was Reprsentative James Elliot of Vermont, who briefly entered into partnership with the *Freeman's Journal* of Philadelphia in 1808.[10]

Given the vagaries of mass communication, members of Congress began to communicate directly with their constituents. Their innovation was to send circular letters directly to various people in their district.[11] Like today's newsletters, the circular was usually one to four pages, printed on stationery-size paper folded and franked, and was often reprinted in local newspapers with the members' tacit approval. Gradually, legislators took greater advantage of the opportunities the letters offered to claim credit before the voters.[12] Senator Samuel L. Mitchill wrote to his wife in 1804, "You might say that packages of these sorts were sent off by the bushel." He went on to say that the reason was that "in many [districts] the intercourse by post-roads is not very convenient nor frequent, and that News-Papers

8. Leonard, *Power of the Press*, pp. 72–75; and Elizabeth Gregory McPherson, "The Southern States and the Reporting of Senate Debates, 1789–1802," *Journal of Southern History*, vol. 12 (May 1946), p. 242.

9. Quoted in Blanchard, *Congress and the News Media*, p. 17.

10. F. B. Marbut, *News from the Capital: The Story of Washington Reporting* (Southern Illinois University Press, 1971), p. 26.

11. An invaluable source is Noble E. Cunningham's edited collection of all extant circular letters from the period, *Circular Letters of Congressmen to Their Constituents, 1789–1829*, 3 vols. (University of North Carolina Press, 1978).

12. Elaine K. Swift, "The Electoral Connection Meets the Past: Lessons from Congressional History, 1789–1899," *Political Science Quarterly*, vol. 102 (Winter 1987), tables 2 and 3.

do not circulate extensively among the people. The Representatives therefore enjoy the double satisfaction of furnishing their constituents with all the good news, and disposing their minds favourably for the next election."[13]

News about Congress reached a limited audience—not surprisingly, considering that politics and suffrage in the first decades of the nineteenth century were largely reserved to the elite. All that would change during the Jacksonian Era, but one thing would not: members of the House were able to control most of the publicity about themselves, either by actual or presumed sanctions over the reporters or by their own independent efforts.

## Beginnings of the Washington Press Corps

With the democratic fervor and partisan debates of the age of Jackson, the consequent development of the penny press in the 1830s, and the inauguration of telegraphic news in the following decade, Washington news was easier to get and easier to reproduce, and egalitarianism made politics a matter of importance to the commoner. As before, news focused on Congress, but now it was written by hired journalists. In 1841, when patronage battles threatened to delay the news, the *New York Herald* showed the value of reports from Capitol Hill when it announced a new policy of mounting "at vast expense, an efficient corps of the ablest reporters that this country can afford, who will furnish us, at the close of every day's proceedings, a report of the debates. This will be transmitted to us by Express mail, and will invariably appear in the second edition of the Herald on the second day after."[14] With the development of the telegraph in the 1840s, congressional news could be quickly reported beyond Washington.

News was still generally marked by the stenographic style of reporting. Most dailies displayed congressional news prominently but in a standard format that began with an account of the previous day's session, followed

13. Quoted in Cunningham, *Circular Letters*, vol. 1, pp. xx, xxv. Although few members were career representatives, neither were they ready to return to private life. Most were ambitious and parlayed their House service into another political office upon their departure. See Allan G. Bogue and others, "Members of the House of Representatives and the Processes of Modernization, 1789–1960," *Journal of American History*, vol. 63 (September 1976), pp. 275–302.

14. Quoted in Frederick B. Marbut, "The Letter-Writers in the Senate," in Blanchard, ed., *Congress and the News Media*, pp. 34–35.

by a summary, in smaller type, of all Senate and House floor activity.[15] Ideas of newsworthiness and methods of newsgathering favored debates. Official floor proceedings were considered more important than what happened in the wings, and reporters had not yet invented the interview (let alone the press conference). Moreover, the understanding of governance was not, as journalists today assume, that the president proposes and Congress disposes. Instead, Congress was seen to decide and the executive to implement. With no White House press corps, presidential news was almost exclusively reported by official pronouncements (it was considered improper for the executive to speak out on the issues of the day). For most of the nineteenth century, the congressional press corps was synonymous with the Washington press corps; Washington news was news about Congress.[16]

But notions of what was fit to print were evolving. Penny papers seeking large circulations had become notorious for covering matters that precursors had thought insignificant if not tawdry—crime, local news, human interest stories. Aspects of Congress that were once ignored were now newsworthy, too. Reporters concentrated on the floor, but almost anything that happened there might be fair game. In 1846, for example, Horace Greeley's New York Tribune inaugurated a gossipy column called "Rumors and Humors in Washington." In its second installment, the pseudonymous author described the habits of Ohio Democrat William Sawyer, who customarily devoured a sausage on the House floor each day at two o'clock: "What little grease is left on his hands he wipes on his almost bald head which saves any outlay for Pomatum. His mouth sometimes serves as a finger glass, his coat sleeves and pantaloons being called into requisition as a napkin. He uses a jackknife for a toothpick, and then he goes on the floor again to abuse the Whigs as the British Party."[17] Such new directions in what was considered newsworthy did not go unnoticed. Indeed, the enraged Sawyer had the paragraphs read into the record by the Clerk of the House. An Ohio colleague then introduced a resolution, which subsequently passed, to expel all Tribune reporters from the House, forcing

15. Vincent Howard, "The Two Congresses: A Study of the Changing Roles and Relationships of the National Legislature and Washington Reporters as Revealed Particularly in the Press Accounts of Legislative Activity, 1860–1913," Ph.D. dissertation, University of Chicago, 1976, p. 42.

16. Samuel Kernell and Gary C. Jacobson, "Congress and the Presidency as News in the Nineteenth Century," Journal of Politics, vol. 49 (November 1987), pp. 1016–35; and Jeffrey Tulis, The Rhetorical Presidency (Princeton University Press, 1987).

17. Quoted in Marbut, News from the Capital, pp. 71–72.

them to cover proceedings surreptitiously from the public gallery until the next session. But the journalists may have had the last laugh; "Sausage" Sawyer was never able to shake his nickname.

The new attention to floor activities also required members to give renewed heed to their speeches. In 1803 Senator John Quincy Adams had gladly agreed to provide the substance of the remarks he made on the floor to an editor; but when he returned to Capitol Hill in 1831 after his presidency, he thought twice about making speeches, noting in his diary that he considered it a "double waste of time—first to speak, and then to report."[18] As his comment implies, in the early republic, members of Congress spoke first and revised later; oral debates continued to take priority over printed publicity. But by the 1850s the members were taking a more public stance. Instead of stressing the give-and-take of legislative deliberation, they read prepared speeches that were then sent to constituents and the press.[19] The altered understanding of newsworthiness had begun to change how Congress went about its job.

## Toward Modern
## Washington Journalism

In the late nineteenth century, journalism became big business. Huge news organizations such as Joseph Pulitzer's empire deemphasized political preoccupations and concentrated on profit, dramatically extending their circulation and power. Linotype replaced movable type, the cylinder press sped up printing, and pulp paper replaced rag paper, lowering prices of newsprint and allowing large editions that needed more news content to accompany the burgeoning number of advertisements. Front page news became more important than the editorial page, and the public's image of the journalist changed from crusading editor to star reporter.

Not surprisingly, Washington news prospered.[20] And because journalists still considered the executive less newsworthy than the legislature, Con-

18. Charles Francis Adams, ed., *Memoirs of John Quincy Adams, Comprising Portions of His Diary from 1795 to 1848* (Philadelphia: J. B. Lippincott, 1874–76), vol. 8, p. 437.

19. Leonard, *Power of the Press*, pp. 83–86.

20. Samuel Kernell, "The Early Nationalization of Political News in America," *Studies in American Political Development: An Annual*, vol. 1 (Yale University Press, 1986), pp. 255–78. For the journalists' perceptions of these changes, see Francis A. Richardson, "Recollections of a Washington Newspaper Correspondent," *Records of the Columbia Historical Society*, vol. 6 (1903), pp. 24–25.

gress continued to hold center stage, and the congressional press corps grew considerably. No longer could an Associated Press reporter recall, as one did in his 1869 memoirs: "Twenty-two years ago, I was, for six weeks, the only newspaper correspondent in Washington."[21]

Ideas of newsworthiness continued to evolve. The reports that presented verbatim texts of floor debate were supplemented and then displaced by stories of what was happening in committees and what was likely to occur in the coming week.[22] Before the end of the century a new convention had arisen, emphasizing color, spectacle, and the drama of what one contemporary journalist termed "intelligent previsions of the course that great questions will take and with the earliest information concerning the plays in the great game of politics."[23]

Other developments conspired to elevate the role of the correspondent. As newspapers became bigger and more profitable, more could afford full-time Washington correspondents. As editors and publishers become more interested in profit than in partisanship, reporters began to view themselves as professionals and sought to settle into Washington careers and become celebrated in their own right. The turnover of reporters was cut in half between the 1860s and the 1890s.[24]

Presidents still thought granting interviews improper—the one exception to the rule had been Andrew Johnson, and the reaction to his public attempts at self-justification hardly made him an example to be followed—but members of Congress were willing subjects. Many dropped by Newspaper Row, that section of 14th Street between Pennsylvania Avenue and F Street where most bureaus were located, and others went so far as to interview themselves, the first appearance of what are now known as press releases.[25] Finally, the dramatic increase in the use of wire services in the 1880s freed Washington correspondents from the ennui of recording de-

21. L. A. Gobright, *Recollection of Men and Things at Washington during the Third of a Century*, 2d ed. (Philadelphia: Claxton, Remsen & Haffelfinger, 1869), p. 400.

22. Howard, "The Two Congresses," pp. 79–84, 96–100.

23. Henry L. Nelson, "The Washington Correspondent," *Harper's Weekly*, April 9, 1892, p. 354.

24. Samuel Kernell, *Going Public: New Strategies of Presidential Leadership* (Washington: CQ Press, 1986), table 3-1. Schudson, *Discovering the News*, chap. 3, provides an overview of this change. Useful contemporary accounts include Ben Perley Poore, "Washington News," *Harper's New Monthly Magazine*, January 1874, pp. 225–36; and O. O. Stealey, *Twenty Years in the Press Gallery* (New York: published by author at Publishers Printing Company, 1906), chap. 1.

25. Richardson credits Representative Benjamin Butler with this invention and adds, "a great many members of Congress . . . speedily 'got on' to General Butler's idea. Many of them don't wait for the asking, but send in lengthy self-prepared opinions." Richardson, "Recollections," p. 33.

bates.[26] Francis A. Richardson, longtime Washington correspondent of the Baltimore *Sun*, noted, "Washington has become so fruitful in gossip and scandal, and intrigue, political and otherwise, that in contrast the ordinary debates can but prove exceeding dry reading. The gentlemen who declaim at the different ends of the Capitol are much aggrieved over this."[27]

As the sanction of denying access to debates lost its punch, the House got out of the business of overseeing the press gallery and making individual decisions on admitting reporters.[28] In the late 1870s the Standing Committee of Correspondents was established to recommend press gallery members to the Speaker and was formally recognized in 1881. The Speaker today retains final say on admitting journalists, but the Standing Committee is empowered to judge whether the applicants are bona fide reporters for daily newspapers, to report violations of the provisions to the Speaker, and to control press gallery employees.

Why did the House give up the direct power to deny access to its proceedings? The history is murky, but it appears that the decision was neither magnanimous nor a bow to the powerful press. For one thing, partisan politics reinforced the power of the Standing Committee when, at the end of the Forty-seventh Congress in 1883, the outgoing Republican Speaker became involved in a feud with the press, provoking a public debate that the Democrats, in the majority in the Forty-eighth Congress, took full advantage of.[29] Moreover, the move was savvy. Oversight of gallery membership had become difficult; sheer numbers hindered House members from deciding case-by-case which applicants were reporters and which were lobbyists who had posed as journalists to gain access to members. And Hill correspondents had professionalized. Making a career out of Washington reporting, establishing press clubs, and generally seeking to shore up their dubious prestige, they could be counted on to judge who were, in the

26. Donald L. Shaw, "News Bias and the Telegraph: A Study of Historical Change," *Journalism Quarterly*, vol. 44 (Spring 1967), pp. 3–12, 31. Virtually every memoir of congressional correspondents from this period records displeasure with the debates. See Gobright, *Recollection of Men and Things*, p. 410; Poore, "Washington News," p. 234; and Stealey, *Twenty Years*, p. 9.

27. Richardson, "Recollections," p. 34. See also Stealey, *Twenty Years*, pp. 2–3.

28. Frederick B. Marbut, "The Standing Committee of Correspondents," in Blanchard, ed., *Congress and the News Media*, pp. 40–49; Stephen F. Mannenbach, "How Broad Discretion? Congressional Delegation of Authority to the Standing Committees of Correspondents," *Administrative Law Review*, vol. 31 (Summer 1979), pp. 367–84; and Stephen Hess, "Policing the Washington Press Corps: The Role of the Standing Committee of Correspondents," Brookings Discussion Papers in Governmental Studies, no. 3 (Brookings, July 1986).

29. Marbut, *News from the Capital*, pp. 147–51; and Howard, "The Two Congresses," pp. 100–04.

words of the Standing Committee, "bona fide correspondents of reputable standing in their business."

Perhaps most important, legislators had more say in newsmaking. Reporters had adopted enterprising but informal tactics, such as interviews with both named and unnamed sources who often sought out friendly journalists. One reporter wrote in 1874, "A Washington chief correspondent is expected to be omnipresent. . . . He must daily visit the White House, haunt the departments, call at the hotels, drop in upon communicative congressmen at their rooms, dine with diplomates, chat with promenaders on the Avenue, listen to the conversation of those who may be his fellow-passengers in the street cars."[30] Another, looking back to the 1870s, noted, "In the phrase then common among Washington correspondents, every one of them had his own senator, representative or cabinet member who came to his office and told him the news."[31] The legislators' implicit ability to withhold that communication potentially allowed them to have a large say in determining what the news from Capitol Hill was all about.

The diminution of newsmaking on the House floor revealed and reinforced new political priorities. The earlier preference for debates, recorded with little interpretation or comment, had been founded on an egalitarianism that opened up the process of the people's branch to all for scrutiny. By the end of the century the correspondent had emerged as one who would make sense of the goings-on of Capitol Hill for a mass audience that was perceived to demand color and excitement more than details of policy disputes. And since journalists had already moved to the wings, they could easily move off Capitol Hill altogether should a political rationale develop to do so—which is exactly what the rise of progressivism at the turn of the century provided.

Progressives sought to impose order on the industrial revolution through professionalism, expertise, nonpartisanship, and unbiased administration in government. This emphasis on clean government by means of direct primaries and secret ballots undercut the power of party nominations and party-line voting. House members could still pursue long careers, but party government had been made impractical. Consequently, the House of Representatives, once the center of national politics and attention, changed from a highly centralized, partisan body where Speakers

30. Poore, "Washington News," p. 234.
31. Richardson, "Recollections," p. 27.

held sway over shifting memberships to an institution that deferred to committees in which members gained expertise and, with time, power through the workings of the seniority system.

Careerism and parochialism meant shunning policy disputes in favor of a quieter inside strategy that would win benefits that could be trumpeted back home. This new emphasis created a vacuum that enterprising presidents such as Theodore Roosevelt and Woodrow Wilson filled with a more energetic approach to the legislative process. Roosevelt and Wilson conceived of the president as protector of the national interest. They wanted not only a more aggressive office but a more visible one.

Roosevelt's accession to the presidency in 1901 was in retrospect the final break from the laconic style of nineteenth century presidents. In some ways, he simply took advantage of opportunities that were already there. Progressive emphasis on administration instead of policy disputes had encouraged the press to transfer its attention from legislature to executive. Events such as President Garfield's assassination and President Cleveland's marriage had fit journalists' new emphasis on spectacle and had taken up considerable news space. In the last years of Cleveland's presidency reporters had already begun to gather at the White House gates to corner those leaving the grounds, and President McKinley had held White House receptions for journalists at the beginning of his term. What Roosevelt did was to welcome reporters into the presidential mansion, inaugurating the White House press corps.[32]

Since Wilson, even such passive presidents as Warren Harding and Calvin Coolidge have dealt with the press in an ever more public manner. The gap between executive and Congress widened as agencies began appointing public relations officers who would crank out official press releases. Congress, with its renascent parochialism and weakened party leadership, was further displaced from the center of journalistic attention. To the extent that reporters noted the activities of the institution, they converged on its leaders; virtually the only attention paid to lesser lights was from the growing number of special correspondents representing regional newspapers.[33] At the beginning of the 1920s, Congress, the presidency,

32. George Juergens, *News from the White House: The Presidential-Press Relationship in the Progressive Era* (University of Chicago Press, 1981), chap. 2.

33. A reporter noted in 1906, "Twenty years ago it was absolutely necessary for the newspaper men to be acquainted with nearly all the members of Congress—otherwise they would not get the news. . . . In the last ten years all that a newspaper man has had to do in order to keep informed on the progress of legislation was to keep in touch with the three members of the House constitut-

and the media had assumed the roles they retain today. The focus on the presidency in the news is not then the inevitable result of television's routines and needs. Instead, it is a product of the Progressive Era's concentration on politics as administration instead of debate. Neither radio nor television needed to invent new journalistic forms; the old ones suited very well.

## Entry of the Electronic Media

The first commercial radio broadcast in the United States occurred in 1920; television followed in 1941. Yet while each expanded its reach dramatically and presidents took advantage of the opportunities they provided, Congress was slow to enter the electronic age. Radio journalists were denied the privileges of the press gallery until 1939. Newspaper reporters on the Standing Committee of Correspondents had refused to admit them, and many had to eavesdrop from the public gallery with pen and paper. Only when radio reporters successfully lobbied Congress for a separate gallery were they accommodated.[34] Still, members of the radio and television gallery could not take microphones and cameras into official proceedings of the House until 1970, when broadcasts of committee hearings were permitted for the first time.

Part of the House's antipathy to broadcasting stemmed from longtime Speaker Sam Rayburn's personal distaste for the media in general and television in particular. After the much-publicized hearings on organized crime that Senator Estes Kefauver chaired in the early 1950s, Rayburn ruled that cameras and microphones would be prohibited from committee hearings, on or off the Hill. This rule received few serious challenges either during his tenure or when it was continued after his death in 1961 by his successor, John McCormack.[35] Little wonder that the Rayburn years were generally known as the high point of the inside strategy, when getting

---

ing the majority of the Committee on Rules." Stealey, *Twenty Years*, pp. 2–3. In the 1930s Leo C. Rosten wrote, "It is not necessary to court more than a few congressmen; the majority are poor news-sources because they are neither men of public interest nor occupants of important committee posts." *The Washington Correspondents* (Harcourt, Brace, 1937), p. 79.

34. Marbut, *News from the Capital*, pp. 210–14.

35. A vivid account of Rayburn's relations with the media is David Halberstam, *The Powers That Be* (Knopf, 1979), pp. 245–50. See also Ronald Garay, *Congressional Television: A Legislative History* (Westport, Conn.: Greenwood Press, 1984), chap. 3.

along was equated with going along and private bargaining was preferred to public pressure.

The press was not, of course, absent from the House. Even members such as Rayburn, who called national correspondents "vultures" and "buzzards," had cordial relations with home-town reporters.[36] Indeed to most members of the House at this time "the media" meant the local press, and their primary use was to help the member get reelected.[37] At that, members seemed to prefer personal contact with voters through letters or trips home. Even in the Rayburn House, however, they were beginning to take advantage of various media. After the studios opened on Capitol Hill, one study showed that just under half the members regularly used television programs to reach constituents. These are hardly overwhelming numbers, but not many more reported using radio programs or sending newsletters or other mass mailings.[38]

The attention to local media did not carry over to the nationals. Senate liberals elected in the Democratic sweep of 1958 and frustrated at the intransigence of the seniority system and the dominant conservative coalition had taken advantage of the chamber's loose rules to develop a style that played down the apprenticeship and specialization valued by the insiders and instead emphasized appeals to the public.[39] Their House counterparts, in a more constraining structure, were unable to do the same. Observers in the 1960s went so far as to note complementarity between the publicity-seeking Senate, which raised issues and set the agenda, and the efficient, diligent House, which followed through with hard legislative work.

Why and how then did the House allow television to cover its floor proceedings in March 1979, well ahead of the Senate?

The House moved toward television in the 1970s in part because of "a remarkable period of congressional introspection—surely the most intense

36. See, for example, Anthony Champagne, *Congressman Sam Rayburn* (Rutgers University Press, 1984), pp. 87–88.

37. See Charles L. Clapp, *The Congressman: His Work as He Sees It* (Brookings, 1963), pp. 389–91.

38. The survey determined that 68 percent of the sample regularly used government bulletins or pamphlets; 36 percent items from the *Congressional Record*; 52 percent letters, exclusive of personal mail; 48 percent meetings; 58 percent newsletters; 4 percent newspaper ads; 76 percent press releases; 34 percent public opinion polls; 41 percent radio broadcasts; and 41 percent television programs. Dorothy Hartt Cronheim, "Congressmen and Their Communication Practices," Ph.D. dissertation, Ohio State University, 1957, p. 112.

39. Michael Foley, *The New Senate: Liberal Influence on a Conservative Institution, 1959–1972* (Yale University Press, 1980).

such period, perhaps the only one, in the history of that institution."[40] For one thing, Congress felt squeezed by the imperial presidency. The president had virtual carte blanche to make a prime-time speech, but opposing members of Congress had no right to respond, despite pleas and even litigation for equal time. Some legislators fretted about the decline of public trust in Congress. House members also became restive about the Senate's domination of the airwaves. So the 1970 Legislative Reorganization Act allowed television to cover House committee hearings, and such access became commonplace after the members decided in 1973 to open every committee session unless a majority of the panel publicly voted to close it.[41] Yet while the media were thought to be crucial to reinvigorating the role of Congress, most members remained skeptical that introducing television coverage beyond hearings could do all this singlehandedly.

Hearings held by the Joint Committee on Congressional Operations in early 1974 are revealing. Few members favored gavel-to-gavel coverage of floor proceedings, which Representative Jack Brooks said would be "similar to continuous coverage of hospital operating rooms for the purpose of improving the image and understanding of the medical profession."[42] Relying on the networks was no more attractive. Members and witnesses suggested that commercial television's preference for conflict and sensationalism would prevent the institution's message from getting out. Senator Edmund Muskie spoke for many: "a clash of opinion is innately more newsworthy than the resolution of those differences. That judgment of what makes news is one we must live with while we do our best to alter it." He went on to add, "When you come to judge what is significant, you cannot leave that to the press, because their view of what is significant is different from the public view and different from ours. We have to find ways of presenting our view of what is significant."[43]

Members began to be convinced of television's benefits, however, when deliberations of the House Judiciary Committee considering impeachment articles against President Nixon were televised in 1974.[44] For the first time

40. James L. Sundquist, *The Decline and Resurgence of Congress* (Brookings, 1981), p. 5.

41. Some 40 percent of committee meetings were closed before 1973, falling off to 16 percent in 1973, and 7 percent in 1975. Norman J. Ornstein, Thomas E. Mann, and Michael J. Malbin, *Vital Statistics on Congress, 1987–1988* (Washington: CQ Press, 1987), p. 134.

42. *Congress and Mass Communications*, Hearings before the Joint Committee on Congressional Operations, 93 Cong. 2 sess. (Government Printing Office, 1974), p. 4.

43. *Congress and Mass Communications*, pp. 16, 19. See also the comments of John B. Anderson, Robert Giaimo, and James O'Hara on pp. 56, 74, 351.

44. Gladys Engel Lang and Kurt Lang, *The Battle for Public Opinion: The President, the Press, and the Polls during Watergate* (Columbia University Press, 1983), chap. 7.

actual committee deliberations and decisions rather than only the hearings were broadcast, and, far from sensationalizing or stressing conflict, television proved easily manageable and positive in its tone, effectively increasing public approval of the committee and Congress.

Committee Chair Peter Rodino fostered an image of bipartisan judiciousness through his deliberately low-key presentation of himself and his chief counsel and by passing along all information through his administrative assistant each morning at 9:00 while the committee met behind closed doors to call witnesses and review evidence.[45] Once deliberations began, the media zeroed in on the swing votes—the Southern Democrats and Republicans who seemingly defied their pro-Nixon constituencies—as most newsworthy. Restricted by Rodino's efforts to maintain consensus and cued by swing vote members' references to their "awesome responsibility," the networks portrayed the congressional process reverently: "off-screen activity received only minimal attention. The big story was in the committee room. This contrasts with network coverage of esoteric debates, particularly of political conventions, during which backstage events are introduced to provide the 'real' excitement whenever proceedings are judged to be boring. Television journalists refrained from creating news and seeking exclusives."[46] House members saw how favorably they could be presented and what could be done with the help of national television.

Once Nixon resigned, of course, the House's moment in the spotlight was over—ABC's Sam Donaldson was reputed to have said, "Now we can go back to the Senate, where news *really* happens." But the House was loath to abandon the attention. The 1974 elections, which created a large reform-minded class of freshman Democrats, increased support for televised proceedings. Most members now supported radio and television coverage of the floor, usually approving a system operated by a pool of the three networks instead of a House-controlled system.[47] Yet some, particularly among the ranks of the Democratic leadership, expressed doubt, and after a long study by an ad hoc subcommittee, the full House Rules Committee killed its recommendation for a network pool. Supporters of televised floor proceedings were thus taken by surprise when, in March 1977, newly elected Speaker Thomas P. (Tip) O'Neill, Jr., announced his inten-

45. Instead of finding such restrictions onerous, reporters said they helped manage the task of a daily story. See Sam Donaldson, *Hold On, Mr. President!* (Random House, 1987), pp. 51–54.

46. Lang and Lang, *Battle for Public Opinion*, p. 175.

47. These results are taken from a mid-1976 poll of 346 House members conducted by Representative Claude Pepper, a booster for television on Capitol Hill since his Senate days in the 1940s. Garay, *Congressional Television*, p. 93.

tion to conduct a ninety-day test of closed-circuit broadcasting from the House floor to a few offices in the Capitol and the Rayburn Building.[48] His action enhanced the likelihood that television would enter the chamber, but he had made sure that it would enter on terms favorable to the party leadership. Closed-circuit transmission emphasized the usefulness of coverage to members rather than to journalists; and, sure enough, the test period evoked favorable comments from members that they were able to keep track of floor debate while attending to other duties. In such a way, the broadcasts became a video equivalent of the *Congressional Record* and, like the *Record*, could be controlled by the House rather than by the news media.[49]

The Rules Committee report recommending a system controlled by the House revealed much of the distrust of network television that had surfaced in earlier discussions. After pointing out First Amendment problems that might accompany a House-controlled system, the report noted

> allegations that network pool control may produce coverage that is unbalanced, biased, deliberately or accidentally unfair to individual Members, and damaging to the dignity of the House . . . that broadcast journalism is prone to judge what is newsworthy on the basis of conflict, drama and humor rather than on the substantive significance of a matter; that television journalists tend to emphasize visual impact over substance because that is the nature of their medium. . . .[50]

Television and radio would be permitted to eavesdrop on the system, but any reach beyond Capitol Hill was to be a mere by-product of maintaining a "complete, uninterrupted and accurate record of the official proceedings and business of the House." In floor debate as well, while many members reminded colleagues of the favorable response to the impeachment debates, others voiced distrust of the networks' ability to decide what news was in a way that would preserve the "dignity" and "integrity" of the

---

48. A full account of decisions in the Ninety-fifth Congress is in Garay, *Congressional Television*, pp. 97–112.

49. Take, for example, the comments of Representative James Cleveland: "for those who may be persuaded that network control of our television cameras is in order or proper, I ask them then if . . . it would be in order and proper to have our *Congressional Record* of proceedings be under the control of *Newsweek*, *U.S. News and World Report*, and perhaps *Time* Magazine." *Congressional Record*, June 14, 1978, p. 17661.

50. *Broadcasting the Proceedings of the House*, H. Rept. 95-881, 95 Cong. 2 sess. (GPO, 1978), pp. 9–10.

House.[51] One worried about being cut off by commercials for toothpaste or dog food, and another noted the absence of network reporters in the gallery. Majority Leader Jim Wright concurred that "Most of what goes on here may not be jazzy enough for [the networks'] purposes," and implied that networks could censor members as much as the other way around. And in language hearkening back to that of Elbridge Gerry, Ron Dellums argued that the media were too selective and biased. "I have stood with many other progressives on the floor of this Congress. . . . Pick up the newspaper. You never see one word about that, and we wonder why. . . . I do not want to see corporate America dominate these proceedings. . . . I dream of the day when many of my colleagues and I can communicate openly with the American people, with no one distorting, no one deciding that Ron Dellums is too radical to quote."[52]

Distortion, of course, is in the eye of the beholder. When the broadcasts from the floor went public in 1979, the cameras were operated under the control of the Speaker. Three cameras were set up, one aimed at the Speaker's rostrum and one each at the majority and minority tables. An employee of the Architect of the Capitol was responsible for switching from one to the next, and a computer automatically focused the image. Such a system effectively removed all discretion, except that of the Speaker.[53]

To appreciate the impact of the decision to place the system under the Speaker's control, imagine how different the coverage would be if the networks had the freedom they have at national party conventions—freedom to break away from official proceedings to interview members on the floor, to have anchor booths within the chamber itself, and so forth. Without

---

51. The key debate occurred on June 14, 1978, on two amendments to the legislative appropriations bill, one introduced by John Anderson that would prevent the purchase of new equipment for televising except by prior approval of the House, and one by Adam Benjamin mandating that funds used on televising floor proceedings could be spent only if cameras were run by House employees. The first amendment failed and the second passed, effectively locking in the Speaker's control.

52. Comments are from *Congressional Record*, June 14, 1978, pp. 17664, 17665.

53. This discretion meant little to anyone except the networks until 1984, when a group of junior Republicans dubbed the Conservative Opportunity Society (COS), led by Newt Gingrich and Robert Walker, began taking advantage of the special order session after the close of formal business to address issues they thought the Democratic majority ignored. Furious at what he saw as an attack on the patriotism of absent colleagues, O'Neill ordered the cameras to pan the almost completely empty chamber during one of Walker's speeches. The resultant flap was punctuated by O'Neill's angry outburst on the floor against Gingrich that earned him a reprimand from the presiding officer; it brought much more attention to the COS and its cause than the special orders ever would have alone.

such access attention is concentrated on official proceedings. What the networks draw from those proceedings may often be excerpts from one-minute speeches or may be atypical but dramatically tinged moments in an otherwise somnolent debate, and journalists may assemble this raw material to fit their own interpretations. The result does not open up the entire process to scrutiny, only the debates, as if to bring back the emphasis that marked nineteenth century reportage from the Hill.

Under the constraints of a House-controlled system, televising the floor has scarcely altered the workings of the institution. Few internal activities have been changed. There has been a slight increase in the number and length of one-minute speeches and special orders after the close of legislative business, reflected in a fatter *Congressional Record*. But fears that televised proceedings would lead to massive numbers of amendments from grandstanding members have not been realized. Amending activity has declined from its high in the Ninety-fifth Congress, which was a response to the earlier introduction of electronic voting.[54] Little wonder Speaker O'Neill himself said the principal effect of television on the House was that his male colleagues showed up "in blue shirts, red ties and stickem on their hair."[55]

## Who Leads the Dance?

The relationship between the journalists and their sources has been characterized by metaphors ranging from open warfare to collaboration, collusion, and sleeping together. But perhaps the most accurate comparison is that of a struggle to lead a dance. In the words of Herbert Gans, "although it takes two to tango . . . more often than not, sources do the leading."[56] Conflict between journalists and politicians is predictable, given their different needs and their distinct roles in unlike organizations, but that conflict is bounded and regulated, whether by a shared presumption of ground rules or by formal mechanisms of conflict management. In the process, no one ends up being consistently dominant.

On one hand the House has worked to channel reporters toward partic-

54. Garay, *Congressional Television*, pp. 136–42; and Steven S. Smith, "Revolution in the House: Why Don't We Do It on the Floor?" Brookings Discussion Papers in Governmental Studies, no. 5 (Brookings, September 1986).

55. Quoted in Garay, *Congressional Television*, p. 141.

56. Herbert J. Gans, *Deciding What's News: A Study of CBS Evening News, NBC Nightly News, Newsweek, and Time* (Pantheon Books, 1979), p. 116.

ular aspects of the legislative process and away from news stories that members consider detrimental to themselves, the institution, or both. None of the decisions that House members have made about the media can be thought of as magnanimous. Subtly or not, these decisions, cloaked by concern for the dignity of the institution, have been self-serving. On the other hand, journalists still have the final say over what is and is not news. Changes in the criteria of newsworthiness and, consequently, in the coverage of Capitol Hill—particularly the loss of interest in debates, the rise of news-storytelling, and the adoption of progressive values—had little to do with what House members did. The changes were much more closely aligned to shifts in the political economy of journalistic enterprises.

In short, each side holds important power—members of the House by controlling whether, when, where, and how to grant access, journalists by deciding whether, when, where, and how to pay attention. The movements in the tango of their relationships are constantly subject to negotiation and renegotiation.

# 3

# House Reporters
and House Reporting

How REPORTERS cover Congress and shape their stories conditions what, when, where, and how House members make news. Reporting on Capitol Hill is different from what it is elsewhere in Washington because of the varied interests of the congressional reporters and the open, collegial nature of Congress that guarantees them access to many possible stories or authoritative sources. Despite the diversity, however, and the uncertain newsworthiness of their subjects, journalists have similar priorities and report news in a predictable manner, which is what offers legislators a chance to devise long-range media strategies.

## A Permeable
## Press Corps

Given the kaleidoscopic varieties of mass communication, it is no accident that *media* is a plural word. Congress has formally recognized the diversity by setting aside four separate galleries for the congressional press corps: the original press gallery for journalists on daily newspapers, the periodical gallery for newsmagazine reporters and those on specialized journals, the radio and television gallery, and a gallery for still photographers. But the variety within the congressional press corps is hardly limited to this basic classification. Reporters converge on Congress for very different reasons, seek out diverse newsmakers, use distinct reporting methods, and consequently present disparate slices of congressional life.

Because of this diversity, the congressional press corps is *permeable*, that is, diffuse in its structure and capable of being penetrated and influenced by the media strategies of House members' press offices.[1] Permeability of the press is thus a key to the tactics of those strategies. It ensures a range of news about congressional activities, provides publicity opportunities for members, and influences the mix of reporters and constituencies that will be the main customers for a House office's news product. To be sure, diversity characterizes other Washington newsbeats, but reporters' work on Capitol Hill is unique, giving members' media strategies their peculiar variety of styles and tones.

## The Nature of the Beat

Understanding the congressional newsbeat is crucial to understanding relations between House members and reporters.[2] A newsbeat is what a reporter is assigned to cover and is the principal way in which reporters interact with their sources and topics. Defined by geography (the White House, Capitol Hill) or subject matter (labor, taxes, environment), it enables news organizations to channel the daily flow of stories.

Newsgathering necessarily varies from one beat to the next, but the unusual nature of the Capitol Hill beat becomes clear when it is contrasted with the White House beat.[3] All agree on the key newsmaker: the president. He is the only person who can make news every day. But reporters' access to him is restricted. The president is rarely reached in settings less formal than carefully choreographed press conferences. And even these opportunities have diminished. Presidents since John Kennedy have deemphasized the give-and-take with reporters in favor of speeches and public appearances.[4] Regular presidential press conferences have largely been replaced by press briefings organized by the White House office and pre-

1. The source of the term in congressional studies is Richard F. Fenno, Jr., *Congressmen in Committees* (Little, Brown, 1973), pp. 278–79. Distinguishing between permeable and corporate committees, Fenno described permeable committees as showing less emphasis on committee expertise, less sense of group identification, less autonomous group decisionmaking, and lower job satisfaction. Though the parallel is not precise, much the same could be said for the press corps on Capitol Hill as contrasted with the corporate press corps at the White House.

2. The best study of newsbeats and their implications is in Mark Fishman, *Manufacturing the News* (University of Texas Press, 1980).

3. For White House media operations, the two classics still are Timothy Crouse, *The Boys on the Bus: Riding with the Campaign Press Corps* (Random House, 1973), pt. 2; and Michael Baruch Grossman and Martha Joynt Kumar, *Portraying the President: The White House and the News Media* (Johns Hopkins University Press, 1981).

4. Gary King and Lyn Ragsdale, *The Elusive Executive: Discovering Statistical Patterns in the Presidency* (Washington: CQ Press, 1988), chap. 5, especially table 5.1.

sided over at scheduled times by the White House press secretary. Together these stage-managed public appearances and briefings allow the White House to influence if not determine the day's top story. Reporters' days are so organized for them that the White House press office even notifies them when a lid goes on for lunch or at the end of the day, when no more news will occur.

The White House beat is geographically centralized. Reporters get most of their information in the White House briefing room (constructed when President Nixon filled in a swimming pool) and in the neighboring press areas, which makes it likely that they will have more contact with fellow journalists than with their sources. They are quickly aware of the stories and angles pursued by their colleagues and cannot help following each other's leads. The closeness is reinforced by their sense of being an in-group; they are recognized as occupying a prestigious position and their assignments are comparatively long-term. Because of the beat, then, the White House press corps is a textbook example of pack journalism, more corporate than permeable.

Reporters often contrast newswork at the opposite ends of Pennsylvania Avenue. Russell Baker described the stifling uniformity imposed on the presidential press corps, which follows the same stories and the same un-cooperative newsmaker day after day. On Capitol Hill, however, he found 535 potential newsmakers that "all *loved to talk*."[5] But there are costs to this freedom. David Broder noted that "reporters working on Capitol Hill have far more choices of how to operate and what to do every day. That makes the congressional beat much more fun, but it also gives it burdens that the White House beat does not have."[6]

The Capitol Hill beat has no agreed-upon principal newsmaker or principal news item. Indeed, it is one instance of the president's dominance in most reporting that, when Capitol Hill reporters do agree on a story, it is often on congressional consideration of a presidential proposal, an attempted override of a presidential veto, the confirmation of a presidential appointment, or an investigation into a presidential scandal. With the wealth of hearings, markups of legislation, and decisions in committees and subcommittees, the deliberations and actions on the floor in both chambers, not to mention initiatives taken in 535 members' offices, Congress has no one story, and it can be difficult to decide what to cover. Even on a single subject, such as an environmental issue, various legislators can

5. Quoted in Crouse, *The Boys on the Bus*, p. 195.
6. David S. Broder, *Behind the Front Page: A Candid Look at How the News Is Made* (Simon and Schuster, 1987), p. 221.

legitimately claim to be experts, and journalists must find a way to choose among them. Finally, Hill reporters differ in their judgments of newsworthiness because of their national or local audiences. National reporters who cover Congress see institutional processes and decisions as crucial. Local reporters pay more attention to the activities and involvement of legislators from their regions, especially when the institutional decisions have already been covered by the newswires.

Again, unlike on the White House beat, access to newsmakers on the Hill is generally straightforward. Congressional decisions, whether in subcommittee, in committee, or on the floor, are accessible to all journalists—since the sunshine reforms of the mid-1970s, a committee chair can no longer easily close a hearing.[7] Deliberations, particularly with the televised floor proceedings fed live to the press galleries and the networks, are open. For more direct access, reporters can use the Speaker's Lobby in the House or the President's Room in the Senate for interviews, or they can waylay legislators in the labyrinthine corridors of the Capitol, in their offices, before or after scheduled hearings, or on their way to or from the floor. Congressional press conferences are also far less formal than the president's. The regular press conferences held by Speaker Tip O'Neill or briefings held by Speaker Jim Wright proceeded without cameras or tape recorders—merely a batch of reporters clustered around the Speaker's desk, almost in the way they had crowded around President Franklin Roosevelt's half a century before. Douglass Cater's 1959 observation still stands: "Even the fledgling correspondent in Washington finds an ease of access to congressional leaders which makes Congress for him a happy hunting ground of journalistic enterprise."[8]

Congress is a fluid news beat not only because of its access but because it is also hard to decide just who is a congressional correspondent. The *Congressional Directory* listed 1,387 journalists registered with the press galleries in the One-hundredth Congress and an additional 1,590 with the radio and television galleries, perhaps the "largest single press corps in the world."[9] But being admitted to the galleries by the Standing Committee of Correspondents serves only as the basic accreditation for Washington jour-

7. This was the sanction most often mentioned by Hill reporters in 1973. See Robert O. Blanchard, "Congressional Correspondents and Their World," in Blanchard, ed., *Congress and the News Media* (Hastings House, 1974), pp. 212–16. This is not to say that many or even most committee meetings are covered by the media. The principal effect of sunshine reforms may well have been to open up deliberations to lobbyists rather than to reporters or the general public.

8. Douglass Cater, *The Fourth Branch of Government* (Houghton Mifflin, 1959), p. 52.

9. James White, "Modern Accommodation: The New Patronage?" in Blanchard, ed., *Congress and the News Media*, p. 53.

nalists. Some never cover Congress at all.[10] Most are based at their news organization's bureau elsewhere in Washington and at best use the cramped spaces of the galleries only as occasional checkpoints. Thus an in-group like the White House press corps has less chance to develop.

Even those using their credentials may not consider Congress their beat. Some national reporters organize their work according to subject matter and attend to Congress only when an issue intersects with congressional decisions. Others may cover another institutional beat, such as the White House or the Supreme Court, and turn to congressional sources only when they require a different point of view. Still others—stringers who work for otherwise unrelated small media outlets or Washington bureau representatives of local news organizations—are usually more interested in local legislators than in the activities of Congress overall. Still, whether or not reporters actually cover it as an institution, Congress is a cornucopia of information. David Broder, for instance, has said that the best way to judge a president's performance is by checking with sources on the Hill.[11] And in general, news from Washington is so dependent on congressional sources that it may well reflect a congressional perspective. In short, the congressional beat is as permeable as the press corps, a diversity that works to facilitate at once the reporters' daily gathering of news and the congressional press secretaries' pursuit of publicity.

## Local Reporters

The most important distinction among reporters on the congressional beat is whether they work for outlets with a national or a regional audi-

10. Estimates vary. In sending out his 1973 questionnaire to congressional correspondents, Robert Blanchard reduced the sample from 2,393 to 722 by removing foreign reporters and "all but known congressional correspondents" working for large bureaus, the wires, and local Washington media. Of the 307 responses he received, 46 percent reported spending less than two-fifths of their time covering Congress; see Blanchard, "Congressional Correspondents and Their World," pp. 166, 226. Broder, Behind the Front Page, p. 208, suggested in 1987 that "not more than one twentieth" of the 4,000 accredited reporters work on Capitol Hill most days. Stephen Hess, The Ultimate Insiders: U.S. Senators in the National Media (Brookings, 1986), p. xv, estimated that "the number of full-time national reporters on Capitol Hill is under a hundred, although at times of heavy activity news organizations will add to the regulars." In The Washington Reporters (Brookings, 1981), p. 48, Hess concluded that more than one-fifth of the Washington press corps worked on the congressional beat, but that included regional reporters. Whatever the precise percentage, only a small fraction of those listed in the Congressional Directory would be likely to consider Congress as their main beat.

11. Broder, Behind the Front Page, p. 209.

ence. Editors for local media generally want news on the legislators who represent part of their circulation area or their television market, or they want news on issues of local importance. A newsworthy story is thus less about what Congress is doing than what individual representatives are doing. As a bureau chief for a chain of regional newspapers commented, "We cover the trees, not the forest." Local reporters can use contacts with members either to generate stories of primarily local interest or to provide a local angle for wire service copy through adding comments from hometown representatives. To national reporters covering Congress, most members of the House are anonymous; to the regional correspondent, they become newsmakers whose newsworthiness is predicated on being a district's man or woman in Washington.

The presence of local news representatives in Washington is an impressive but recent development. One survey of congressional correspondents in the early 1970s showed that most spent no time reporting local or regional angles.[12] Now, because of the increasing ownership of local newspapers by chains and because of technological developments that have brought communications costs down, most of the congressional press corps is made up of correspondents for local outlets. Indeed, Congress has been termed the "center of regional coverage."[13]

Consider, for example, reporters for daily newspapers. Some 580 dailies and 27 weeklies had a Washington reporter linked to them in 1987.[14] Ninety-seven, ranging from the *New York Times* and the *Wall Street Journal* to the Enid, Oklahoma, *Daily News and Eagle* and the Bangor, Maine, *Daily News*, operated Washington bureaus containing at least one full-time reporter.[15] Other local media may not be able to afford a full-time Washington correspondent but they need not be shut out; they can always sign up with a stringer. Thus in 1987 Virginia Robicheaux represented newspapers in Lewiston, Idaho; Opelousas, Louisiana; Sparks, Nevada; and Salt Lake City. Other entrepreneurial reporters can concentrate on regional papers, as Alan Schlein has done with his one-man bureau for

12. Blanchard, "Congressional Correspondents and Their World," table 11. However, regional reporters (then known as special correspondents) received attention as early as the 1930s as "an extension of the city desk" searching for "local aspects of national events." See Leo C. Rosten, *The Washington Correspondents* (Harcourt, Brace, 1937), pp. 127–37.

13. Hess, *Washington Reporters*, p. 40.

14. Computed from information in Howard Penn Hudson and Helene F. Wingard, eds., *Hudson's Washington News Media Contacts Directory* (Rhinebeck, N.Y.: Hudson's, 1987).

15. This number includes newspapers with their own bureaus and chain newspapers with reporters assigned exclusively to them rather than shared with other members of the chain.

papers in Texas and Colorado. Perhaps most important, Copley, Gannett, Knight-Ridder, Newhouse, Thomson, and other newspaper chains hire correspondents especially to cover a state's or a region's representatives for their subsidiary organizations. Eighteen such chains provided Washington coverage for 475 newspapers in 1987, usually by assigning reporters to work for a group of their papers. Finally, although wire services have few regional reporters based in Washington, there are now news services designed explicitly to supplement AP and UPI coverage of Congress with coverage of local members. Most prominent since its inauguration in 1973 has been States News Service, which had twenty-five reporters generating stories of local interest and locally oriented sidebars to national stories for about fifty subscribing newspapers in 1987.[16]

Broadcast news organizations have similarly changed. With the development of the minicamera and the widespread use of satellite connections, many local television stations can now send a reporter to Washington or join with other stations to use a common reporter in States News Service's video equivalents, Potomac News Service or the Conus system.[17] Frequently, these reporters will file consecutive reports with virtually the same script except for a special interview or a few sentences about the effect of the news on a particular locality. Via satellite the networks can uplink excerpts from House or Senate debates to serve as raw material for local affiliates either as part of a package of national and international news clips assembled by the network or, in special circumstances, at the request of the local station.

Membership in the radio and television galleries has been growing far more quickly than in the other galleries, doubling between 1968 and 1978 and again between 1978 and 1988. But the growth has been concentrated among local media as much as among the major networks. Data compiled by the Senate radio and television gallery show that 232 journalists were from ABC, CBS, or NBC in 1973, and 385 were from Washington televi-

16. I am indebted to Richard Wilde for providing the results of his 1986 research on States News Service.

17. William J. Drummond, "Is Time Running Out for Network News?" *Columbia Journalism Review*, vol. 25 (May–June 1986), pp. 50–52; and Carol Matlack, "Live from Capitol Hill," *National Journal*, February 18, 1989, pp. 390–94. Conus was founded in 1984 and operates a Washington bureau through which raw footage, full reports, and interviews with sources can be sent by satellite. In 1989 Conus employed three reporters serving about 85 stations; Potomac employed four for about 150. Oddly enough, this nationalization of local news was happening at the same time as CBS's much-publicized attempt under Van Gordon Sauter to localize (or at least de-Washingtonize) the national news.

sion stations, foreign broadcasters, or independents. In 1981 the three networks contributed 380 journalists to the galleries, while 681 came from the
other categories.[18] Television's increasing presence in Washington in general and on Capitol Hill in particular serves to reinforce the local reporters'
majority in the congressional press corps as a whole.

The tendency is important because local correspondents necessarily see
the congressional beat differently from national correspondents. For local
reporters the beat consists of making the rounds of the offices of representatives whose districts fall within their circulation areas or media markets.
Likewise, when covering a national story, local reporters are less interested
in comments from congressional or party leaders than in the reactions of
representatives who can give local color.[19] For example, to accommodate
all the members who wanted to comment after the president's 1987 State
of the Union message, television cameras were moved to Statuary Hall,
where legislators prowled in search of appropriate (usually local) television
outlets among the twenty-eight allocated camera positions.[20] Of the 458
interviews conducted that evening, 372 were done for 116 stations by
groups of local bureaus or by independents such as Conus on behalf of
local stations; the networks, individual programs, and public television
combined conducted the rest.

This example is not unique. Even if they can attract national media
attention, most House members will necessarily interact more with their
hometown journalists. For most of the members most of the time, the only
regular customers are the local outlets. One survey from the early 1980s
showed that, though their press releases were divided about evenly between subjects of national interest and those of more local concern, press
secretaries estimated that 71 percent of their time was spent dealing with

18. My thanks to Jane Ruyle of the Senate radio and television gallery for providing these
figures.

19. After the 1987 revelations of Supreme Court nominee Douglas Ginsburg's marijuana use,
Tony Mauro wrote, "It was a hard news event that seemed to cry out for follow-up—but what
kind? In the vast stratum of Washington journalism known as 'regional reporters' . . . the most
typical response was the one that came most naturally: call your local congressman for reaction."
But as Mauro noted, this "peg in search of a story" created discomfiture for local reporters unac-
customed to putting their sources on the spot. See "Marijuana II: Reporters Opt Out," *Washington
Journalism Review*, vol. 10 (January–February 1988), p. 10.

20. There were more organizations than positions because local crews from the Eastern time
zone would be replaced by ones from the Pacific zone. A vivid description of the 1986 post–State-
of-the-Union media vigil is found in Hedrick Smith, *The Power Game: How Washington Works*
(Ballantine Books, 1988), pp. 128–30. My thanks to Beverly Braun of the House radio and television press gallery for supplying these data.

media from their congressional districts, 18 percent with national media, and 11 percent with state media.[21]

Yet even here there is variability. One reason is that the boundaries of many districts do not coincide either with circulation areas for major newspapers or with television markets. The United States is divided into 211 media markets, each comprising the counties or parts of counties that receive television signals primarily from one city. These markets range from New York City's 6.7 million viewing households to Glendive, Montana's 5,000.[22] The median population of a market is close to that of a House district—about 530,000—but they rarely overlap, since district lines have seldom been drawn with attention to communities or natural geography. Most districts are thus not favorably positioned for television coverage of their representatives. The district may be lumped with many others in a single metropolitan market, or it may be made up of several tiny rural markets without the resources to cover Washington, or it might comprise bits and pieces of larger urban markets.[23] Although circulation areas for daily newspapers present similar if less stark problems, the newspapers with the largest circulations within a given district are most often also distributed in other districts. Journalists reporting local matters may thus have to choose between several House members (not to mention senators) for comments on an issue, and variety lessens the possibility of a lasting collaboration. Local exposure is by no means automatic.

### National Reporters

If local reporters are mostly interested in legislators who represent certain circulation areas or television markets, national reporters who cover Congress are more interested in particular issues or in the institution itself and the legislative process. For them, members of the House become newsworthy only by their association with such national issues or their importance to the legislative process.

21. Robert E. Dewhirst, "Patterns of Interaction between Members of the U.S. House of Representatives and Their Home District News Media," Ph.D. dissertation, University of Nebraska, 1983, p. 142.

22. These are 1985 figures taken from The Broadcasting/Cablecasting Yearbook 1986 (Washington: Broadcasting Publications, 1985).

23. See James E. Campbell, John R. Alford, and Keith Henry, "Television Markets and Congressional Elections," Legislative Studies Quarterly, vol. 9 (November 1984), pp. 665–78; and Richard G. Niemi, Lynda W. Powell, and Patricia L. Bicknell, "The Effects of Congruity between Community and District on Salience of U.S. House Candidates," Legislative Studies Quarterly, vol. 11 (May 1986), pp. 187–201.

Yet the national press corps is also diverse. In 1988 some organizations—the *Washington Post*, National Public Radio, ABC, and NBC—split congressional reporting into separate Senate and House beats. (Should a story overlap beats, as the joint hearings of the House and Senate committees investigating the Iran-contra scandal did, the Senate correspondent usually lands the assignment.) Others such as the *New York Times* and CBS covered Capitol Hill as a whole, allocating stories, when necessary, on the basis of subject matter and tracking events as the stories work their way through both chambers. Under such circumstances, the Senate gallery is usually home base, being (by Capitol Hill standards) more spacious and comfortable.

Congressional reporters for the wire services, who contribute most newspaper coverage of the two houses, operate under different deadlines and conditions.[24] A reporter for a national newspaper can spend an entire day writing one story, and thus may have the luxury of sitting through testimony and tracking down sources. Wire reporters must meet successive deadlines on a variety of stories that often recycle copy from previous versions. Wire stories thus tend to be dry, colorless indications of what happened or who said what in public, with neither analysis nor a sense of the behind-the-scenes drama of lawmaking.

The most notable occupational division in the national press corps, however, is between those journalists who work for print outlets with a national audience and those who work for radio and television networks. Not only do they occupy separate press galleries, which are organized differently, but their means of newsgathering necessarily differ, partly because electronic news media need visuals and sound bites but also because Congress has restricted access to cameras and microphones in a way that has no equivalent for print reporters.

The similarities and differences of print journalists and radio and television reporters become apparent on visiting the galleries. The press gallery is like something out of *The Front Page*, with tiny desks crammed into a medium-sized room. Reporters telephone around Capitol Hill or back to the bureau while monitoring the televised floor proceedings and exchanging banter with would-be rivals. When they are not on the phone or deep in the details of the story on their terminals, they genially trade information, perhaps repeating what other reporters have missed at a news conference so that they can do fills to the home office. The radio and television

24. Charles M. Tidmarch and John J. Pitney, Jr., "Covering Congress," *Polity*, vol. 17 (Spring 1985), table 2, provides empirical evidence on the role of wire service coverage.

gallery is no more modern, but correspondents occupy private offices, each about the size of a small walk-in closet. Most have three television sets, one with the feed from the House floor, another with the Senate feed, and a third available for other material, such as CNN's continual news updates. Unlike print reporters, who are constantly coming and going, radio and television reporters tend to be, in the words of one of them, "electronic prisoners." "I'm sitting here like a stenographer," one network reporter commented, "and I'm locked in by the time, taking notes, talking to producers, coordinating and structuring. You get past two in the afternoon and you're hostage here. You can't stake out people; you have to do all your legwork early in the morning."[25]

Broadcast reporters are electronic prisoners in another sense. Their access to legislators is more restricted and their options more limited than those of print journalists. The members gave control of the cameras on the House floor in 1979 not to a network pool but to the Speaker, largely because of their skepticism about the fairness of television news. Much the same sentiment would seem to govern the rules on television cameras and microphones not only in the Capitol, where limited space makes an excellent excuse, but in the halls of the various office buildings and even on the Capitol grounds, where cameras with tripods for stand-up shots may be set up in only six places without advance permission.[26] As one employee of the Senate radio and television gallery noted, "Every square inch up here is controlled by someone." Inside the Capitol, stakeouts, where reporters await participants coming from confidential proceedings such as party caucus meetings, require advance permission, especially since there may be limited room for cameras, and a clear rule against "walking and shooting" with minicameras prohibits reporters from pursuing recalcitrant members. Linda Ellerbee, NBC House correspondent in the mid-1970s, described the import of these restrictions:

> Congress was able to enforce a handful of stupid rules it would never have tried with print journalists. For example, not only could I not take my camera crew—my equivalent of pen and notebook—into the

25. All unattributed quotations are from interviews with reporters that mostly took place over two weeks in March 1988. Since I wished to strike a balance with the not-for-attribution rules I follow elsewhere, these reporters are listed only in the acknowledgments.

26. The information in this paragraph comes from *Rules and Procedures for Broadcast Coverage of Congress*, prepared under the direction of the Executive Committee of the Congressional Radio-Television Correspondents' Galleries, January 1982, and from information provided by that gallery in March 1988.

chamber of the House or Senate. I could not take my camera crew to some places in and around the Capitol that were, at the same time, open to tourists with their cameras. . . . If I wanted to make pictures walking down the hall of one of the congressional office buildings around the Capitol, I needed to get permission from the occupant of every office whose door I would pass. Some halls have twenty or thirty offices along them. Try getting permission from each. If I wanted to take my camera crew and wait outside some congressman's office to ask him a question he did not want to answer, I needed the permission of the congressman who didn't want to answer what I wanted to ask. Figure that one.[27]

Print and broadcast journalists often gather information the same way, but the ability of radio or television reporters to present this news with sources being quoted on tape or film is hampered. Many occasions when leaders might be quizzed, such as at the Speaker's daily briefing, bar cameras and tape recorders, and there is no guarantee that there will be other opportunities.[28] Using the telephone to solicit reactions, as print journalists routinely do, does not provide high-quality sound bites even for radio reporters. Broadcast reporters thus lack flexibility. And following recent budget cutbacks at the networks, the amount of footage shot on speculation has declined considerably, further narrowing the range of possibilities. If all else fails, file footage or computer graphics can illustrate the spoken text, but producers' demands for quality visuals may also push the story later in the broadcast or out of the news flow altogether.

Radio and television correspondents must therefore rely much more on floor proceedings, committee hearings deemed important well enough in advance to arrange for stationary cameras, and interviews with sources who wish to get on the news and whose cooperation is essential for producing a good story in a way that producing good copy for print is not. Broadcast news sent from Capitol Hill is then even more routine than that in the newspapers, as dependent as print may be on the agreed-upon authoritative sources and official proceedings.

27. Linda Ellerbee, "And So It Goes": Adventures in Television (G. P. Putnam's, 1986), pp. 64–65.
28. One network reporter fumed, "On the House side, we've got a deplorable situation with the Speaker [Jim Wright]. He does not like television, he doesn't like the press at all but especially television. Unlike O'Neill, he doesn't cooperate in stakeouts. We used to be at the law library door [to the Capitol], calling Chris Matthews [O'Neill's press secretary] to find out when the Speaker was arriving; and he'd be coming out of the car and talking to us. I never, never recall him snubbing us."

### Consequences of Permeability

By contrast with those covering other newsbeats, there is about as much pushing congressional reporters apart as drawing them together. Some cover the institution itself, others cover hometown legislators in action, and still others find that their beats on issues or institutions overlap with the interests of Congress and turn to congressional sources for enlightenment. Even among full-time congressional correspondents, the differing standards of access for print and electronic media may push journalists toward different parts of the process and different sources.

With such a permeable press corps, members of Congress have many potential points of access to publicity. Even the lowliest House member will be considered newsworthy by someone somewhere. Dealing with reporters, and getting a story out, is then simply part of any House member's job description. But what is the story the reporters will favor? Even if representatives are newsworthy to their hometown reporters, permeability of the congressional press corps does not mean that any House member can find someone in the national press to cover his or her activities and concerns. A welter of competing stories faces congressional correspondents. Floor activity in each chamber encompasses a great many bills on disparate subjects. Lots of House members make speeches every day. There are hearings and markups by committees and subcommittees on both sides of the Hill, not to mention press conferences, briefings, and the like. Capitol Hill reporters, unlike their counterparts in the White House, must choose among these offerings to come up with the big story of the day, leading House members who seek national publicity to pay attention not only to *who* but to *what* the media are likely to report, and *when* that is likely to occur.

## What and Who Become News

How do congressional journalists decide who and what to cover? After all, if potential newsmakers and stories are legion, an easy choice would seem impossible. But a permeable press corps does not imply rugged individualism, with each reporter single-handedly defining his or her own work. Although reporting on Congress is a more flexible activity than reporting on the White House, it does show predictable patterns.

For local and regional reporters, decisions on coverage are relatively easy—local representatives and the issues of concern to the district. Of course, not just anything a House member does instantly becomes news. The wire services suggest the most important stories of the day, and reporters choose those that have local interest or need a local angle. The best hometown placement is reserved for a local member's action or statement on an issue before Congress that has local consequences—restricting footwear imports in New England, raising air quality standards in Southern California, tightening space program funding in Florida. Any attention to these issues in Washington will interest one or another local reporter. Because including material on a local representative can heighten the story's exposure at home, reporters have an incentive to encourage members to emphasize parochial concerns and members have an incentive to anticipate such sources of newsworthiness.

Congressional correspondents for national media do not have so straightforward a task. They find few legislators worth covering except as they are connected to what is happening in Congress or in Washington. What Congress as a whole is doing is deemed more newsworthy than what individual members are doing.[29] But what happens then? Who and what do they choose to write about?

### National Correspondents and the Big Story

The range of possible stories and sources for a national journalist is at once exhilarating and unsettling. Reporters prize the variety of subjects and sources and the ability to choose among them because it increases their control over the final story and makes their work more satisfying.[30] "The accessibility is fabulous," one exulted. "You can get to these people, they want to talk to you, they're interesting and fun to talk to. More important, you can check yourself. . . . I'm never in the position of asking myself if they're trying to use me for something. Because I can literally walk down the hall and get the other point of view."

Correspondents might be tempted to stay on the Hill if the White House beat were not more prestigious and a more reliable way to get stories published or on the air. Often they express exasperation about persuading editors and producers of the import of what is happening in Congress. "I

---

29. A study of the 1978 coverage of Congress in ten metropolitan newspapers, including stories about local members, concluded that from two-thirds to three-fourths of the items referred to institutional matters more than individual actions and statements. Tidmarch and Pitney, "Covering Congress," p. 473.

30. Hess, *Washington Reporters*, p. 9.

could do a story a day out of the House, but I can't get it on the air," one network correspondent griped. "Congress will get on where there's a vacuum of power elsewhere. It might be an element of someone else's story. Just look at my assignment sheets if you want to see how much the networks care about Congress."

Congressional activities per se are not considered as important as many other Washington stories. What makes Congress newsworthy to editors is its involvement with other institutions. Capitol Hill correspondents routinely lose stories to their counterparts in the so-called Golden Triangle—the White House, State Department, or Pentagon beats. Even new information or a catchy quotation may be incorporated into someone else's front page story—a process known as the weave—or appended in the newspaper as a reefer, a short article that accompanies the story's continuation on the back page. Max Frankel, executive editor in the *New York Times*, defended this practice: "There's a peculiar habit in Washington of breaking stories down into geographical divisions. . . . If the president makes a comment, then they've always done separate reaction stories from the Hill, say, and the Pentagon. But I'll be damned if I'm going to present three stories to the readers."[31] Such attitudes are, of course, distasteful to journalists, who pride themselves on attributed authorship, on prominent placement, and on control over a story. So Hill correspondents must sell their story ideas if they are to be budgeted a decent portion of the newshole and awarded a leading spot in the newspaper or broadcast. In presenting ideas to superiors they often choose a topic already circulating and thus presumed newsworthy.[32] They then emphasize how their coverage will provide the most encompassing and important perspective on the subject. For example, in 1988 when I accompanied a Hill reporter for a national newspaper, David Boren, chair of the Senate Intelligence Committee, was testifying on the Intermediate-Range Nuclear Force (INF) Treaty before the Senate Foreign Relations Committee at the same time that Soviet Foreign Minister Eduard Shevardnadze was visiting Washington in prepara-

31. Quoted in Bruce Porter, "The 'Max' Factor at the *New York Times*," *Columbia Journalism Review*, vol. 27 (November–December 1988), p. 32.

32. This is not to say that congressional coverage is merely a by-product of topic coverage, as some have alleged—see, for example, Susan Heilmann Miller, "Congress and the News Media: Coverage, Collaboration and Agenda-Setting," Ph.D. dissertation, Stanford University, 1976, p. 59. For reporters on issue beats, congressional involvement may be an indicator of the importance of a particular topic. For Capitol Hill reporters, hot topics may help in deciding which are the most important things that Congress is doing. On selling stories, see Herbert J. Gans, *Deciding What's News: A Study of CBS Evening News, NBC Nightly News, Newsweek, and Time* (Pantheon, 1979), pp. 90–93.

tion for a summit meeting.[33] In the middle of the senator's statement the reporter stepped out to a phone booth to alert the paper's bureau chief: "This is going to be a vehicle for tying everything together. It'll be broad rather than narrow." The strategy was necessary to avoid the fate of a previous story, which became a reefer. As the correspondent told me, "It may happen again. Or the best quotes may be taken out of *my* story and put in the Shevardnadze story. Or the other way around. The trick will be to write it as broad as I can. Get into the top of the story that the markup begins today. Stress the importance of getting the treaty through without amendment."

As the comment suggests, a national reporter's trump card is the ability to cover legislative processes. Not only might institutional decisions be considered the most newsworthy occurrences in Congress, but such an approach works in reporters' own interests by getting their work prominently displayed. One network congressional correspondent illustrated the strategy:

> Contra aid pops up all the time. The story is institutional; the White House can't force contra aid. They can contribute to it, but they can't pass it on their own. That's surely a congressional story. INF, catastrophic health insurance, child care—all these issues that Congress will deal with, these are things where Congress has to decide. Take the cease-fire in Nicaragua today. That's a story all over town. More often than not, it ends up at the White House. I guess we've got an institutional bias toward the White House on how we cover stories. But the others are particularly and peculiarly congressional actions.

But congressional reporters must still choose what and who to cover. They necessarily lack the certainty of White House correspondents that they are focusing on what everyone agrees is the right story. Such assurance is important for a reporter, because nobody quite knows what is and what is not news; as Leo Rosten said fifty years ago, "News in the last analysis is what newspapers choose to print."[34] Reporters feel pressure not necessarily to get the exclusive or the scoop but to get the story everyone else is covering. In their cost-benefit calculations, they worry more about the embarrassment of having missed a story than the satisfaction of having beaten everyone else to the punch. And with all the activity in Congress, chances are rela-

33. This correspondent was mostly following Senate action, but there is no reason to expect that my conclusions would be different if the job that day had been House action.

34. Rosten, *Washington Correspondents*, p. 261.

tively high that they could be accused of missing the big story. They must therefore determine the most authoritative source despite the permeability of the congressional press corps that hampers receiving cues from colleagues.

Outwardly, congressional correspondents are surprisingly blasé about their choices. In the 1970s, when Robert Blanchard asked reporters what their chief sources of ideas for stories were, the responses were singularly uninformative: *what's happening on a given day . . . the stories of the day, what breaks that day you work on . . . the flow of news itself—what the big events of the day happen to be . . . something happened or it didn't . . . the legislation before Congress.*[35] The reporters I talked to held similar sentiments: *Breathing the air tells you it's coming . . . If you have to figure out what to cover, you shouldn't be up here.*

Who dictates what the big events will be? The daybooks of the wires, listing what they consider the most important scheduled events, suggest every evening what may be worth paying attention to the next day. Correspondents also study the prestige papers, especially the *Washington Post*, the capital's newspaper of record, and weekly specialized journals such as *Congressional Quarterly Weekly Report.*[36] So as one CQ reporter noted, "If we don't cover it, it doesn't get covered." Network reporters are well known to scrutinize the press, and those newspaper reporters who are still in the press galleries may flip the television dial at 6:30 or 7:00 P.M. from House or Senate floor coverage to a network broadcast. As one network reporter explained:

> You start out with an idea of the story of the day . . . by looking at the *Washington Post*, the *New York Times*, the *Wall Street Journal*, the *Washington Times*, *USA Today*. I guess I read five papers every day. I get the *Post* at home and it's the first thing I see, so it shapes my impression of what might be the flow of news today. I look at how we might move the story farther down the road, beyond where it's already been.

Even though congressional correspondents cannot be thought of as members of a pack, they converge toward the same stories to reduce uncertainty and routinize their work. The 1930s practice of blacksheeting— sharing carbon copies of stories—has fallen into desuetude, but national reporters' coverage of Congress by no means lets a thousand stories

---

35. Blanchard, "Congressional Correspondents," pp. 183–84 and following.

36. Evidence on the *Post* as gatekeeper is provided by a study of ten metropolitan newspapers in 1978; see Tidmarch and Pitney, "Covering Congress," p. 468.

bloom.[37] Shared understandings emerge of the newsworthiness of particular issues. The importance of a bill is measured, as with other news items, by the number of people likely to be affected by its passage. Tax reform might become newsworthy, while unemployment programs might not. Journalists also assume that less complex issues or ones that are more clear-cut will be more comprehensible and interesting as well as easier to present in a shorter amount of space. Clear-cut issues are especially felicitous if they can be dramatized by two (and only two) distinct sides and an easily reported conflict. This situation is not, however, easy to come by. Politicians send out diffuse rather than specific appeals. They may also prefer to shift the fight to more favorable grounds rather than argue on terms set by opponents.[38] Although such strategies are rational, reporters tend to see them as indecisive or evasive, confusing the issues or, in a favorite journalistic metaphor, muddying the waters.

If a bill can be characterized in a phrase or provokes familiar divisions, such as those between party blocs or between presidential supporters and opponents, it will probably receive more attention than a more complex bill about which the lines are less clearly drawn. In the early days of the One-hundredth Congress, for instance, the highway bill achieved prominence because one clause allowed states to increase speed limits to sixty-five miles an hour on interstate highways in rural areas. This ease of characterization, which belied the hodge-podge of pork-barrel projects that the bill really was, and the threat of a presidential veto, encouraged the media to give it extraordinary attention as it progressed through Congress. Likewise, reporters covered tax reform in the Ninety-ninth Congress only when they could concentrate on who was for or against reform per se rather than the various ways the tax code could be altered. When a complex issue has become news because of a dispute between president and Congress or because it is considered important regardless of its complexity, the clearer

---

37. Rosten, *Washington Correspondents*, p. 90, claimed that most reporters in the 1930s took advantage of blacksheeting, with "no effort to conceal or deny the practice. Correspondents who cover the same events, eat together, think alike, meet socially, discuss news, share leads and consult one another can hardly be blamed for extending their reciprocity to its logical conclusion: the exchange of news dispatches." Of course, if they do all the rest (as they still do today), why do they even need to exchange stories?

38. On reporters' preference for clear-cut issues, see Thomas E. Patterson, *The Mass Media Election: How Americans Choose Their President* (Praeger, 1980), chap. 4. On politicians' strategies, see E. E. Schattschneider, *The Semisovereign People: A Realist's View of Democracy in America* (Holt, Rinehart and Winston, 1960); and Benjamin I. Page, *Choices and Echoes in Presidential Elections: Rational Man and Electoral Democracy* (University of Chicago Press, 1978).

information is given a more prominent place in the story in hopes that its presence will improve its placement in the newspaper or the broadcast.

Choosing what to cover is not enough. A reporter must also know when to cover it. Such a decision becomes especially difficult when reporters confront processes that have no clear beginning or end. According to Mark Fishman, a participant-observer in a medium-sized city council press corps, reporters decide when to cover a process by constructing an idealized "phase structure" that can be broken down into discrete steps.[39] Newsworthy points occur when the process moves from one phase to another. A bill's being reported from subcommittee to committee or passing the floor would be newsworthy; its being bottled up in committee would not. Inaction becomes newsworthy only when a deadline provides dramatic possibilities that the government will (at least briefly) have to shut down, that automatic spending cuts will occur, or that a program will expire. (Roger Mudd's nightly vigil on Capitol Hill for CBS on the stalemate over the 1964 Civil Rights Bill is a legendary exception that proves the rule.) Otherwise, without movement news by definition does not exist. As one congressional reporter noted of the issues she had been covering, "I made the judgment that the contras were going [today] to be a White House story, that there's nothing happening, that things muddled along, that there's no news. . . . The House is taking up the budget resolution so we should have a story. With the contras, there's nothing on the level of a story because nothing's been decided."

By anticipating an orderly process, reporters endow decisionmaking with more regularity, clarity, and rationality than it actually has.[40] The pitfalls of such idealization become clear when decisionmaking, as it often does, defies lock-step progression. Early in 1985, for instance, as a measure to allow moderate Democrats to vote for some sort of aid to the Nicaraguan contras, Democrats Michael Barnes and Lee Hamilton proposed that $14 million be appropriated, $4 million to implement a Central American peace treaty and the remainder to go to the International Red Cross for humanitarian aid to Nicaraguan refugees. On April 24 the amendment was adopted by the House as a substitute for President Reagan's original proposal. On CBS, during the first broadcast at 6:30 P.M. eastern time, anchor Dan Rather dutifully mentioned this vote as an "effort to compromise" but did not mention that another vote was forthcoming on final passage of the overall bill. The bill itself was defeated by a

39. Fishman, *Manufacturing the News*, chap. 3.

40. David L. Paletz, Peggy Reichert, and Barbara McIntyre, "How the Media Support Local Governmental Authority," *Public Opinion Quarterly*, vol. 35 (Spring 1971), pp. 80–92.

coalition of liberal Democrats and conservative Republicans during Rather's 7:00 P.M. broadcast. When he interrupted with this breaking news, Rather looked visibly confused: this outcome had not been expected and so was inexplicable.[41] If reporters' expectations are not fulfilled, the event is cast as an upset or a reversal, when in fact it was easily interpretable and predictable from another angle.

If the legislative process is presumed to operate in an inexorable progress toward enactment, the most newsworthy moment would be a bill's final passage. Such an emphasis is encouraged by televised floor proceedings, which are easily monitored and more readily accessible than committee deliberations. And this technological consideration is reinforced by the presumption that a less provisional, more decisive action is more newsworthy.[42] Indeed, final passage is the ultimate in congressional coverage; the less that newspapers cover Congress the more they concentrate on floor proceedings.[43]

Editors and producers and, to a lesser extent, reporters see earlier stages as opportunities for political posturing, delay, and obstruction of the quasi-natural unfolding of the process. Moreover, issues and battle lines are too vague then to allow crisp reporting. Final passage enables the newsworthy institutional action to be reported: what Congress did, not what its subunits or its members did. A national congressional correspondent revealed this bias upon filing a story on the override (by the Senate in the morning and the House in the afternoon) of President Reagan's veto of the Civil Rights Restoration Act in 1988: "It's nice to have been able to use some action verbs, to have had a story that begins in the morning and ends in the afternoon."

Such an emphasis has its costs. As another national Capitol Hill reporter noted, "It's a struggle to get it onto page one when it's passing the House and the issues are still unfocused and unsettled. Editors ask, 'Is it going to pass?' Well, it may be uncertain if it's going to pass and then the editors will wonder if it's so important. But one way to govern is to pass legislation, another way is *not* to pass." And according to a third reporter, "Editors see Congress as a troublesome intrusion into the otherwise orderly

41. Information on the 6:30 P.M. broadcast is from the *Vanderbilt Television News Abstracts and Indices.* I watched the 7:00 P.M. news in Washington.

42. As ABC's Sam Donaldson, invoking his news president, said, "The Roone Arledges of this world do not pay us to stand on the White House lawn night after night and say, 'Gee, I haven't a clue as to what's going to happen here. Beats the hell out of me how things will work out.'" Donaldson, *Hold On, Mr. President!* (Fawcett, 1987), p. 106.

43. Tidmarch and Pitney, "Covering Congress," p. 478.

affairs of state. Editors see Congress as 535 people with their own agendas. It's not neat. It's not *supposed* to be neat. . . . It's difficult to convince editors that the key decision might be made at the subcommittee level. . . . They aren't aware that by the time final action occurs, it might be too late."

### The Authoritative Source

After reporters have found a newsworthy event—a what and a when—they must decide who will serve as an authoritative source for information and commentary on it. How journalists choose sources reveals a lot about how they cover the legislative process.

Because what individual House members do is less important for national correspondents than what the institution does, the best sources are those crucial to moving the process along. One reportorial rule of thumb is to focus on designated leaders—or committee leaders—whose institutional position is taken as a sign that they have greater influence than the average member. Leaders may not always be considered newsworthy, however, even if they enter a fray spouting colorful quips. A leader who seems mostly to be pushing a personal agenda is less newsworthy than one who speaks and acts on behalf of a committee or a party. For example, one day I accompanied a national newspaper correspondent at hearings of the Senate Foreign Relations Committee on the INF Treaty. In the morning Senators David Boren and William Cohen of the Intelligence Committee testified. From the outset, the reporter was leery of Boren's motives in announcing potential problems of verification, noting that an earlier story had been buried by editors' suspicions that the senator had an ax to grind. The story as it was ultimately written strongly emphasized Cohen's concurrence with Boren and then only after a committee staffer had established that the recommendations did not reflect what the reporter called Boren's "waving his own flag versus consensus on the committee."[44]

In congressional deliberations, especially those open to public scrutiny, nonleaders can also become newsmakers. Merely participating in the formal legislative process, as long as they seem to be advancing its resolution, can give nonleaders a legitimacy in the media that they would not otherwise have, and can make them more influential. Swing votes, for instance, may be newsworthy in ways that dependable votes are not, as Senator Terry

44. This concern about authoritative sources emerged again later in the day when we arrived in the midst of Senator Sam Nunn's testimony. The correspondent scribbled a note to a colleague, reading in part, "Am I right that . . . Nunn's testimony is the soapbox stuff that is part of his longstanding personal agenda and therefore ignorable?"

Sanford found to his chagrin when he was the necessary (and indecisive) last vote for overriding President Reagan's veto of the 1987 highway bill. In contrast to the House as it was before reform, when junior representatives were expected to defer to senior colleagues, all members now expect to participate equally in hearings, markups, and floor deliberations. In December 1986, for example, the House Foreign Affairs Committee conducted the first public hearings on the Iran-contra scandal. In a live morning telecast Secretary of State George Shultz responded to questions from committee members in descending order of seniority. Because time ran out before all members could pose their questions, Committee Chair Dante Fascell promised that the remaining members could submit questions in writing. When former National Security Adviser Robert McFarlane, a more central participant in the scandal, appeared in the afternoon, the order began where the questioning of Shultz left off, with Representative Tom Lantos, thirteenth in seniority among the Democrats, so that most of McFarlane's answers were in response to junior committee members. Besides the publicity accorded by live television, members had a fairly equal chance to receive attention in the news; that evening the only member who was shown directly interrogating either witness on any of the networks was Larry Smith, then in his second House term.[45]

Yet while nonleaders potentially enjoy equal access to the media, their ability to make news hinges on reporters' belief that their participation is helping to advance the legislative process and thus move a story to a new phase. I witnessed an instance of this in the summer of 1985 at a House-Senate conference of the two budget committees. By chance, although as a congressional fellow I entered as a staffer, I was seated in the press section between reporters for two well-regarded daily newspapers. Up to that point, speculation had been high over how the House conferees, led by William Gray, and the Senate conferees, led by Pete Domenici, would resolve their deadlock. The reporters listened intently whenever Gray or Domenici spoke, although most of their statements consisted in little more than Domenici's insistence on percentage cuts and Gray's emphasis on policy before numbers. But when other conferees, such as Representatives Bobbi Fiedler or George Miller, spoke up on particular aspects of the budget that bothered them—Miller, for example, decried the way the budget skirted the problems of the "poorest of the poor" and began a disquisition

45. Fascell's announcement of the policy of questioning appears in *The Foreign Policy Implications of Arms Sales to Iran and the Contra Connection*, Hearings before the House Committee on Foreign Affairs, 99 Cong. 2 sess. (Government Printing Office, 1986), p. 102. Smith's question was shown on CBS that evening.

on the concerns of the homeless—the two reporters between whom I was seated exchanged glances, sighed, rolled their eyes, and doodled on their steno pads. In the room overall the whispering and fidgeting became so loud that Miller was scarcely audible above the racket. The reporters had, in effect, rendered a verdict that reinforced their news judgments. Miller was wasting their time by pushing a personal agenda and doing something other than break the stalemate. That he was discussing an important matter was beside the point; his comments constituted a nonevent.[46]

Sometimes, congressional correspondents cannot rely on the cues provided by phase structures, especially when they are assigned to cover an issue of continuing interest and require congressional commentary to fill out a story. One way of choosing a source is then to look at all members participating in the legislative process, even those giving one-minute speeches at the start of a day or participating in the so-called special orders after the close of business when they may enter into long disquisitions by themselves or with colleagues on topics of their choice. Such participation gives a modicum of legitimacy to all members. "Anyone who speaks up in a debate is involved," one network reporter commented.

But not just anyone speaking on the floor can make news. When there is a choice among potential sources, a reporter may have to rely on another criterion of newsworthiness—being interesting. One way to be interesting is to be quotable. A pithy quotation from a source may give a story additional credibility, even though the response may have been set up by a reporter's question. And given journalists' commitment to factuality, any hunches or colorfully phrased pronouncements are usually found in quotations rather than in the language of the ostensibly impartial reporters.[47]

Radio and television reporters place a higher premium on quotability than print journalists. One network correspondent's report on the House debate over aid to the Nicaraguan contras included only two quotations, one from the flamboyant ex-sheriff, James Traficant, comparing the contras to the Three Stooges, and the second the angry response of the bill's manager, Mickey Edwards. "You work with sound bites to make them say what they're trying to say—or, rather, complete *the* thought they're trying to say," the correspondent said. "Traficant . . . talked about Larry, Moe and Curly. Edwards both *explains* what Traficant was talking about *and* rebuts it in seven seconds. These are complicated stories, so you've got to

46. For ways in which phase structures prevent occurrences from being noticed as newsworthy events, see Fishman, *Manufacturing the News*, pp. 76–84.

47. Gaye Tuchman, "Objectivity as Strategic Ritual: An Examination of Newsmen's Notions of Objectivity," *American Journal of Sociology*, vol. 77 (January 1972), pp. 660–70.

link them, thread them together." Of course, whether this exchange informed the viewers is open to question.

Vivid quotations are also structurally useful to print journalists. Reporters for national newspapers customarily quote as a way to move a story from one item to the next or to capture a particular reaction. One correspondent, in the course of a story on the contra debate, quoted Representative Edward Markey's quip that Ronald Reagan had gone south to let off Oliver North, who was the subject of the next paragraph. "Get something said in a quote," the reporter commented, "and get something which saves me words."

Good sources must be more than clever or glib, however. As one newspaper correspondent observed, "A colorful quote in a debate on the floor . . . will get covered—at least if it's colorful and reflects a sentiment that's there." Because individual representatives are less newsworthy than the institution, they must be able to articulate ideas considered widely held in Congress. "You only give voice to a constituency that deserves reputation," a newspaper journalist noted. "Traficant is quoted only as a liberal who'll always vote against contra aid, but never as someone [who can provide] an idea of how the House would go, versus [Representative David] Obey, who's someone trustworthy. There's a difference between people who stand up on the floor and people you seek out. You're choosing people who can give you information."

When reporters covering a given subject need a reaction and are without a committee hearing or floor proceeding to draw on, they have to determine an authoritative source. As their stories indicate, they often choose a legislator of some institutional prominence—a party leader, committee chair, caucus member, or so forth. Not only does choosing a leader ease the problem of selecting among potential sources, but implying the reason for the selection by being able to identify the member by title also rationalizes it before potentially skeptical superiors.

Reporters may winnow their sources by trying to maintain parity among Democrats and Republicans, though the majority party, presumed more responsible for legislative action, usually is first to be covered. Among rank-and-file members of a particular committee, reporters may seek out a swing vote or a member who bridges factions, such as Dave McCurdy, who willingly responded to the wishes of the media to take advantage of his middle-of-the-road position in the Armed Services Committee in the early 1980s and later during the debate over contra aid. Reporters are also drawn to the sponsor of a bill that occasions debate, so that Romano Mazzoli emerged out of nowhere when the Simpson-Mazzoli immigration reform bill began to win headlines in the Ninety-eighth Congress. Even representing particular kinds of districts can make a source attractive. For a television story about the Sikorsky military helicopter that experienced three times as many crashes as other helicopters, Robert Badham of California was sought out as "the congressman of the district where the crashes have occurred."[48] At the very least, reporters may state that their source is a "congressional expert" on a given subject, an appellation that may mean as much to the legislator as to the reporter.

If correspondents must cover a matter about which they are uninformed, they can turn to members of the committee with jurisdiction over it. "You work from the general to the specific," a network correspondent said. "Start with the committee that has oversight. . . . Start with the chairman or the majority staff director. Say, 'Look, I've got an issue I know nothing about, what should I do and where should I go?' It's amazing how many knowledgeable people there are here on completely arcane subjects."

Although leaders are preferred, reporters can also come to rely on non-leaders as authorities on particular issues or, in rare cases, on a wide variety of topics. For example, on the day in 1985 that White House Chief of Staff James Baker and Treasury Secretary Donald Regan unexpectedly announced their intent to switch jobs, I visited one senior correspondent for a national newspaper who was desperately seeking congressional reaction. He called predictable names—Senate Majority Leader Bob Dole, House Speaker Tip O'Neill, House Majority Leader Jim Wright, and House Ways and Means Chair Dan Rostenkowski—and then Newt Gingrich, a fourth-term Georgia Republican with inconsequential committee assignments. "Why Gingrich?" I asked. The correspondent, taken aback, hurriedly pointed out that the representative, who had pushed the agenda of a group of junior House Republicans known as the Conservative Opportunity Society, had emerged as a spokesman for a significant wing of the Republican party. "Good reporters know where power comes from," he added; "they gravitate toward it, follow the flow, seek it out. And they seek out information and insight. No one can market themselves over a period of time unless they have power—by that I mean power of position—or information." Still, his discomfiture revealed that few legislators lacking power of position are accorded the status of speaking authoritatively on a wide variety of issues.

When journalists are aware that they have highlighted someone whom most people would not consider a leader, they may second-guess their

48. "CBS Evening News," March 13, 1987.

choice or stop using the material from those, such as Barney Frank, Henry Hyde, or Edward Markey, whose quotability often exceeds their institutional position. And if a source seems to have made news too frequently, they may cultivate other sources. But second-guessing occurs with protestors and demonstrators, not with the officeholders being demonstrated against. Reporters rarely ask if they are giving too much attention to the powers that be: there is never a moratorium on covering House leaders. After all, in the determination of newsworthiness, interest takes a back seat to importance. A quotable person who is not considered authoritative is generally less newsworthy than an authoritative source who is not so quotable.

## The Shape of Congressional Coverage

Of all the House members and activities that could be potential subjects, reporters attend to relatively few. By the time their stories get budgeted and edited, even those selections are winnowed down, so that the audience receives an exceedingly small sample of congressional goings-on and personalities. The sample is by no means representative, any more than the goals and fistfights that sports coverage extracts from sixty minutes of hockey. Reporters may assert that they have brought the most important information to public attention, but selection can bestow importance at least as much as reflect it.

The shape of congressional coverage is crucial to legislators not only because it sets the context in which they pursue publicity—indicating what, where, and when they may be able to make news—but because it also certifies some activities as more important than others. The conception of Congress held by most Americans most of the time is heavily influenced by the news. Though the local news may well be responsive to a local representative, it leaves the institution itself to national media and wire service reports. Not surprisingly, then, House members try hard to influence its portrayal. But their attempts are directed at an increasingly small newshole.

It is impossible to pin down one or two news outlets as most typical of national coverage of the House, especially as the media's diversity increases. A few are very influential in establishing for other reporters what is and what is not newsworthy. Among those, I have chosen two for study. The *New York Times*, which views itself as a newspaper of record, has long been watched for cues. More recently, network television evening news broadcasts, partly because they reach large audiences, can bestow importance. What they do not cover may no longer be thought of as front-page material.

In recent years, national news, especially on television, has begun to depend less on Washington news and more on varied (and homier) coast-to-coast coverage. And within the Capital Beltway the president continues to set journalists' agendas. The news from Capitol Hill has gradually become a less valuable commodity. These trends are most noticeable for television, but the declining news value of Congress has also been evident in newspapers of record. The shape of congressional news has an ironic dimension: more members are making more news at the same time that the institution itself as a newsmaker seemingly fades slowly in the west.

## A Shrinking Public Image

In 1959 Elmer Cornwell remarked on "the expanding public image" of the president. And as presidents have become more media oriented and more skilled in the use of publicity, Congress's share of the news has dwindled.[49] By one estimate the number of network evening news stories from Capitol Hill decreased by half between the late 1970s and 1980–84.[50] In a typical month (September 1985) of the three networks' evening broadcasts, Norman Ornstein and Michael Robinson identified a hundred stories or so—one out of ten—that mentioned Congress in some way, about half the percentage noted ten years before. And only forty-one focused on Congress. "Clearly," they concluded, "all three networks have systematically deemphasized their Capitol Hill coverage; they all seem to agree that the Congress of the 1980s isn't nearly as newsworthy as the Congress of the 1970s."[51] Not only is Congress less visible vis-à-vis other federal institutions, it is newsworthy largely as an impersonal entity reacting to presiden-

49. Elmer E. Cornwell, Jr., "Presidential News: The Expanding Public Image," *Journalism Quarterly*, vol. 36 (Summer 1959), pp. 275–83; and Lynda Lee Kaid and Joe Foote, "How Network Television Coverage of the President and Congress Compare," *Journalism Quarterly*, vol. 62 (Spring 1985), pp. 59–65.

50. Greg Schneiders, "The 90-Second Handicap: Why TV Coverage of Legislation Falls Short," *Washington Journalism Review*, vol. 7 (June 1985), p. 44.

51. Norman J. Ornstein and Michael J. Robinson, "Where's All the Coverage? The Case of Our Disappearing Congress," *TV Guide*, January 11, 1986, p. 5. Similar findings from a sample of television and newspaper stories are presented in Richard Davis, "News Coverage of American Political Institutions," paper presented at the annual meeting of the American Political Science Association, August 1986, table 2.

tial initiatives. And while most news from Capitol Hill is bland, the few items that do editorialize, openly or not, are almost never positive.[52]

Representatives seeking publicity are further handicapped because the Senate, despite some fluctuation from year to year, is more frequently covered than the House. The contrast is even stronger when individual House and Senate members are compared. In the Ninety-seventh Congress (1981–82), the recent apogee of House members' television visibility, all House standing committee chairs were less visible in network news than their Senate counterparts.[53] In addition, news media are concentrating on less varied stories. Selectivity itself is not surprising, and subjects considered newsworthy, such as foreign policy, civil rights and crime, health, and the environment, can make the House committees on foreign affairs, the judiciary, and energy and commerce more prominent.[54] But in the 1980s, for example, television focused on only a handful of big stories; in the 1960s, broadcasts, which were more closely restricted to Washington and New York, covered many more aspects of congressional decisionmaking.

## Members on Television

Table 3-1 shows the number of members mentioned and the total number of mentions in network evening news broadcasts for 1969 through 1986, all the years for which information is available. However it is measured, the visibility of House members has not declined since the late 1960s and early 1970s.

From 1969 through 1973 only a quarter of the House members were mentioned at all each year. That percentage increased in 1974 with the intense attention to the House Judiciary Committee's deliberation on impeaching President Nixon and increased again in 1975 with the large influx of class-of-1974 reformers. The recent height of members' visibility was the Ninety-seventh Congress (1981–82). With the Senate newly in

52. Michael J. Robinson and Kevin R. Appel, "Network News Coverage of Congress," Political Science Quarterly, vol. 94 (Fall 1979), pp. 407–18; and Tidmarch and Pitney, "Covering Congress," pp. 463–83.

53. Joe S. Foote and David J. Weber, "Network Evening News Visibility of Congressmen and Senators," paper presented to the Association for Education in Journalism and Mass Communication, August 1984, table 4. See also Kaid and Foote, "How Network Television Coverage of the President and Congress Compare"; and Davis, "News Coverage of American Political Institutions," table 3.

54. Steven S. Smith and Christopher J. Deering, Committees in Congress (Washington: CQ Press, 1984), pp. 66–67, calculate the number of minutes from 1969 to 1980 that evening news broadcasts devoted to topics within committee jurisdictions.

TABLE 3-1. Number of House Members Mentioned on Network
Evening News, 1969–86

| Year | Members mentioned | Total mentions | Average per member |
|------|-------------------|----------------|--------------------|
| 1969 | 110 | 573 | 5.21 |
| 1970 | 110 | 442 | 4.02 |
| 1971 | 102 | 456 | 4.47 |
| 1972 | 114 | 553 | 4.85 |
| 1973 | 126 | 438 | 3.48 |
| 1974 | 150 | 1,699 | 11.33 |
| 1975 | 174 | 932 | 5.36 |
| 1976 | 160 | 830 | 5.19 |
| 1977 | 189 | 715 | 3.78 |
| 1978 | 181 | 617 | 3.41 |
| 1979 | 178 | 661 | 3.71 |
| 1980 | 168 | 865 | 5.15 |
| 1981 | 245 | 1,237 | 5.05 |
| 1982 | 232 | 1,087 | 4.69 |
| 1983 | 199 | 996 | 5.01 |
| 1984 | 186 | 837 | 4.50 |
| 1985 | 200 | 749 | 3.75 |
| 1986 | 205 | 1,066 | 5.20 |
| Average | 168 | 820 | 4.88 |

SOURCE: Author's calculations from the *Vanderbilt Television News Abstracts and Indices*. Figures exclude major presidential and vice presidential candidates in presidential election years, and any seats occupied by more than one person during that calendar year. Major candidates, as defined by Gary King and Lyn Ragsdale, *The Elusive Executive* (Washington: CQ Press, 1988), table 7.3, are those candidates who received more than 0.5 percent of the vote in more than one state or received federal matching funds. Major candidates from the House included John Ashbrook, Shirley Chisholm, and Paul McCloskey in 1972; Morris Udall in 1976; Philip Crane and John Anderson in 1980; and Geraldine Ferraro in 1984. Figures differ slightly from those reported in Timothy E. Cook, "House Members as Newsmakers: The Effects of Televising Congress," *Legislative Studies Quarterly*, vol. 11 (May 1986), table 1, which are derived from the yearly index; these figures are taken from the monthly indexes.

Republican hands, the Democratic House became the site for much-publicized battles over President Reagan's budgets, and more than twice as many members received coverage than had been the case ten years before. Although the high levels fell off, evening news during the Ninety-eighth and Ninety-ninth Congresses covered some 200 members a year.

Once members passed the threshold of visibility, the average number of mentions they received was the same in 1986 as in 1969. After the extraordinary attention in 1974, members' visibility did not simply return to previous levels, but gradually waned through 1978, with only a slight increase in interest following the start of televised floor proceedings in 1979.[55] The

55. Likewise, the number of network stories from the House went up only slightly between 1977 and 1979, but the 1979 stories were longer and more likely to use filmed excerpts. Kaid and Foote, "How Network Television Coverage of the President and Congress Compare," pp. 64–65.

political context of the 1981 budget battles boosted visibility much more than did the televising of proceedings.

How does the growing television presence of House members square with the declining prominence of the institution? Part of the answer lies in the changing techniques of covering the news. In the 1960s, reports were filmed instead of videotaped, and camera equipment was bulky and not easily transported. Consequently, reporting on Congress usually entailed attending a single event such as a committee hearing. Correspondents might introduce a discussion among legislators or an interrogation of a witness and would reappear—frequently they were not seen at all—only with the tag-line close. In recent years, however, the sound bites, which have been shortened (ostensibly to keep the attention of the viewers), are stitched together by the reporter, who is prominently seen and provides the interpretation. Because minicamera video technology enables Washington news to be shot all over town, journalists off the Hill can spice up reports with legislators' reactions, on the floor or elsewhere. In the reports' most extreme form, legislators provide one-second snippets or questions that become part of a collage of commentary, almost in the manner of a Greek chorus. Many more House members are seen, although each appearance means less.[56] And even so, half the members never appear on network evening news.[57]

The evening news is only one outlet among many—morning news shows, call-in shows on C-SPAN, or discussion-format shows such as the "MacNeil-Lehrer News Hour" or ABC's "Nightline." But though these broadcasts have proliferated, House members are not heavily represented. From calculations made by Stephen Hess, only 145 representatives sitting in the Ninety-eighth Congress appeared in such broadcasts from January 1983 to June 1984.[58] Most are simply unable or unwilling to appear on national television news. The proliferation of avenues for exposure has not increased exposure.

56. Compare Edward Jay Epstein, *News from Nowhere: Television and the News* (Random House, 1973); and Daniel C. Hallin, "The Coming of the Ten-Second Sound Bite: Changing Conventions in Television News, 1965–1985," unpublished paper, University of California, San Diego, 1987.

57. Virtually every senator, however, appears sometime during a given year. Timothy E. Cook, "House Members as Newsmakers: The Effects of Televising Congress," *Legislative Studies Quarterly*, vol. 11 (May 1986), table 1.

58. Unpublished data provided by Stephen Hess from the Senate Republican Conference's "Network Roundup," a survey of the guest lists of the previous day's broadcasts; see Hess, *Ultimate Insiders*, pp. 17–18.

TABLE 3-2. Number of Mentions and Percent of Total on
Network Evening News, by Member Classification, 1969–86

| Year | Party leaders[a] Number | Percent | Committee leaders[b] Number | Percent | Candidates for office[c] Number | Percent | All others Number | Percent |
|------|------|------|------|------|------|------|------|------|
| 1969 | 133 | 23.2 | 128 | 22.3 | 26 | 4.5 | 286 | 49.9 |
| 1970 | 117 | 26.5 | 73 | 16.5 | 81 | 18.3 | 171 | 38.7 |
| 1971 | 80 | 17.2 | 151 | 32.4 | 8 | 1.7 | 227 | 48.7 |
| 1972 | 77 | 13.9 | 150 | 27.1 | 36 | 6.5 | 290 | 52.4 |
| 1973 | 110 | 28.5 | 71 | 16.2 | 16 | 3.7 | 241 | 55.0 |
| 1974 | 214 | 12.6 | 458 | 27.0 | 149 | 8.8 | 878 | 51.7 |
| 1975 | 176 | 18.9 | 237 | 17.1 | 42 | 4.5 | 477 | 59.5 |
| 1976 | 235 | 28.3 | 107 | 12.9 | 68 | 8.2 | 420 | 50.6 |
| 1977 | 162 | 20.9 | 167 | 21.5 | 29 | 3.7 | 417 | 53.8 |
| 1978 | 133 | 21.6 | 88 | 14.3 | 51 | 8.3 | 345 | 55.9 |
| 1979 | 120 | 18.1 | 87 | 13.2 | 12 | 1.8 | 442 | 66.9 |
| 1980 | 139 | 16.1 | 171 | 19.8 | 34 | 3.9 | 521 | 60.2 |
| 1981 | 351 | 28.4 | 268 | 21.7 | 33 | 2.7 | 585 | 47.3 |
| 1982 | 329 | 30.3 | 201 | 18.5 | 72 | 6.6 | 485 | 44.6 |
| 1983 | 236 | 23.7 | 199 | 20.0 | 44 | 4.4 | 517 | 51.9 |
| 1984 | 270 | 32.3 | 97 | 11.6 | 64 | 7.6 | 406 | 48.5 |
| 1985 | 229 | 30.6 | 139 | 18.6 | 29 | 3.9 | 352 | 47.0 |
| 1986 | 228 | 21.4 | 216 | 20.2 | 146 | 13.7 | 476 | 44.7 |
| Total | 3,339 | 22.5 | 3,008 | 20.3 | 940 | 6.3 | 7,536 | 50.8 |

SOURCE: Author's calculations from *Vanderbilt Television News Abstracts and Indices.*
a. Includes Speaker, majority and minority leaders, majority and minority whips, and chairs of the Democratic Caucus, the Republican Conference, campaign committees, the Republican Policy Committee, and the Republican Research Committee.
b. Includes chairs and ranking minority members of standing and select committees.
c. Includes candidates for offices such as senator or governor, but not major presidential or vice presidential candidates.

## The Dominance of Leadership

Congress watchers have argued not only that more members can now make news but that backbenchers, especially mavericks, rather than party and committee leaders are the ones who have swelled the numbers. On the other hand, however, leaders might be holding on to their proportion of the expanding coverage by continuing to serve as authoritative sources, even if competition from nonleaders forces them to run harder to stay in the same place. To help examine the ideas, table 3-2 divides members mentioned on television from 1969 to 1986 into four categories: party leaders, committee leaders, candidates for such other offices as senator or governor (but not president or vice president), and all others, which in effect encompasses nonleaders. If backbenchers were more prominent, the leaders' share of mentions should have decreased and the nonleaders' share increased. This does appear to be the case through the 1970s. But after 1980 the trajectories are reversed. Still, nonleaders won considerable television visibility in both decades. Even in the prereform Ninety-first and Ninety-second Congresses, nonleaders who were not candidates for other office received half the mentions in any year. If anything, that percentage declined after 1981.

Party leaders' share of mentions has increased relative to the shares of both committee leaders and nonleaders. Although party leaders were frequently less prominent than committee leaders during the Speakerships of John McCormack and Carl Albert, they generally received more attention after the accession of Tip O'Neill in 1977. All, however, were outnumbered by nonleaders, especially in the Ninety-sixth Congress (1979–80), the first to be televised from the floor and also one dominated by scandals such as Abscam.[59] The impressive expansion of House news in 1981 strengthened the leaders' media presence.

If half the mentions of House members in any year went to those who were neither House leaders nor candidates for higher office, how could party leaders, with a quarter of the mentions, dominate the news? Because there are only eleven of them and forty-five or so committee leaders; the half that goes to the nonleaders is shared among hundreds. The ability of any nonleader to make news on a regular basis is far less than the capacity of any leader to do so.

The dominance of leadership becomes clearer in appendix table B-1, which lists the fifteen most prominent House members on evening network television news for each year from 1969 to 1986. These rankings are so similar to those determined from the New York Times that they seem to be measuring the same phenomena.[60] There are, however, some differences. In some cases, subject matter was too arcane or complex for television. Thus Henry Reuss, a House expert on the economy, was routinely prominent in the Times in the 1970s but was only sporadically visible on television, even after becoming chair of the House Banking and Currency Committee in 1975. More recently, the Times highlighted the slow progress of complex immigration reform proposals in the Ninety-eighth Congress, pushing Romano Mazzoli, the House sponsor of the Simpson-

59. Of the 521 television mentions of noncandidate nonleaders in 1980, those accused of ethical misconduct accounted for 151.

60. For example, in the Ninety-first, Ninety-second, Ninety-fifth, and Ninety-sixth Congresses, the intercorrelations of mentions in the network news and mentions in the New York Times were respectively .55, .73, .73, and .68. Rankings from the Times are available from the author upon request.

Mazzoli bill, to the fore in print but not on the networks. Legislators favored more by the networks than by the *Times* have been those at the height of the dispersion of powers in the House who sought to make news with no base in the institution. Examples include George Hansen, with his quixotic attempt to negotiate with the Iranians holding American hostages in 1979, Richard Nolan and his 1979 campaign to draft Ted Kennedy for president, and Edward Markey, who led the nuclear freeze campaign in 1983. But the networks have sometimes covered leaders more thoroughly.[61] Despite some divergences, then, the newsmakers favored by television news are also favored by the *New York Times*, and neither medium is more or less inclined than the other to cover either leaders or backbenchers.

In each medium, party leaders have become more prominent. Speaker O'Neill and Minority Leader Robert Michel became spokespersons for their parties in the 1980s and achieved a consistently higher profile than their predecessors. Extended party leadership positions, such as majority or minority whip, or chair of the Democratic Caucus or Republican Conference, gained visibility, potentially putting out the leadership's line through a media version of the strategy of inclusion.[62] Committee chairs, prominent newsmakers early in the 1970s, have become less visible, while chairing a subcommittee, which was rarely important in the late 1960s and early 1970s, has become a good way to make news. Those involved in scandals or accused of ethical misconduct also became more newsworthy in the late 1970s but faded through 1986, a rise and fall that was directly tied to the member's role in the House. (The upswing of the scandal story in 1988 and 1989, when those under suspicion included Speaker Wright, Majority Whip Tony Coelho, Minority Whip Newt Gingrich, Democratic Caucus Chair William Gray, and Julian Dixon, the chair of the Committee on Standards of Official Conduct, also suggests scandals are judged important only when newsworthy members become involved.) Finally, enterprising free-lancers who raised their issues and increased their own

61. Thus in the same period, networks were more attentive than was the *New York Times* to Majority Leader Jim Wright in 1978, Minority Leader John Rhodes in 1979, and Minority Leader Robert Michel in 1984.

62. The strategy of inclusion, whereby leadership ranks are expanded to bring in those with potentially independent bases of power, is well portrayed in Barbara Sinclair, *Majority Leadership in the U.S. House* (Johns Hopkins University Press, 1983). Some of this prominence may be due to the inclusion in the leadership of ambitious national figures such as 1988 presidential candidates Jack Kemp (chair of the Republican Conference from 1981 to 1987) and Richard Gephardt (chair of the Democratic Caucus from 1985 to 1989), yet their leadership posts also indicate the value of bringing in those who would be visible on the outside.

prominence regardless of their position in the House are no more common or typical today than they were in the 1970s.[63]

The late 1960s and early 1970s found House members and their leaders at a low ebb in newsworthiness. In the Ninety-first Congress (1969–71), John McCormack, in his last term as Speaker, was indifferent to publicity and made news largely because of a controversy over the bribery indictment of a former staffer that ultimately precipitated his own retirement. When Carl Albert succeeded him, coverage remained much the same; in fact, on the networks in 1971 Albert was far less visible than his majority leader, Hale Boggs. Old-style committee chairs such as Mendel Rivers on Armed Services, Emanuel Celler on Judiciary, and Wilbur Mills on Ways and Means were routinely covered, whether or not they sought publicity. The newsworthiness of committee leadership was even attested to by the continuing saga of Adam Clayton Powell, the flamboyant black former chair of the Education and Labor Committee, who had been denied his seat by the House in 1967 but was reelected in 1968 by his Harlem constituency.

The best way to win visibility without an institutional base was to run for other office. In particular, the 1970 Senate elections attracted considerable attention because of President Nixon's hard campaigning for numerous Republican House members he had persuaded to run. Opportunities for junior members to attract attention within the institution were rare. Subcommittees were not institutionalized, and few had substantive jurisdictions or significant legislative responsibilities. Their chairs were most prominent when the subcommittee was conducting an investigation—as for example in 1969 when William Moorhead, chair of the Government Operations Subcommittee on Foreign Operations and Government Information, disclosed evidence of government deception in the Lockheed affair.

But even these Congresses saw free-lancers gaining coverage. Richard McCarthy made news in 1969 for what was then pointedly termed "his own investigation" of the Defense Department's secret stockpile of biological and chemical weapons.[64] In the Ninety-second Congress the media prominently featured three newly elected representatives. Robert Steele went to Vietnam to investigate drug use among American soliders. Bella Abzug, assisted by her mediagenic collection of wide-brimmed hats, became a lively symbol of contemporary feminism. Les Aspin began sending

63. The term *free-lancer* is that of Burdett Loomis, *The New American Politician: Entrepreneurship, Ambition, and the Changing Face of Political Life* (Basic Books, 1988).

64. "Poisonous Gas Disposal," *CQ Almanac*, vol. 25 (Washington: CQ Press, 1969), p. 799.

out press releases disclosing mismanagement in the Pentagon and received heavy coverage in the *New York Times*. Well before television entered the House, members could use their own resources to gain publicity with virtually no base of power in the institution.

The Ninety-third Congress might represent the watershed of modern coverage of the House as two big stories changed how members and reporters viewed each other. The impeachment proceedings in the Judiciary Committee elevated many otherwise obscure members to prominence and reminded reporters of the possible newsworthiness of the House. Next was the attention given in 1974 to Wilbur Mills's companionship with Argentine stripper Fanne Foxe, particularly after Washington police found her wading in the Tidal Basin, where she had flung herself with Mills in pursuit. Before 1974, reporters noticed House scandals, such as the indictments and convictions of John Dowdy in 1971–72 and Bertram Podell in 1973–74, only after proceedings had begun. Official action is still a prerequisite for coverage, but the criteria have loosened to include an investigation by the House Committee on Standards of Conduct (or a request for one), FBI inquiries, or involvement with the police.[65] Until there are official inquiries, even open secrets in Washington such as Jim Wright's shady financial dealings do not become breaking news.

Mills's fall from power—he resigned the chair of the Ways and Means Committee and underwent treatment at Bethesda Naval Hospital for acute alcoholism—validated scandals as news not because such peccadillos were important per se but because the chair of the House Ways and Means Committee was newsworthy. Scandal stories accentuate rather than undercut journalists' reliance upon leadership, though the stories scarcely reflect well on those leaders. Accounts of ethical misconduct receive more play the higher the accused is in the House hierarchy. So, in 1976 when Wayne Hays, the powerful head of the House Administration Committee and chair of the Democratic Congressional Campaign Committee, became enmeshed in a scandal focusing on his lover, Elizabeth Ray, whom he had hired as a secretary even though she could not type, sex scandals became major House stories. Only then, with the media on alert, did smaller, unrelated incidents gain prominence as part of a continuing story about

65. At this point the dynamic noted by a French journalist can begin: "Scandal in Washington plays out in four acts. First act: rumors and leaks to the press. Second act: the tearful televised confession. Third act: the devastating 'report.' Fourth and final act: exile from power or redemption." François Sergent, "Le syndrome Tower frappe à la Chambre des représentants," *Libération*, April 18, 1989, p. 26 (my translation).

members' misdoings. Thus later that year another scandal involved an obscure first-term Utah Democrat, Allen Howe, who was arrested in Salt Lake City for propositioning a policewoman disguised as a prostitute. The brouhaha made Howe the fourth most prominent House member on evening network news, right behind Hays, retiring Speaker Albert, and Majority Leader O'Neill.[66] Similar scandalmongering occurred in 1989, when conservative Republican Buz Lukens's conviction on contributing to the delinquency of a minor made national headlines as part of the preoccupation touched off by the misbehavior, this time financial, of Speaker Wright and Majority Whip Coelho.

Howe and Lukens notwithstanding, ethics and scandals have never been the good stories they have sometimes been considered, at least unless already newsworthy individuals are implicated. It is true that before Watergate, Fanne Foxe, and Elizabeth Ray, individual scandals might have garnered scant press. Afterward, scandals gained considerable attention: Dan Flood's indictment and trial in 1978–79 on bribery charges, Robert Bauman's arrest for soliciting an underage Washington go-go boy in 1980, or allegations of Charles Wilson's cocaine use in 1983. But all three had elements of already newsworthy stories; both Flood and Bauman had been regarded as important Washington figures, and drug abuse is always a news item. Otherwise, unless the accusations of misconduct occur when a leader has made scandal notable (as in 1976 and 1989), members either remain obscure after allegations surface or they become known in the media only by large conflict-of-interest scandals that involve many offices—the Koreagate investigation into the financial dealings of lobbyist Tongsun Park in 1978, the Abscam bribery stings by the FBI in 1980, and the investigations of sexual liaisons with congressional pages in 1983.

Whether the leaders are involved in favorable or unfavorable events, they have a better chance of making news than the average House member. The rankings for both the networks and the *Times* show no trend toward equal access. If anything, since O'Neill became Speaker, party leaders have been more prominent than they were during McCormack's and Albert's time. Without a post in the House or candidacy for other office, members have become newsworthy only when they have sponsored im-

---

66. Even the *New York Times* coverage placed Howe among the top fifteen. His arrest may have made a good man-bites-dog story, given his Mormonism. For evidence of the extent to which the local media pounced on this story, see Milton Hollstein, "Congressman Howe in the Salt Lake City Media: A Case Study of the Press as Pillory," *Journalism Quarterly*, vol. 54 (Autumn 1977), pp. 454–58 and following.

portant bills, such as the Gramm-Latta budget proposal and the Conable-Hance tax cut in 1981. High-profile free-lancing is no longer effective in winning publicity if the legislator lacks insider credentials.

The sole new boost to coverage in the 1980s was chairing a subcommittee. Before 1981, virtually the only subcommittee chairs that received network coverage were on the House Government Operations Committee investigating misconduct. Similar investigations, of course, may still attract television: James Scheuer's examination of the mishandling of toxic waste cleanup funds in the Environmental Protection Agency and Donald Albosta's investigation into how Jimmy Carter's 1980 debate briefing papers ended up in the hands of the Reagan campaign won both members considerable if fleeting visibility in 1983 despite the obscurity of their posts.[67] More intriguing are the subcommittee chairs that receive attention as powers within policy-oriented committees such as Foreign Affairs, where Michael Barnes and Stephen Solarz became authorities on Central America and the Philippines because of their respective subcommittee posts, and on Energy and Commerce, where Henry Waxman and Timothy Wirth gained exposure through their subcommittees' jurisdictions over, respectively, health and telecommunications. The new prominence of subcommittee chairs is not solely a result of media routines; the chairs have become increasingly important in managing and advocating bills sent to the committee and to the floor.[68]

Doing something out of the ordinary may once have been sufficient to win publicity, but now gaining a subcommittee chair may be a necessary precondition for nonleaders to make national news. Both before and after the reforms that dispersed power within the House, leadership position and seniority have determined visibility.[69] A member's base of operation within the institution has become more crucial in seeking and gaining publicity.

67. Scheuer chaired the Subcommittee on Natural Resources, Agriculture Research and the Environment of the Science and Technology Committee; Albosta chaired the Subcommittee on Human Resources of the Post Office and Civil Service Committee.

68. See Christopher J. Deering, "Subcommittee Government in the U.S. House: An Analysis of Bill Management," Legislative Studies Quarterly, vol. 7 (November 1982), pp. 533–46; and Richard Hall, "Participation and Purpose in Committee Decisionmaking," American Political Science Review, vol. 81 (March 1987), pp. 105–27.

69. Evidence from multivariate equations predicting visibility in the evening news and the New York Times for the Ninety-fifth and Ninety-sixth Congresses is reported in Cook, "House Members as Newsmakers." I have also replicated these results on the Ninety-first and Ninety-second Congresses. In all four, party leadership status and years of service significantly predicted visibility. Member-controlled resources, with the exception of running for other office (and for the Times, liberalism), rarely predicted visibility except in a hit-and-miss manner.

## Localizing
## and Specializing

Media coverage of Congress is full of paradoxes. As attention to the institution has declined, coverage of members has increased. Backbenchers' share of that coverage was highest when the overall membership was least visible. In the 1980s, at the height of the recent prominence of House members, leaders claimed a higher portion of this attention than ever before.

Journalists cover representatives because of, not in spite of, their position in the House. Reporters search for a predictable legislative process and identify important participants most often by their designated position of authority. In today's House, what one does in office seems less important for attracting coverage than who one is.

The news media do not provide many opportunities for House members to gain national publicity. But should we concur with Stephen Hess's conclusion for the Senate, that most members get so little attention that the national media are "irrelevant in affecting their elections or promoting their policies"?[70] Does the leadership dominate the news so much that it would be irrational for backbenchers to try to influence policy through the national media?

Not necessarily. Reporters covering the House exercise considerable leeway in choosing whom to cover. Leadership is not synonymous with publicity, because indicators of importance do not always guarantee interesting news.[71] Nonleaders consistently garner a large part of the attention paid to House members. And though a nonleader is far less likely than a leader to be mentioned, a nonleader may not require much to enable a press strategy to assist a legislative strategy. Even tangential coverage can call attention to an issue and link the member's name with it. One story on the network news or a well-placed mention in the *New York Times* or the *Washington Post* can influence attentive colleagues and others in Washington, or at least start the process moving.

Most members might wish to be generalists, making their marks on a variety of issues, but the size of the House precludes such a role for all but the party leaders and a handful of others. So, just as local journalists' con-

70. Hess, *Ultimate Insiders*, p. 5.

71. Equations predicting media visibility rarely explain more than is unexplained. In statistical terms, either there are other predictor variables to be discovered or the process is subject to considerable randomness.

cern with local matters reinforces members' parochialism, national journalists' search for authoritative sources encourages specialization. Members realize that to make a mark they must concentrate on narrowed topics. But to be able to get into the national news, nonleaders also have to cope with the shrinking coverage of Congress. Enterprising members can no longer expect reporters to be interested in what Congress is doing. Publicity-seeking, then, has to go beyond Capitol Hill. Members may have to latch on to stories that are, in the words of a network reporter, "all over town," the big stories elsewhere in Washington.

The national media thus give mixed signals. On one hand they encourage members to specialize and work up the ladder of the House hierarchy. On the other they push members to be responsive to forces off Capitol Hill that they can ride for stories. Insofar as gaining national attention becomes an important part of wielding influence in Congress, legislators cannot be satisfied with bargaining in some smoke-filled room. But a strategy depending on publicity may not be enough to win much attention if a legislator is not an authoritative source. Those wishing to meld media strategies and legislative strategies must become public insiders, simultaneously playing by the not-always-compatible rules of both the media and Congress.

# 4

# Press Secretaries and Media Strategies

MEDIA STRATEGIES in the contemporary House of Representatives are administered if not decided by a newly important individual in members' offices: the press secretary. Most representatives now have a full-time press assistant on their staff, whereas before the reforms of the 1970s, working with the media was simply one aspect of a generalist's job. The presence of a press secretary is important not merely because it provides another person for dealing with the press but because the position integrates journalistic perspectives into the House office. Just as reporters have become more professionalized through journalism schools, press associations, codes of ethics, and emphasis on individual autonomy and public service, so too have the people they deal with in Washington, who go through standard patterns of recruitment and take up clearly delineated tasks. More precisely, the position of press secretary can best be understood as a boundary role between politicians and reporters, much like political consultants in election campaigns and public information officers in federal bureaucracies.[1] House press secretaries, while employed by and directly accountable to House members, have many affinities with reporters, and their consequent dual loyalty serves to tie government and the media more closely together.

1. The concept of boundary role is taken from Jay G. Blumler and Michael Gurevitch, "Politicians and the Press: An Essay on Role Relationships," in Dan D. Nimmo and Keith R. Sanders, eds., *Handbook of Political Communication* (Beverly Hills: Sage Publications, 1981), p. 485.

71

## The Professionalizing of Press Secretaries

The position of press secretary, at least as an explicitly designated post, has evolved from a luxury in the early 1970s to a commonplace component of most members' staffs. As the numbers of staff people soared in the past twenty years, offices became miniature enterprises that are now the most basic subunits of Congress.[2] Today's House office is divided into jobs with precise tasks: legislative assistant, legislative correspondent, computer operator, caseworker, press secretary.

Of course, merely naming someone press secretary is not necessarily a sign of a sophisticated press operation. Nor does failing formally to assign press responsibilities mean that no one performs these functions. Still, a formal designation is far from irrelevant. The irregular and informal production of news, continually redefined by newsmaker and reporter, can become a more stable and manageable process. The existence of the position also establishes newsworthiness as a central criterion for decisionmaking in a House office; after all, a press secretary is there to be used.

From 1970 to 1986 the number of House members designating a press secretary increased rapidly (table 4-1). These are conservative estimates, since surveys reveal that virtually every office has someone responsible for press relations. Eighty-four percent of House offices listed no person with press responsibilities in 1970; only 24 percent did so in 1986. This growth was propelled primarily by new generations of House members vigorously using the new perquisites of office, but even members who had already accumulated seniority added press assistants to their staffs.[3] The ascent of the press secretary is not merely the product of a new batch of media-conscious newcomers; it is a reaction at all levels to resources made generally available and to the presence of the news media in the contemporary political world.

Nearly all of these press secretaries are based in the Washington offices.

2. See Burdett A. Loomis, "The Congressional Office as a Small (?) Business: New Members Set Up Shop," *Publius*, vol. 9 (Summer 1979), pp. 35–55; and Robert H. Salisbury and Kenneth A. Shepsle, "U.S. Congressman as Enterprise," *Legislative Studies Quarterly*, vol. 6 (November 1981), pp. 559–76.

3. Richard Born shows that new members replacing retirees were significantly more likely to add a press assistant than were holdovers, and that the proportion of the latter with a designated press secretary consistently but slowly grew from 1960 to 1976. "Perquisite Employment in the U.S. House of Representatives, 1960–1976," *American Politics Quarterly*, vol. 10 (July 1982), table 1.

TABLE 4-1. Press Secretaries Listed in House Offices, Selected Years, 1970–86

| Staff arrangement | 1970 | 1972 | 1974 | 1976 | 1978 | 1980 | 1982 | 1984 | 1986 |
|---|---|---|---|---|---|---|---|---|---|
| Person listed only as press secretary in Washington | 54 | 92 | 135 | 148 | 185 | 197 | 226 | 245 | 243 |
| Person listed as press secretary with other responsibilities in Washington | 2 | 6 | 17 | 29 | 31 | 29 | 32 | 47 | 45 |
| More than one person listed with press responsibilities in Washington | 3 | 3 | 4 | 3 | 6 | 4 | 7 | 6 | 15 |
| One press person in Washington and one press person in district | 1 | 3 | 5 | 4 | 1 | 6 | 1 | 1 | 4 |
| One or more press persons in district, none in Washington | 9 | 9 | 11 | 16 | 19 | 20 | 15 | 13 | 16 |
| No listed press person | 366 | 322 | 283 | 235 | 193 | 179 | 154 | 123 | 112 |

SOURCES: *Congressional Staff Directories*, 1970–86.

Even though the most common customers for House members' news are the local media, the press secretaries are not farmed out to the district, as are some staffers, such as caseworkers, whose work is judged as necessary but onerous.[4] Press secretaries are not only common but apparently valued. Despite a fair amount of variation, their average salaries are exceeded only by the big guns in House offices: administrative assistants, chief district representatives, and chief legislative assistants. Thus in 1984 the average press secretary made around $26,000, compared with the average House office salary of $22,761.[5]

In some ways the press secretaries are much like the typical Capitol Hill staffer. To judge from my survey of 124 Democratic press secretaries, they tend to be young men, unmarried and highly educated.[6] They are also locals, with 59 percent of them coming from the same state and 35 percent from the same district as the representative for whom they work. Like most House staffers, they are not permanent congressional bureaucrats; on average, those surveyed had been on the job a little more than two years. But they differ from other House staffers by their professionalism. They spend

4. See John R. Johannes, *To Serve the People: Congress and Constituency Service* (University of Nebraska Press, 1984), pp. 63–73.

5. Burdett A. Loomis and others, *Setting Course: A Congressional Management Guide* (American University, 1984), pp. 208–09.

6. In the survey, 64 percent were male; the average age was 31; only 33 percent were married; and all but 3 percent had graduated from college, with 42 percent having done some sort of graduate work.

most of their time on press-related matters; they estimated only 36 percent is taken up by other functions. Most also had previous journalistic experience; 48 percent had worked for newspapers or magazines, 27 percent had been employed in broadcasting, and 32 percent in public relations or advertising. Only 26 percent had not worked in any of these fields. In addition, 41 percent had majored in journalism in college. In short, most press secretaries have experience working with the people who are sometimes considered their adversaries—a pattern of recruitment that distinguishes them from their fellow staffers and provides them with different insights and understandings of the job to be done.[7]

These raw figures hide wide variations among offices. To study what press secretaries do, and how that is linked to the contexts and goals of House members and their offices, I interviewed a representative sample of forty House press secretaries from both parties and administered a questionnaire through the auspices of the Association of House Democratic Press Assistants (AHDPA) that received 124 valid responses. (Further discussion of the samples and the interviewing techniques appears in appendix A). Press secretaries are useful sources for understanding the media operations of an office. Choosing to focus on the post was prompted initially by the lack of knowledge about the role itself. While their responses cannot be surrogates for those of their bosses, they do reveal the offices' goals and priorities. Moreover, most members rely on press secretaries' expertise so much that these aides' responses to interviews and surveys provide straightforward information on the activities they pursue, perceptions of their media operations, and the strategies preferred by those working most closely with reporters on a routine basis.[8]

A day in the life of most press secretaries begins as early as breakfast. They may get rolling by reading the *Washington Post* or the *New York Times* in search of ideas for statements or staged events. Once they arrive

7. In 1977 press secretaries were considerably less likely than other staffers to have had previous Hill experience. Although David W. Brady concludes that the more important the staff position, the more important it is for that staffer to have Hill experience, this complements the argument that the skills brought to the press secretary post are those from off the Hill. See "Personnel Management in the House," in Joseph Cooper and G. Calvin Mackenzie, eds., *The House at Work* (University of Texas Press, 1981), p. 156.

8. Susan Heilmann Miller came to similar conclusions in 1975 from interviews with members and staffers. "Members relied on their aides to handle virtually all of their media contacts. Therefore, it is aides, rather than members, who constitute the appropriate subjects for interviews about the nature of media-Congress relationships, the understandings that exist, and the techniques that are employed in exchanging information." "Congress and the News Media: Coverage, Collaboration and Agenda-Setting," Ph.D. dissertation, Stanford University, 1976, pp. 8–9.

at the office, a press release may be set to go out and last-minute information may need to be added, cleared, and checked before hundreds of copies are mimeographed. Next comes telephoning the usual contacts for hometown news outlets (whether in the district or in Washington) and scurrying around Capitol Hill to drop off stacks of releases at the various press galleries. After that they may escort their representatives down to the recording studio to rehearse and tape a cable television show or over to the "swampside" area in front of the Capitol for a stand-up interview (the aides themselves are often the ones asking the questions) to be beamed by satellite back to their districts by their party's House campaign committee. Press secretaries are often responsible, too, for redrafting op-ed pieces and speeches written by the member or by staffers. Aides may have to squeeze in other activities—thinking up ideas and possible formats for the next postal patron newsletter, for mail targeted to specific groups in the district, or for the weekly newspaper column—between answering reporters' telephone inquiries or meeting with them as they make their rounds. And then there is always a fast-accumulating pile of district papers to be clipped for the boss's portfolio. Of course, as soon as matters seem under control, something happens that is either a ripe opportunity for generating publicity or cries out for aides to call and urge reporters to follow up, and the endless attempts to manage the work load begin anew.

Press secretaries' responsibilities vary from office to office, but most would agree with the job description that one press assistant composed (see appendix C). Amid the multiplicity of tasks, however, the heart of the job is what one aide termed the "care and feeding of the media." Not only must they feed journalists with information and releases, but they must take care that the relationship prospers.

### Dual Loyalties

Press secretaries are no longer journalists, but they have not left their training and experience behind. Although one aide confided, "Having been an observer, I wanted to see if I could be a manipulator," most of those interviewed were not fully comfortable with their new roles and anxious not to be portrayed as flacks. There is bound to be strain as they find themselves pushing releases, events, and stories with marginal news content, which they must do because, given the competition for coverage, their job consists much more of trying to get the members' names in the news than keeping them out of it. But if they serve as representatives' ambassadors to the press, they must also plead the media's case in the House office. "The press aide walks a fine line," said the press secretary to a four-term Republican. "He has to maintain credibility with the press *and* with the congressman. . . . I've got to please everybody."

Few press secretaries see their relationship with reporters as fundamentally adversarial. House offices emphasize cooperation more than opportunism, so that an exchange relationship evolves in which officials get publicity and reporters get copy. This symbiosis is not a deliberate agreement to trade favors; instead, it grows out of the continuing needs for both journalist and source to produce news. Maintaining a long-term relationship may override temptations on the part of either reporter or official to make news that could jeopardize this mutual understanding. Reporters take care not to cover their authoritative sources too frankly for fear of losing their access; officials seek to facilitate the reporter's job by providing information that can indeed be considered newsworthy, and in a timely, concise manner. The press secretary to a senior Eastern committee chair noted, "Anyone can know about deadlines. But you must have respect for the press. . . . The best advice I ever got is always to think of the reporter and what would make their job easier—would you write for this story or cover this event? You have attention for a mutually beneficial relationship, not an adversarial one."

Press secretaries' comments that they write a press release as they would write a story must be generously discounted, given that the point of a release is not accuracy so much as showing the representative in a good light. Still, being aware of the needs of reporters can be crucial to getting as much coverage as possible on the most favorable terms possible. One press secretary to a five-term New England Democrat moved the boss's name out of the first headline and the first paragraph of a press release altogether; though the member protested, his demotion facilitated the verbatim publication of the release as if it were hard news. "There's the temptation to do something making us look good this week," a press secretary to a senior Southern Democrat commented. "But all that [members] have is their word and reputation with journalists and other members. If you blow that, it's done. . . . We feed [reporters] tips and we try to get the story out *and* to make friends. You may have a story that isn't as important to them as it is to you—and you get more from them if you're nicer to them."

Although press secretaries do their best to get as much coverage as possible, reporters must be convinced of the member's newsworthiness. So aides will sometimes fall back on marketing, emphasizing the legislator's good points and playing down drawbacks, all in terms of journalistic priorities. A press secretary, with a public relations background, to a three-term Southern Democrat seeking statewide visibility presented the analogy this way:

> Some stations don't want to carry something canned. You have to antic-ipate news—if there's an issue we can get the jump on. In advertising school, we learned about the unique selling point of a product—the one characteristic that separates your product from the rest. . . . I con-centrate on the one thing that [X] has which the [state] delegation doesn't have—what things he can do that will get him exclusive cover-age. Like a bill coming out of his committee, or if he chaired the hear-ing on the topic, that can be mentioned right away in the lead para-graph or we can get a media interview.

Despite the conspiratorial sound, proper marketing requires an awareness of the audience. Some marketing can reach voters through newsletters and targeted mail, but the media are no unobstructed conduit. Marketing the member must then take into account how to make reporters receptive to providing coverage.

"I'd rather miss a press opportunity than antagonize the press. . . . It's a soft process, not a hard sell," commented the press aide to a three-term Eastern Republican. The work must not only get publicity today but en-sure that reporters return tomorrow. Some of this necessitates reaching out. Several aides spoke of "schmoozing" with reporters to keep them aware of the member. Others answered questions unrelated to the member's work in hopes that the favor would eventually be returned. The press secretary to a freshman Midwestern Democrat said, "The ideal situation is to have the press call you, to have them *want* to call you. If I didn't have to write releases enough because *they* called *me*, I'd be doing my job. Sure, it'd be nice if they printed my releases verbatim; I always get a charge when I see my work in print. But it's not my objective to get it printed but to generate interest."

A press aide's primary loyalty, like those of most House staffers, is of course necessarily to the member. But this sensitivity to the needs of the media and the pressures from reporters make the position so different from others that one should ask how well integrated into the enterprise are the press secretaries and the presswork they pursue.

As some press secretaries realize, their job requires more versatility than most other staff positions. They must know the issues receiving attention within the office to describe them effectively to the press. Thus they frequently become involved not merely in publicizing what has already been decided but in determining what the office's efforts will be. Media strategies are not then an afterthought to legislative strategies; they are often intimately connected. Press secretaries play a valuable part in shaping strategies by bringing the journalistic perspective to bear during decisions. The concern about how to win media coverage influences what legislative course to take. As one press secretary to a five-term Western Democrat noted, "Reporters hate it when called in on a story which is in fact a nonstory. . . . The press secretary is to all intents and purposes an editor, deciding the basis on which releases are made or press conferences scheduled." Whether press secretaries term themselves the "no-man" or the devil's advocate, their anticipation of media reaction to a proposed initiative promotes the media's idea of worthiness.

Press secretaries often have to educate fellow staffers on the methods and preferences of the press. Sometimes this task involves cautioning them to avoid glutting the media with too many releases and losing credibility with reporters. At other times the press aide encourages greater aggressiveness, such as urging recalcitrant members to start using the opportunities they have. The lessons are different, but in either case the House offices achieve a greater awareness of the needs and interests of the news media that potentially translates into a symbiosis of newsmakers and newswriters.

Above all, just as journalists' reliance on routines shapes the final news product, so does the routine relationship between newsmaker and newswriter on Capitol Hill. Press secretaries have to meet unpredictable and wide-ranging demands of both national and local journalists, usually single-handedly. Like all laborers, they seek to make their work loads as manageable as possible. So isolated chances to increase a member's visibility, such as can occasionally be achieved when network news uses clips from televised House debates, are not highly valued if they do not help manage a routine. Press secretaries are more interested in what makes reporters more receptive to future news from and about the member, and that is usually summed up by credibility.

### The Search for Credibility

House offices' media strategies assume that, for reporters to follow through, members must be seen as providing a reliable newsworthy product, especially by the editors and producers who pass judgment on the quality of reporters' work. At home, a representative's activity can provide a local angle, but such local reporting is not automatic. As the press aide to a junior Midwestern Republican noted, "There's the problem of what the media force you to do. There's pressure to go do something, maybe to undo it. . . . They won't cover you just for being there." So representatives interested in local attention must either pepper their comments on national issues with references to their districts or focus on parochial matters such as post office closings, federal grant applications, and the like.

Establishing credibility is more delicate with the national reporters, who can easily turn elsewhere for sources. If a relationship is to be achieved, a legislator must claim to be an authoritative source on the issue at hand. Press secretaries do not consider this authority easy to establish unless the legislator has verifiable signs of expertise, such as a committee post. In the absence of a post, other legitimating titles, roles, and activities must be pulled out of the hat. The cochair of the Pro-Life Caucus circulating a release on abortion or the prominent sponsor of a proposal seeking to stop the closing of military bases is unlikely to point out to the press that committee assignments have nothing to do with the topic. Occasionally, members do become spokespersons without the cachet provided by a House position, but the media's probable lack of interest in a member without some official institutional base makes press secretaries chary of trying such promotion.

Sometimes, a press secretary realizes that a member has little credibility or newsworthiness. Press aides to freshman members generally agreed that there was little point in wooing national correspondents until their bosses were better positioned to make news. Staffers to more senior members concurred that their bosses' credibility could be damaged by seeking publicity on issues on which they could not be regarded as authoritative sources. Some issues are considered more natural sources of credibility, usually those their bosses examine in their committees. Of course, they realize that once credibility has been established, it can become self-reinforcing; press attention confirms a role of "someone in a position to know," both among congressional colleagues and among other reporters. A press aide to a two-term California Republican sighed, "It's so much easier when you're seen as plugged in." How plugged in—and on what issue—can be in part a product of a media strategy, provoking coverage that reinforces its own judgments as reporters continue to turn to the same sources.

Such credibility extends only to those matters that seem related to a member's expertise, even if the connections are tenuous. A bemused press secretary to a representative who built a name on nuclear arms control issues noted, "We've gotten questions on anything to do with anything nuclear—the MX missile, nuclear energy, reacting to *The Day After*, the death of Buckminster Fuller. We even got onto Phil Donahue on Grenada. . . . Once you're on track, you have to work hard to get off." Reporters' tendencies to ask about a limited range of subjects encourage members to specialize. Press secretaries attempt to link a member with an issue, so that when and if the issue becomes prominent, the reporters will turn to that member. But they recognize that members stand out most convincingly when their positions in the House boost their credibility.

### Punching Up the Product

A member's institutional importance is crucial to power, but to become a newsmaker he or she must also be interesting. Press secretaries who want to win additional publicity for their bosses must remind them of the demands on journalists. Instead of restraining legislators and fellow staffers from pursuing the press too aggressively, some press secretaries must take the product they have and punch it up to make it more attractive. The reasons are many: "He's not a very good politician; he's more of a statesman, and he opens his mouth when he's got something to say." "He's not a headline grabber." "He's not comfortable with talking on his feet." "He's mediocre at hyping something." "He doesn't talk in quotes."

Punching up the product often involves accustoming politicians to television. But retraining pols can reach comic levels. One press assistant to a freshman Western Democrat reviewed videotapes of the member's television appearances and provided lengthy comments: "Once I told him, 'Don't look into the lights; it makes you squint.' The producer said, 'What did she say?' and when I told him, he said, 'Great! Good for you!' Because otherwise it makes it look like he's got something to hide. On the average, I write down about eight pages of notes per activity—phrases said improperly, bad English, bad concepts. And I prompt him to smile; it gets rid of his deep-set eyes." Coaching may meet resistance, and pseudoevents may have to be arranged to help the member get practice. The press secretary to a Western Republican noted, "With all the people I've worked for, it's been a constant battle to educate them on the impact of television. . . . Since last November, we've had four joint press conferences. It's a good way of getting his feet wet."

Reeducation goes beyond teaching legislators to be comfortable in front of microphones and cameras. Punching it up can apply equally to teaching conciseness to politicians more inclined to speak in pages than paragraphs, let alone ten-second sound bites. "I've gotta remind him to keep his sentences short," said an aide to one would-be intellectual Republican.

"On some things, reporters say, 'I can't cut that tape.' One job I've got is to take his thoughts and put it in a phraseology attractive to a reporter. . . . Reporters want that, they need the copy. So I've got to say, 'Joe, are you saying this?' And he says yes or no. Then you get it short, you get the hit."

## Local and National Newsmaking

Press secretaries' jobs gain much of their complexity from the diversity of the press corps they face. After all, as both national and local politicians, members of Congress are in an anomalous, often frustrating situation. They may perceive their main job as legislating on national policy, but the demands of the district pull them toward more parochial and less interesting work. Consequently, members spend much of their time trying to win leeway from constituency concerns, a task that becomes both more pressing and more onerous as their legislative responsibilities in Washington increase. And since their seats do not become automatically safe after a few elections, incumbents cannot stop worrying about reelection and spend their full time working in Washington.[9]

Few are more aware of the disjuncture than the press secretaries, who must deal with the divergent needs of national and local media. Separate strategies must be developed for the two, and given the limited time and resources available to media operations, an office may have to choose between focusing attention on one or the other. How do members and their press secretaries decide?

First, House members and their staffers might find local outlets fairer than the relatively tough national ones. Michael Robinson, for example, has argued, "One of the more widely shared opinions on Capitol Hill is that the local media behave less 'seriously,' less 'aggressively' and less 'sensationally' than the national media. . . . Members also tend to define the nationals as 'hostile' and the locals as 'gentlemanly.' "[10] According to Robinson, national coverage has been more negative and unfriendly since the

9. Robert S. Erikson, "Is There Such a Thing as a Safe Seat?" *Polity*, vol. 8 (Summer 1976), pp. 623–32; Richard F. Fenno, Jr., *Home Style: House Members in Their Districts* (Little, Brown, 1978); and Thomas E. Cavanagh, "The Two Arenas of Congress," in Cooper and Mackenzie, eds., *Congress at Work*, pp. 56–77.

10. Michael J. Robinson, "Three Faces of Congressional Media," in Thomas E. Mann and Norman J. Ornstein, eds., *The New Congress* (Washington: American Enterprise Institute, 1981), pp. 76–77.

advent of the investigative reporting that became fashionable following the Watergate scandal. If local news organizations are perceived as more open, fair, and cordial, House offices may gravitate toward them.

Regardless of how friendly the members may consider them, local media might simply be more accessible. Most legislators do not matter much to national journalists, but a representative who can emphasize a local angle can achieve attention back home. Because districts vary in their access to local media, however, some members can dominate a newspaper circulation area or a television market while others remain almost as anonymous as they are to network television—in which case they may as well spend their resources wooing the national news outlets.

Finally, national and local media may serve different uses. Although in the 1970s some scholars assumed members of Congress were "single-minded seekers of reelection," more recent observers have concluded they are not seeking any one thing.[11] House members pursue reelection, good public policy, influence in Washington, and nurturing their own ambition. The values they accord to national and local publicity depend on the mix of these motives.

### The Primacy of Local Media

In the questionnaire, I asked the press secretaries to rank, on a scale from one to ten (highest), the utility of various media outlets and media strategies (table 4-2). The highest values, on the average, were awarded to home district newspapers, especially dailies. Local television news was rated slightly less highly. National print and electronic media were rated significantly less useful, although press secretaries disagreed more about their value.

Similar results emerged from interviews. Frequently, the press aides mentioned nothing about the newspapers of record or television network news until I asked whether the national outlets help in getting the job done. The responses were often incredulous, some aides indicating specifically that nobody in their district reads the *Washington Post* or the *New York Times*. Only one disagreed with the statement I encountered early on:

11. Compare David R. Mayhew, *Congress: The Electoral Connection* (Yale University Press, 1974), p. 5; and Richard L. Hall, "Participation and Purpose in Committee Decision Making," *American Political Science Review*, vol. 81 (March 1987), pp. 105–27.

TABLE 4-2. Press Secretaries' Evaluations of the Effectiveness of
Media Outlets and Strategies[a]

| Outlet | Mean | Standard deviation | Outlet | Mean | Standard deviation |
|---|---|---|---|---|---|
| Local dailies | 9.0 | 1.5 | Recording studio | 4.9 | 2.9 |
| Local weeklies | 8.2 | 2.0 | Weekly columns | 4.8 | 3.2 |
| Press releases | 8.1 | 1.8 | *Washington Post* | 4.7 | 3.1 |
| Newsletters | 7.8 | 2.0 | Network television news | 4.4 | 3.2 |
| Local television news | 7.4 | 2.6 | *New York Times* | 4.3 | 3.1 |
| Targeted mail | 6.7 | 2.7 | Televised floor | | |
| Radio actualities | 5.6 | 3.3 | proceedings | 3.8 | 2.7 |

SOURCE: Calculated by author from Democratic press secretaries' questionnaire.
a. Number greater than 120. Descending order of value (ten highest).

"We'd rather get in [the hometown paper] than the front page of the *New York Times* any day." Even press secretaries of members pursuing national visibility agreed. As the aide to a senior Southern Democrat said, "You have to lay the groundwork—every house's got to have a good foundation, every tree's got to have a good stump."

The orientation toward local news outlets should not be surprising except perhaps in its unanimity.[12] Beyond the fact that other aspects of press secretaries' jobs, such as preparing newsletters and directing targeted mail, all focus on the district, the local press can provide crucial information and images to complement direct communications. So if the press secretary must answer a pile of telephone messages, the local reporter will get called back first. Part of the reason is the primacy of reelection. "Unless it's for a specific purpose, like getting a bill through Congress, we don't worry about the national media," the press aide to a senior Eastern Republican said. "It's nice for [X's] ego. But he's not here to become a senator, he's not here to run for president. Periodically, someone comes to Congress who doesn't understand where their bread is buttered—the national media doesn't mean a damn back in the district."

Yet few members are so suspicious of national journalists that they would discourage attention from them. When asked whether local reporters are fairer to members than the national correspondents, 59 percent of press secretaries neither agreed nor disagreed; only 26 percent agreed. Another survey of press secretaries in 1981–82 showed 21 percent rating the

12. The member's reelection is the goal that all House offices share. Consequently, on a scale of 1 to 10, with 10 being high, building name recognition was 8.4; by contrast, becoming spokesperson on an issue of national importance was 6.3, constituent liaison 5.3, creating a national constituency for an issue 5.2, and progressive ambition 4.9.

national media as fairer, 24 percent rating the district media as fairer, and the remainder reporting no difference.[13]

Some press secretaries are suspicious of the national media, considering them uninformed and uninterested in an accurate account of either the member or the district. One aide to a three-term Midwestern Republican admitted becoming gun shy of the national press after a two-minute phone call from a well-known columnist led to an article depicting the poverty of the district. That experience was echoed by the press aide to a two-term Southern Democrat: "The national media just aren't familiar with [the situation], can't just move into the district and report it. The local media are already savvy about local issues . . . so the local nuances are picked up. You run the risk of being criticized by the national media and then having your opponents use this information." Others felt that being visible nationally implicitly distances the member from district concerns in the minds of constituents. "I'm not sure [network news] can help but I think it can hurt," said the aide to a freshman Democrat. "What the network news does to news is something like what the big screen does to TV movies—it's larger than life, it's not the same story."

However, a number of press secretaries considered the national media fair, informed, and ready to present a positive portrait. One aide to a senior Southern Republican pointed out, "The local media expect you to run around and do all the work for them; they don't know what the bill is or how something gets done." Several also suggested that national visibility can convince constituents of the member's importance. An appearance on a network program might receive a greater reaction back home than if the member had been covered by a local television station. Even attention from national newspapers or magazines, which normally goes unnoticed by constituents, can help press aides win points back home. A senior Southern Democrat's press secretary whose boss was quoted in a variety of national newspapers was able to package a portfolio to show in the district: "Then you've got a guy out on Route 3 in Kazoo City who reads where his congressman is in the Washington Post and U.S. News. . . . If it starts at the local level, there's a one-in-a-million chance of trickling up. But at the national level, there's a big chance of trickling down." This trickling down is abetted by the attentiveness of local and wire service reporters to national coverage, especially to papers of record that provide cues on newsworthiness.

13. Robert E. Dewhirst, "Patterns of Interaction between Members of the U.S. House of Representatives and Their Home District News Media," Ph.D. dissertation, University of Nebraska, 1983, p. 142.

Press secretaries prefer to have attention from both local and national media. The staffer who coined the phrase about preferring the local daily was quick to add, "Obviously, we salivate any time we can get on the networks." But dealing with both is seldom simple, because local and national media definitions of newsworthiness diverge.[14] A press release on the award of a highway improvement project, for instance, might be spectacularly effective with a local paper but would easily be dismissed as parochial by a national reporter. A House member's participation in inside baseball might be grist for the mill of the "Washington Talk" page of the *New York Times* or the "Style" section of the *Washington Post* but would be considered inconsequential by the reporters back home. Most important, even if the member is newsworthy to both, the national media's needs deemphasize a member's personal role in favor of the issue or controversy. After all, national news can often get covered without attention to the member who addresses the issue or convenes the hearing. The press secretary to a senior Southern Democrat on Appropriations summed up,

Anybody who calls, we'll call back, whether it's a high school newspaper or NBC. We don't often go to [the national media] and say "We've got a story for you." Stories of national significance deal with his bills, and they're coming to us, so we don't need to. [Q: Do they help in your job?] If it's positive coverage, yeah. But they tend to focus on his legislation, his appropriation rather than on him.

The national media are, then, not closely attended to by most legislators because their interest in a member is unpredictable, likely to be short-lived, and may not result in a story that attributes its sources. If press secretaries must see that their bosses get covered routinely in as many media as possible with as personal a press as possible, the national media provide uncertain prospects. "The frustration is greater on the national level," one aide to a senior Southern Democrat commented. "Everything we want to get on the local media, we can get in. It's a lot tougher to get [the nationals] interested in you and . . . in what you're doing. You can put in a tremen-

14. Donald R. Matthews documented this phenomenon in the 1950s. "To send the same kinds of stories to reporters operating on the two different levels of reporting can result in loss of confidence by both kinds of reporters in the senator's news sense and the downgrading of the importance attached to all future releases. . . . Most of them learn what is 'news' and how to make it. In other words, they behave in accordance with the reporters' expectations." *U.S. Senators and Their World* (University of North Carolina Press, 1960), p. 204.

dous amount of work, and then something uncontrollable can happen, and all your work goes down the chute."

### Pursuing the National Media

Why then would members have any interest in national media visibility at all? The answer: they have goals in addition to reelection. An effective press operation can help a member achieve not only reelection but also public policy expertise and influence in the House and in Washington. Legislators can take advantage of the fact that national newspapers and network television provide crucial information on what is going on in the House, in Washington, in the nation, among the public, and in the world.[15]

The national media can be especially important to members because they influence the legislative process. They can determine which issues receive the most attention. They can also establish how an issue should be best understood. Finally, they can boost a legislator's reputation as someone worth paying attention to. Such visibility may, of course, be helpful in running for higher office, but the attention can also advance a member's policy agenda. As the press secretary to a prominent House Republican noted, "Promoting the ideas is the same as promoting him. Even a personality column mentions ideas."

Through the media, House members may introduce proposals for which they can act as authoritative sources. They can seek reputations that can eventually be translated into influence within the institution. Attention from the press can mobilize outside groups, further boosting coverage—a bandwagon effect that can become even more pronounced as other elected officials join the crowd.

Despite press secretaries' general awareness that national media attention can be a potent legislative tool, not many see their work as directly involving them in legislative strategies. Even those who spoke highly of the opportunities for publicity often had other payoffs in mind—the trickle down of general name recognition to local press or preparation for a possible statewide candidacy. Since press secretaries are already working full-time, the constant distraction of the local media undercuts efforts to construct a national strategy. Still, fifteen of the forty press secretaries interviewed—seven among Republicans and eight among Democrats—spon-

---

15. Even in the clubbish, personalized Senate of the 1950s, Donald Matthews found senators turning to the media to find out what they, as a body, were doing. *U.S. Senators and Their World*, p. 206.

taneously noted the utility of the news media in the legislative process, a sizable minority that in time should grow.

## Who Deals with the National Media?

Although the impact of media strategies on legislative strategies will be evaluated later, it is worth asking now which House offices find the national media useful. First, it must be understood that members have unequal access to national and local outlets. Those characteristics that might make a member more newsworthy—liberalism, perhaps, or seniority— should increase the utility of national coverage, while competition from other media, occasioned by a close overlap of television markets with the House district, should decrease it. Members' strategies can also mesh with activities they pursue elsewhere in Congress. Those who take positions on many issues or sit on policy-oriented committees, which are traditionally inclined toward more individualistic approaches to policymaking, should find national publicity more valuable, as would younger members, who are presumably more media-conscious.

National coverage may also be made more attractive by strategic considerations. Allocating more of the press secretary's time to press matters or hiring a campaign consultant may indicate a more sophisticated operation that would include pursuing attention from the national outlets. Among the five long-term goals rated by the press secretaries, making the member spokesperson on an issue of national importance and building a national constituency on an issue are highly intercorrelated. Along with ambition, they increase the worth of national media in a congressman's strategy. Finally, those who consider the local media fairer should be less inclined to value the nationals.

Which offices gravitate toward the national media among Democrats? The press secretaries of more liberal Democrats and members of policy committees seem to value attention from the national media more than others (see appendix table A-3). The crux is the importance of the goals of speaking for and building a national constituency for an issue. For press secretaries, then, national media are valuable for helping members pursue goals of national importance. This value, moreover, is not directly conditioned by seniority or the district's media market, conditions beyond the members' direct control. Robinson's argument that press operations consider national news coverage unfair receives no support here. Instead, they are valued because of the different uses they serve—for liberals and policy individualists but above all in advancing the possibility that a member will become spokesperson on a nationally prominent issue.

## The Importance of Being an Authoritative Source

In considering whether to pursue attention from the national media, House press operations must assess whether their bosses want to become authoritative sources on issues that could find a national constituency. As it turns out, those members who want to become spokespersons are likely to find both national news and local television more valuable than newsletters and targeted mail. But having answered this question, another appears: What causes House members' press operations to pursue such goals? Much of this is undoubtedly not susceptible to systematic measurement. Some members, wanting to discuss a locally pertinent issue, may seek out forums that would provoke favorable publicity back home; national attention on this issue may be a pleasant by-product. Claude Pepper's longstanding advocacy of the needs of the elderly, boosted by his years as chair of the House Select Committee on Aging, won immense national publicity both for him and his cause—none of which could have hurt his reelection chances in his Miami district full of retirees. Others may have a pet problem or a pet solution that requires the validation of media attention if it is to rise to the public agenda and become enacted legislation.

More generally, one would expect the more ambitious, the more senior, the younger, the members of policy-oriented committees, and those from competitive media markets to be most likely to want to become an authoritative source. If members are attracted to speaking for an issue in order to win higher office, ambition might play a part. Certain members may also be better placed to become spokespersons. Insofar as seniority enables representatives to devote increasing attention to Washington concerns, it would increase the importance of speaking for an issue. Greater age would dampen it if younger members are less inclined to go along and get along. On the other hand, availability of local media, such as when congressional districts and television markets largely overlap, may distract press secretaries from working on national issues.

The decisions to attempt to become a spokesperson are indeed patterned (see appendix tables A-5 and A-6). In part they reflect particular goals, especially interest in winning higher office. But they also show logical adaptations to conditions. Members with greater seniority deemphasize reelection concerns and become more interested in setting the policy agenda. Media markets that are less competitive provide so much work for press secretaries that there is little time left for national concerns. And youth, as always, permits the dream of political promotion.

House offices overcome the typical indifference to the national media when they emphasize building a national constituency. In the absence of those goals, press secretaries will emphasize dealing with the locals, the sine qua non of House media strategies. Even if the local outlets were not seen as so crucial for getting reelected, they provide the most dependable way to gain favorable, attributed publicity for the member on a day-in, day-out basis. Still, to a growing number of members and their staffs, the national outlets constitute important objects of pursuit. This national publicity is sought not only for its own sake or for advancing the member's career. The importance of becoming an authoritative source says as much. Instead, it is now an important tool in accomplishing policy goals in Congress and Washington.

## Media Strategies in the High-Tech Era

After having determined the balance they seek between national and local news coverage and public relations, House press operations must then decide which medium is best for their message. Strategies that seek national attention do not make many distinctions between major newspapers and television networks; they are equally useful. The varieties of media for reaching local audiences, however, push different members in different directions, depending on which outlets can best present the publicity and how available they are.[16] But contrary to many speculations, local newspapers remain the focus of most House members' media strategies. Although high-technology means of reaching constituents and circumventing the press have gained in popularity, costs and drawbacks prevent them from displacing print. Instead of supplanting attention paid to the press, the growth in such media as cable television has paralleled growth in other forms of self-publicizing. As publicity becomes more important for members, so have *all* the ways to pursue it.

16. In an oblique factor analysis, for example, I found that the rankings for the *Washington Post*, the *New York Times*, evening network news, and televised floor proceedings were explained best by a single factor, while ranking of other outlets and methods, largely aimed at local audiences, were explained by several separate factors. See appendix A.

### The Medium and the Message

The question of which medium press secretaries prefer to get their job done becomes important because each presents information in a necessarily different way, and people seeking publicity must accommodate their activities to fit its priorities. The differences between television and print are particularly important. Although television news programs and newspapers largely concur on newsworthy events, persons, and angles, television news is inevitably more selective and more superficial.[17] As ABC's Sam Donaldson said when covering Capitol Hill in the 1970s, "I spend most of my time telling the audience why I'm having trouble trying to tell them something. . . . In TV you have to reduce the story to the simplest possible terms without crossing the line between fact and nonsense."[18]

Television reports are less anonymous and more immediate than newspaper stories. Sources appear on television not as impersonal quotations but as individuals who can be judged on how they come across. Although much has been made of television's immediacy as a predominantly visual medium, it is more correct to say that it presents several not always complementary kinds of information at the same time—a broadcast without the sound is considerably less comprehensible than one heard but not seen. Still, the visuals give information lacking in print accounts and may provide a different, more vivid, and thus more memorable message.

Without good visuals, stories may be demoted in the lineup or deleted altogether. Conversely, good visuals can make a story more important on television than in a newspaper. When Representatives Dan Mica and Olympia Snowe traveled to the Soviet Union in 1987 to inspect an apparently bugged American embassy, they symbolized their concern by carrying children's magic slates on which they could write notes to each other under electronic surveillance. They captured considerably more attention on television than in the national prestige press, although television attention eventually resulted in some admiring newspaper coverage.

Given the possibilities opened by television, no wonder most portentous critiques of the media focus on their presence and availability. If the search for publicity is dominated by the desire to get on television, press secretaries' strategies should become increasingly susceptible to the needs of reporters attempting to present a coherent, dramatic, and visually appeal-

---

17. For concurrence on newsworthiness, see Herbert J. Gans, *Deciding What's News: A Study of CBS Evening News, NBC Nightly News, Newsweek, and Time* (Pantheon, 1979), pp. 157–62.
18. Quoted in Miller, "Congress and the News Media," p. 33.

ing story. In short, they should have pushed Congress to become less substantive, more personalized, and more inclined toward symbolism.

## Communication at Government Expense

For all the time that aides and their bosses spend wooing the press, they
also have a great many opportunities to communicate directly with audiences in the district and the nation. Technological developments have en-
abled members to take advantage of perquisites of office to send canned
"news," which scarcely relies on reporters at all, through so-called in-
House media.[19] Such high-tech communication at government expense is
commonly portrayed as a very effective device for publicity. As one assessment in *Newsweek* observed: "Scores of congressmen pipe self-serving
cable TV programs to their districts. Another favorite scheme is to video-
tape committee meetings, then transmit by satellite craftily edited 30-
second sound-bites to the local 'Eyewitness News' program. This tech-
nique works particularly well for the more than 150 subcommittee heads
on Capitol Hill, who can show themselves being addressed impressively as
Mr. Chairman."[20] Another observer added, "Except for those congressmen
with national ambitions, senators and representatives are now far less re-
liant on reporters. They once battled with their colleagues for attention
from the press; now, through the marriage of electronic conduits and political privilege, politicians can speak to their audiences directly."[21]

The most venerable congressional perquisite for communicating with
constituents is the franking privilege. By 1984 the number of pieces mailed
from Congress at government expense was almost 925 million annually,
up from 300 million in the early 1970s. Only the strictures of the Gramm-
Rudman-Hollings Act prevented the numbers from topping a billion in

19. I will not discuss replies to constituents' letters, although they were once considered the
crucial means of communication with voters. Insofar as the audience for each letter is one correspondent, it is not a mass-mediated message. Besides, press secretaries are rarely responsible for
answering the mail, which is more often the task of the legislative correspondent, another new
position in House offices.

20. George Hackett and Eleanor Clift, "For Members Only," *Newsweek*, November 14, 1988,
p. 22.

21. Anne Haskell, "Live from Capitol Hill: Where Politicians Use High Tech to Bypass the
Press," *Washington Journalism Review*, vol. 4 (November 1982), p. 48. See also Paul West, "The
Video Connection: Beaming It Straight to the Constitutents," *Washington Journalism Review*, vol.
7 (June 1985), pp. 48–50; and Carol Matlack, "Live from Capitol Hill," *National Journal*, February 18, 1989, pp. 390–94.

1986.[22] Most of what is mailed under the privilege consists of unsolicited communications.[23] Each office may mail up to six four-page newsletters a year to every residence in its district. Virtually every office sends its maximum allotment every year; and if the newsletters are reprinted in newspapers, legislators get twice the mileage from them.

Recently members have discovered a high-technology loophole in these restrictions. Mailings that are mass-produced but individually addressed are exempt. The computerization of House offices in the late 1970s permitted the massive use of computer-generated letters aimed at constituents sharing a given interest. If something should happen on Capitol Hill that might be noteworthy (or perhaps if the member should make something happen), an update can be quickly sent to all constituents who wrote to the member about the issue. Sometimes separate responses are drafted for those who are for and those who are against some proposal or position. Mailing lists may be built by including with the postal patron newsletter a form on which constituents can check off issues of interest. Publicity operations can also borrow or buy lists of names from government sources (licensed drivers, registered voters, veterans) or interest groups and lobbyists (dentists, environmentalists, those against abortion). From these lists categories of constituents are isolated and sent "for your information" updates on a rotating basis to make sure that as many as possible get a specialized mailing focusing on their particular interest at least once a year.

Since the late 1950s, representatives have also had access to the facilities of the House recording studio, which has seen increasing use, particularly by junior House members.[24] Because the studio is heavily subsidized, the cost of taping is far lower than commercial rates. In the mid-1980s the

22. There are some restrictions, which are overseen by the Commission on Congressional Mailing Standards, better known as the Franking Commission. Newsletters may not be sent sixty days before an election and franked letters may not be used for fundraising. Unofficial communications such as birthday cards are no longer permitted, and personal references are rationed in newsletters. See Stephen E. Frantzich, *Write Your Congressman: Constituent Communications and Representation* (Praeger, 1986), pp. 26–27. For volume figures, see Norman J. Ornstein, Thomas E. Mann, and Michael J. Malbin, *Vital Statistics on Congress, 1987–1988* (Washington: CQ Press, 1987), table 6-8.

23. I have found no estimate for the House, but the somewhat less constantly constituency-oriented Senate provides a baseline. Charles Mathias told his Senate colleagues in March 1985, "If we answered every single constituent communication, we would still be talking about 3 or 4 percent of the total [outgoing] mail. . . . Another 4 percent is committee–related. . . . Ninety-two percent is what we generate on our own." *Congressional Quarterly Weekly Report*, October 19, 1985, p. 2109.

24. Robinson, "Three Faces of Congressional Media," p. 63.

Democratic and Republican campaign committees got into the act, becoming "full-service broadcast bureaus for members," who are able to produce tapes in their studios and beam them back to the district via satellite.[25] The expansion of cable television has allowed many members to furnish the video equivalent of a newsletter intended for a showing on local-access channels. A broadcast may last from a few minutes to a half hour or more, with presentations ranging from editorial-style speeches to a talk show format that includes House colleagues, for whom the favor will be returned.

An additional way of reaching an audience directly is C-SPAN, which as of 1987 served 2,700 cable systems with a potential national audience of 33 million households, one-third of them at least occasional viewers of its live, gavel-to-gavel coverage of House floor proceedings.[26] Through these broadcasts, members may publicize themselves and their opinions, not only by participating in the debates but also by speaking during the two times each day that are set aside expressly for them to address topics of their own choosing—the one-minute speeches at the start of the session and the special orders at the close of the day when one or more members may hold forth for an almost unlimited time. Some sort of audience is known to be out there. Most House offices have some anecdote about phoned-in responses to something their boss said on the floor. Because C-SPAN viewers are more politically engaged and active, and because of the existence of groups such as the Watchdogs of Congress (elderly women in Sioux City who gathered weekly to watch the House broadcasts) members may consider floor proceedings as a way not merely to persuade their colleagues but to address a larger audience and ultimately to create a public mood that will land their concerns on the House agenda.[27]

### Pros and Cons of Television Publicity

In an ideal world, press secretaries would love to receive television attention. In my survey 61 percent agreed that if they had to pick one medium to use to sell a story, it would be television. Yet few House offices are exclusively or even principally oriented toward television. Only a third

---

25. Matlack, "Live from Capitol Hill," p. 391.

26. Data provided by C-SPAN from fact sheets and affiliate updates. Televised Senate proceedings have not yet succeeded in winning as large an audience; in 1987 the C-SPAN II network that carries them reached a potential 12.6 million households through 485 cable systems.

27. On viewers, see Diane Granat, "Televised Partisan Skirmishes Erupt in House," *Congressional Quarterly Weekly Report*, February 11, 1984, p. 246.

have regular broadcast programs, while more than half write weekly columns. Likewise, a 1978 survey revealed that while managers of House campaigns considered television the most persuasive medium, campaigns seldom bought TV ads.[28] And as table 4-2 shows, press secretaries rated attention from local television news as generally less useful than that received in local daily or weekly papers. Methods of pursuing publicity using the House television studio and radio "actualities" (audio press releases) were also deemed less valuable than the tried-and-true press release.

These findings fly directly in the face of the presumption that television is the medium of preference for today's legislators. When I asked press secretaries which medium they considered the most effective for getting their message across, some chose television, but most chose other media. The reasons are as varied as the choices.

First, access to television is considered more difficult to achieve than access to print. Many press secretaries, especially those working for non-leaders or members whose districts did not correspond to media markets, shrugged that neither national nor local television was much interested in their bosses' activities. Consequently, television exposure is time-consuming to pursue. With members from urban or suburban districts crammed into one market, television is unlikely to give much coverage to any one member's activities. Smaller towns often lack the technology and staff to tape reports on members' activities, particularly when they are in Washington. Pooled satellite arrangements such as the Potomac News Service or Conus may help, but they are mostly used by stations in larger markets. Few offices have the funding to bridge this technological gap. Because the House recording studio must be reserved well in advance, it is used by most press secretaries only for weekly cable shows or responses to scheduled events such as State of the Union messages. Then too, copy for television is more cumbersome to produce and distribute than radio statements and press releases. "To do an interview here," said a press aide to a senior Southern Democrat, "takes up thirty to forty minutes just to get set up and then some more to do it and then he gets seven seconds of time."

A press release can be assembled and distributed quickly and inexpensively, sometimes without direct involvement by the legislator who is ostensibly being quoted; but an appearance on screen demands involve-

28. Jon R. Bond, "Dimensions of District Attention over Time," *American Journal of Political Science*, vol. 29 (May 1985), p. 337.; and Edie N. Goldenberg and Michael W. Traugett, *Campaigning for Congress* (Washington: CQ Press, 1984), table B-1.

ment.[29] Again, offices own word processors, mimeographs, photocopiers, and tape recorders to facilitate distributing press releases and their audio equivalents, but as the press aide to a class-of-1974 Western Democrat observed, "You can't do feeds for TV. You send press releases to print, you've got paraphernalia to do radio, but have you got cameras, tripods, sticks? There are no technical accoutrements for sending the message out."

Finally, television's format makes it more selective and interpretive, less likely to present the member's views verbatim. Print reporters do search for particular angles, but print's inverted pyramid composition, which moves gradually from most important point to least important so that editors can more easily cut stories to fit available space, hides this process. By contrast, television accounts are coherent stories with a clear beginning, middle, and end to establish tension that is then resolved to keep viewers tuned in. Television correspondents comment on the significance and meaning of what even authoritative sources say. And at the close they present a final line akin to the moral of the tale, a practice rarely seen in print.

Press secretaries realize these limits. "TV is the best way to go but you've got less control," one said. "[With print] there's a better chance to get *your* statements in, whereas the editor in [hometown] television has more control over what goes on and what stays out." Sometimes such selectivity results in what House offices see as the cardinal sin of journalists—presenting information without attribution. Radio is also considered easier to work with than television. One press secretary to a four-term Midwestern Republican from a sparsely populated district noted that radio stations gratefully take a whole statement and "don't cut it up very much. Those newspapers take a grant announcement and take your name out—no attribution at all, which is infuriating because we've worked on it, and we don't get the message that the congressman is working for them. But television for us is probably the most picky."

In addition, despite the influx of representatives who are at ease with cameras, many are not. If the press secretaries must, as they aver, work to highlight whatever talents the members have and downplay their drawbacks, television may not provide the best medium. Then too, the issues that concern a member may not lend themselves to the condensed format of television. The press assistant to a senior member of the Judiciary Committee said that in an interview the member will "explain an issue for ten

29. About the involvement of legislators, I witnessed one key staffer in a Senate office admonish the rest of the staff, "The senator doesn't really mind you speaking for him, but he'd like to know what he's said before he reads it the next day in the papers."

minutes but he doesn't give the quick and concise ten-second news bite, so they won't use *any* of it. . . . Some things translate into TV if you try to make a point about a particular issue. Like with an environmental issue, nothing's more effective than the toxic dump with the skull and crossbones sign. Our issues don't translate into visuals."

Finally, press secretaries are sensitive to other failings of television. Some noted its inability to go into much detail, others its ephemeral quality. "Some say without TV you can't get anywhere. I would trade one paragraph in the *Times*, the *Post*, for any story in the morning news. It's there, it can be recycled, it's more credible, it can cover more. Television *evaporates*." Sometimes, such fleetingness makes it difficult for press secretaries to justify their work. "It helps to get [press] clips in so that we can *see* what we've done," one observed. "With radio or TV, the congressman might not see what it is we're doing even though they're maybe more important nowadays."

Overall, the survey results corroborate these conclusions. Press secretaries find local television news more valuable than other outlets only when their bosses come from media markets that overlap with their districts and when they consider the local media fairer than the networks (appendix table A-4). Local television is useful when it is ready to air the legislator's communication. The member's goals and style are less influential in affecting press secretaries' evaluations of local television. Legislators inclined to take positions have press operations that appreciate the twenty-second sound bites on television. In addition to its value in communicating with constituent groups, the importance of being a spokesperson on an issue serves as a marker of a more active and sophisticated media operation geared more toward using local television.

Press secretaries realize that, despite the conventional wisdom that television is Americans' main source of news, methods of getting informed are haphazard at best. Viewing television news is not a daily ritual; it occurs sporadically and accidentally. And even this audience is not as large as popular wisdom would predict. Indeed, while the number of U.S. newspapers has decreased steadily in recent decades, not only is total circulation about as high as it ever was, but more people (67 percent or so) say they read a newspaper every day than say they watch a television newscast. [30]

30. Among others, see Doris A. Graber, *Processing the News: How People Tame the Information Tide* (Longman, 1984); and John P. Robinson and Mark R. Levy, *The Main Source: Learning from Television News* (Beverly Hills: Sage Publications, 1986).

In addition to all this, because members pursue cautious media strategies, press secretaries try to use as many different means of communication as possible. "You have to have all three," one observed. "TV is image, the newspaper is name recognition and the 'continuing to serve' message, radio is the close touch." Another contended, "To get the message totally across, you have to get the message reinforced, get it more widely dispersed." Thus press operations supplement printed press releases and newsletters with their electronic counterparts and with columns intended for small-circulation weeklies. Their choices in media strategies are rarely either-or. To the extent that House members are using sophisticated methods of public relations, they have grafted them on to tried-and-true methods, and operations using one media resource are more likely to use others.[31]

### Pros and Cons of In-House Media

What is true of television use applies to high-technology, printed in-House alternatives. While press aides almost unanimously use newsletters and targeted mail, these options are still considered less useful than getting mentioned in local dailies. So are recording studio interviews, radio actualities, and televised floor proceedings. It would be unfortunate to pass up any opportunities for publicity, but for all that press secretaries complain about the press, few conclude that a strategy of trying to avoid it completely would work.

The electronic end-run to avoid journalists is, like television, time-consuming and cumbersome. A strategy using the recording studio or floor broadcasts is more closely linked with working through the media than around them because the same proliferation of channels that makes the members' own shows and the House broadcasts on C-SPAN possible also cuts down on the potential size of the audience. After sketching the advantages of canned television messages, the press assistant to a three-term California Republican noted, "The problem is that not everybody gets cable, and when you have twenty-odd channels to choose from, you're also competing with more."

Moreover, what might work well in reaching an audience directly is not likely to be picked up by local television stations. Material from the record-

31. Bond, "Dimensions of District Attention over Time," p. 342; and Timothy E. Cook, "Press Secretaries and Media Strategies in the House of Representatives: Deciding Whom to Pursue," *American Journal of Political Science*, vol. 32 (November 1988), p. 1055.

ing studio may seem too canned, revealing the overt cooperation of House member and news organization. As for the C-SPAN broadcasts, press secretaries often try to notify local television stations of a legislator's appearance, but the unpredictable schedule of the House limits the usefulness of the strategy. And the now-common practice of cutting to a shot of empty seats in the midst of a statement also decreases the visual appeal of these speeches. While the national networks or press may occasionally pick up a member's comment from the floor, their willingness to consider a comment catchy enough to include is impossible to predict. The expenditure of a press aide's resources is once more high and the payoff uncertain, and press operations see these methods only as adjuncts.

Postal patron newsletters and targeted mail thus remain the most popular of direct communication tactics, but even they are rarely centerpieces of media strategies. Although newsletters ensure that sometime during the year a member has made passing contact with every resident of the district, press secretaries are under no illusions about how many recipients have paid attention to them. But as one aide to a Republican whose victories are razor thin boasted, "The way I lay it out, any way you throw it away, [X's] name appears on top. That's how I designed it." Another was also philosophical: "You *know* that the postal patron goes into every home. Maybe the constituents won't read it, but at least they will see that it's from [Y]. Now if it's written to be interesting, you can get impact that way."

If the newsletter is used to maintain name recognition, targeted mail can serve more specific functions. "What's grown up are interest-area newsletters—crime, senior citizens, the environment," said a press assistant to a two-termer. "This way, you target what you're saying to who's interested. Now, I think we may be doing more than we need to; it's a very secure district. But if you win by 51 percent, these newsletters are great for keeping coalitions together by adding them up."

A disadvantage in using newsletters and targeted mail is the same that discourages all direct communications: they may not be as persuasive as press coverage because constituents see them as self-serving documents. A tenet of social psychology picked up by press secretaries is that to be persuasive a source must have credibility. A story in the local daily seems more objective and gives a member's message more legitimacy, even if a favorable cast is tempered. One press secretary to a Western Democrat said, "If you go to the news, you get the balance of it—you can say you're wonderful and get someone else saying it, and then maybe someone else saying you're a dirtbag." But since local media rarely portray the member in a bad light, attempting to attract their attention is relatively painless.

In-House media become most useful when the circumstances favoring the use of local television are reversed (appendix table A-4). The less time press secretaries spend on media-related matters, the less the member seeks to become a spokesperson on an issue, and the less the television market and the district overlap, the more useful newsletters and targeted mail seem. Far from an end-run around the press, turning to in-House media is no more than a fallback option. They are valued precisely when press operations are less important to the functioning of the House office and to the achievement of the member's goals.

## Complementary Publicity

As far as local news outlets are concerned, dailies and weeklies are the focus of almost all House media strategies. Press secretaries recognize television in the abstract as the most effective way to reach the audience. But although they might like to get their bosses on the air as frequently as possible, given the multiple problems of selectivity and access, typical media strategies do not focus on television. For most House members, print is the surer bet.

Media strategies that prefer direct communications with audiences are also rare. Press secretaries are not using high-technology in-House equipment to circumvent journalists. Certainly postal patron newsletters are now taken for granted and, along with targeted mail, are valued more the less that an office pursues the press. But the reduced credibility and persuasiveness of member-controlled communications make them no substitute for the favorable and more influential coverage most members get through the local press.

Similarly, members use the House recording studio or C-SPAN's broadcasting of floor proceedings not to bypass the press but to woo it. Audiences for cable television shows are smaller than those for an appearance on local news programs. So the studio is valued only moderately, and then for video press releases or talks sent to news organizations rather than beamed directly to constituents. Even here, the time and expense that television requires continue to make other publicity options more attractive.

Similarly, the value of broadcast floor proceedings is not C-SPAN's audiences around the country but the networks' feeds or the reporters who tune in. C-SPAN became renowned in early 1984 when Newt Gingrich and other conservative Republicans took to the floor to address issues they considered bottled up in committees. Gingrich estimated 200,000 viewers were tuned into C-SPAN at any one time, commenting, "That's not a bad crowd. . . . This is the beginning of the ability to have a nationwide town hall meeting."[32] But after his strategy provoked an explosive response from Speaker O'Neill, the ensuing publicity suggested that he was less interested in the town-meeting audience than in getting through to the press. He admitted as much in early 1985: "Think of me as a backbencher who used to work very hard trying to figure out how can I articulate something in a flashy enough way so the press can pick it up."[33]

Press secretaries do pursue alternatives to print media, but these other options do not detract from the importance of local dailies, which they continue to consider the primary conduits to a mass audience. If House offices are to win publicity, they must take these traditional values into account. Press secretaries rarely rely on any one medium because none satisfies all four of their crucial criteria: access, a large audience, high credibility, and control of the final product. It would then have to match the particular goals of the office, most notably the extent to which the member seeks to become an authoritative source on a national issue. Outlets with large audiences and high credibility, such as television, offer less access and control over the final message. Those that provide easy access and substantial control, such as local weeklies or newsletters, offer small audiences and only moderate credibility. The one medium that performs least poorly in all these criteria is the local daily newspaper. But press secretaries cannot concentrate exclusively on them: getting publicity is simply too uncertain a process. As far as House press operations are concerned, the more lines of communication, the better.

## The House in the Media Age

In December 1984 Steven Roberts of the *New York Times* began a story with a paragraph that in its entirety read, "'I grew up watching television,' Rep. Richard A. Gephardt remarked recently, 'I watched Howdy Doody.' Last week, the lawmaker from Missouri was chosen as chairman of the House Democratic caucus for the 99th Congress, the No. 4 job in the

32. Granat, "Televised Partisan Skirmishes," p. 246.
33. Lois Romano, "Newt Gingrich, Maverick on the Hill," *Washington Post*, January 3, 1985, p. B2.

party leadership."³⁴ Roberts's opener would be a non sequitur if it did not point up the importance that House leaders and their observers have begun placing on legislators' adeptness in using the media in general and television in particular. At the top, whether in the selection of new leaders or in attempts to retrain old-time stem-winders such as former Speaker Jim Wright or Minority Leader Robert Michel for television, the media have taken on new prominence. The many battles of succession for the Democratic leadership in the House that resulted in the Foley-Gephardt-Gray troika completed the transformation to a media-conscious Congress and revealed the extent to which the Democratic Caucus chose its leaders according to their skills with television.³⁵

Within individual House offices, too, news organizations have become objects of increasing concern. Now that most members have a full-time press secretary who brings professional skills and new perspectives, the priorities and preferences of journalists can be anticipated. Most of this attention turns to local news outlets that are considered crucial for reelection. But House press operations are increasingly aimed at national audiences as part of a legislative strategy that attempts simultaneously to set a given issue on the agenda and to increase a member's reputation as a spokesperson on that issue.

Has the House then entered the television age? Yes and no. As long as people think television reaches and persuades the largest possible audience, skill using it can only help a member's career. Such help does not occur in a vacuum, however, because television applies not only the criteria for quality that are peculiar to it, such as good visuals, but also requires the same standards found elsewhere in journalism, most prominently that news be important and interesting. As an aide to a three-term Southern Democrat who had recently acceded to a subcommittee chair put it,

You have to have a jump-off point on a consistent basis. If you're not newsworthy every two months or so, no charm or personality can

34. Steven V. Roberts, "The New Wave Starts to Crest on Capitol Hill," *New York Times*, December 9, 1984, sec. 4, p. 2.

35. Republicans in the House recognized as much. Steve Gunderson, chief minority deputy whip, commented of the three, "They are all young, dynamic and photogenic. . . . It gives a real challenge to Republicans to be creative in developing alternatives and articulate in selling them." Quoted in Janet Hook, "Gephardt, Gray Join Foley on Leadership Team," *Congressional Quarterly Weekly Report*, June 17, 1989, p. 1445.

launch you as a spokesman. If you've got the combination of reassuring television presence and a position within the House, you're a really good candidate for it. One without the other is not very helpful. Presence without power doesn't make you interesting, and power without presence doesn't make you interesting. But the combination makes you a national figure.

Ability to use the media successfully, then, adds a new criterion for advancement inside or outside the House. Within the legislature, success now depends as much on a member's perceived ability to play an outside media strategy as a mastery of the inside hands-on strategy counted several decades ago. Yet ironically, access to that outside strategy still depends on the ability to gain the institutional bases of power necessary to win the attention of television, and reaching those bases may be at least as dependent on negotiation, bargaining skills, or the slow workings of the seniority system. Television, radio, and newspapers become useful to members not merely when there is presence but when there is institutional power behind that presence.

# 5

# Getting Reelected

WHATEVER THEY and their staffs might wish to accomplish in Washington, it is all for nothing if House members fail to be returned to office. Consequently, reelection is the fundamental task of every House office, and legislators are becoming increasingly sophisticated in campaigning. The increase in the size of personal staffs in the 1970s allowed members to create full-fledged reelection teams at government expense, teams that would seem to be working very efficiently. In 1984 and 1986 few members lost seats. In 1988 a record 98.6 percent of those seeking reelection were returned—the only losses were sustained by members accused of some sort of ethical impropriety.

Press secretaries could well be a crucial part of the reelection process. After all, even in those offices that pursue national publicity as the basis of legislative strategy, press secretaries spend at least as much time and energy—and usually more—servicing the local media and communicating directly with constituents. Their levels of activity are impressive; they estimated sending out an average of eighty-five press releases a year, thirty-five radio actualities, and a smattering of video press releases, in addition to overseeing postal patron newsletters and targeted mail.[1] The popular image has been that this activity is rewarded by ample publicity back home and an adoring electorate. Indeed, in a famous 1973 article Ben Bagdikian accused House members and local news outlets of being "partners in propaganda." "Hundreds of press releases," he asserted, "are sent to the media by members of Congress, and hundreds are run verbatim or with insignif-

1. These estimates come from my 1984 survey of Democratic press assistants, but the figures from Robert E. Dewhirst's 1981–82 study of both Democrats and Republicans are similar. See "Patterns of Interaction between Members of the U.S. House of Representatives and Their Home District News Media," Ph.D. dissertation, University of Nebraska, 1983, pp. 138–39.

icant changes . . . with only rare calls to check facts and ask questions that probe beyond the pleasant propaganda."[2]

It would make sense, then, for press secretaries to devote extraordinary energy to working with local journalists. But given all this effort and given Bagdikian's portrayal of local media as unfiltered conduits for members' publicity mills, why is it that voters show such widespread ignorance of their representatives' activities? The rate of reelection obviously does not reflect constituents' respect for their representatives, whose names they cannot recall and whose records they cannot recount. But voters do not resist or ignore information about House campaigns. When information is available to them, they use it to evaluate the candidates and to make their decisions. So what is going on?

Ideally, the chain of representation should link members' activities to local coverage of the activities to voters' evaluations of the members, and would result in informed voting decisions. The missing link in this chain has to be between what members do and what the media report. When people pick up hometown papers or tune into local radio or television news broadcasts, chances are that they will see little about their representative. But this is the very situation that seems to favor reelection. Incumbents may not really profit from publicity if it calls attention not only to them but also to their reelection contest and their challengers. The sort of neglect that House members and their staffs complain about is a form of benign neglect. They may not receive much publicity, but what they do get is on their terms, and their challengers receive even less.

Still, if it is in the self-interest of House members to avoid too much coverage back home, why do the press secretaries work so hard to get them into the news?

## Press Secretaries' Priorities

House office staffs are very sensitive to the possibility that their bosses might not be reelected. As a district becomes less safe, a press secretary in particular is more active and devotes more time to working with the media,

2. Ben H. Bagdikian, "Congress and the Media: Partners in Propaganda," *Columbia Journalism Review*, vol. 12 (January–February 1974), p. 5.

even if the member has considerable seniority.[3] Strategies of reelection focus above all on making sure that people know who their representative is. When asked to rate the importance of five long-term goals for the office, press aides awarded the highest average ranking to building name recognition of the member in the district. Even acting as a liaison to constituent groups was considered less important than getting the name out there and linked to favorable publicity.

In helping their bosses get reelected, press secretaries leave few possibilities untouched. Media strategies seem to be predicated on the presumption that the more avenues to the constituent, the better. (The principal exception is the national media. Not enough constituents are thought to pay enough attention to them for the average House member to bother pursuing national exposure.) The strategies are reinforced by the attitude that different media send different messages to different audiences. Competing with other candidates for a newshole is difficult enough that press aides cannot always predict which stories will be taken up by which outlet and with what play. As the aide to a five-term New England Democrat pointed out, "The media are fickle—some stories bomb that you think will be great. What I'd call throwaways are used, boom! by five different papers." A press operation must err on the side of generosity, both in its attempts to receive publicity and the range of potential outlets it tries.

The most welcoming district news outlets are tiny operations. Weekly newspapers sometimes republish news from the member with minimum editing—the resources to do their own newsgathering and writing simply are not available. One press secretary to a two-term Midwestern Republican noted with a chuckle, "It's not as hard as I thought it'd be. You take a picture on the steps of the Capitol of someone visiting my boss from Squareville—and they will publish it. At first, I thought, you've *got* to be kidding." The same relative ease of access is also provided by small local radio and television stations. A press aide to a four-term Midwest Republican said, "The little stations are most helpful. They're not too big to deal with a local member of Congress."

But the reach of such small operations is limited, so it is difficult to

3. In the survey the correlation between the electoral margin in the 1982 election and the estimated percentage of work time spent on press-related matters ($r = .21$) was significant at the .05 level, after controlling for years of service. This result is especially striking since few other studies show a relationship of electoral margin to office activities. See Lyn Ragsdale and Timothy E. Cook, "Representatives' Actions and Challengers' Reactions: Limits to Candidate Connections in the House," *American Journal of Political Science*, vol. 31 (February 1987), table 3.

build a media strategy on their good will. With other more influential local outlets, press secretaries try harder, but the greater competition over the newshole allows even less knowledge of how much play they will receive. Deluging the district with daily press releases is not a solution: they would lose value in the eyes of reporters, and the sheer volume could itself become an unfavorable story. Press secretaries must therefore move by trial and error, adjusting their methods depending on their success in getting the right messages into the local outlets over the long haul.

## Campaign Coverage

Local radio, television, and newspapers are constituents' most important sources of information on congressional elections. Not only do most voters pay more attention to them than to the national outlets, but the national outlets pay almost no attention to campaigns for the House of Representatives.[4] Every four years, of course, the presidential election dominates coverage, and in the other even-numbered years, Senate races are more newsworthy than House races, even when House contests may be better indicators of the political landscape.

This neglect is greatest on the part of the three television networks. If spinning the dial during the networks' broadcasts of the 1986 election results was a reliable indicator, only a handful of contests were covered at all, and each involved some sort of celebrity who had little to do with its political significance. Races featuring the candidacies of two children of Robert Kennedy, two sports figures, and two former television actors were all spotlit.[5] The only other House contest receiving any attention was the rematch of the 1984 squeaker between Frank McCloskey and Richard McIntyre in Indiana's Eighth District. In the month before election night, too, there had been little network coverage of House contests: NBC presented no stories on them and ABC presented one two-minute segment on the races' insignificance for shaking Democratic control of Congress. In the week before, CBS broadcast four reports on four consecutive evenings: on the

4. In the 1980 elections, less than 4 percent of UPI's column inches and less than 2 percent of CBS's newstime was devoted to congressional elections. Of that, most coverage emphasized the Senate. Michael J. Robinson and Margaret A. Sheehan, *Over the Wire and on TV: CBS and UPI in Campaign '80* (New York: Russell Sage Foundation, 1983), p. 173.

5. These were Joseph Kennedy II in Massachusetts and Kathleen Kennedy Townsend in Maryland, Tom McMillen in Maryland and Jim Bunning in Kentucky, and Fred Grandy (late of the "Love Boat") in Iowa and Ben Jones (formerly of "Dukes of Hazzard") in Georgia. Robinson and Sheehan, *Over the Wire and on TV*, p. 173, noted similar trends in 1980 coverage.

hoopla over candidates' drug tests, featuring two House candidates; the evangelical factor, focusing on the North Carolina race of Bill Cobey and David Price; the attempts of the American Medical Association to oust two hostile Democrats, Pete Stark and Andrew Jacobs; and an almost four-minute story on the Louisiana race between a black Democratic woman, Faye Williams, and a conservative white male Republican, Clyde Hollo-way.[6] In the entire month no more than eight races were covered even in passing by the three networks' evening news programs.

Metropolitan newspapers are no better—one analysis has called their coverage of House elections the "missing beat."[7] With multiple nearby contests to choose among, they cope by more or less bypassing them all, giving far more space and better placement to races for senator or governor. Smaller papers do show more attention to House campaigns, but the level is never high, even in rural areas where such a story has less competition.[8]

There are three laws press secretaries must remember about the coverage of House elections. First, none of the news media pay much attention to the contests in any locale, and the attention that is paid goes to tighter races and districts that closely match media markets.[9] Second, hoopla and strategies, the matter of who is ahead and who is behind, get more coverage and better placement than do candidates' positions on issues or other more central matters.[10] Third, at all levels of competitiveness, incumbents get more publicity than challengers, and the tone and focus of the coverage resembles that of incumbents' campaign materials. Thus, for example, incumbents were left out of only 4 percent of newspaper articles on the 1978 House campaigns, while challengers went unmentioned in 40 per-

6. These stories were taken from the *Vanderbilt Television News Abstracts and Indices* for October 1986 and November 1–3, 1986.

7. Charles M. Tidmarch and Brad S. Karp, "The Missing Beat: Press Coverage of Congressional Elections in Eight Metropolitan Areas," *Congress & the Presidency*, vol. 10 (Spring 1983), pp. 47–61.

8. Jarol B. Manheim, "Urbanization and Differential Press Coverage of the Congressional Campaign," *Journalism Quarterly*, vol. 51 (Winter 1974), pp. 649–53; and Jan Pons Vermeer, "Congressional Campaign Coverage in Rural Districts," in Vermeer, ed., *Campaigns in the News: Mass Media and Congressional Elections* (Westport, Conn.: Greenwood Press, 1987), pp. 77–89.

9. Edie N. Goldenberg and Michael W. Traugott, *Campaigning for Congress* (Washington: CQ Press, 1984), pp. 124–25.

10. Tidmarch and Karp, "Missing Beat," table 3. Tidmarch elsewhere points out, however, that issues were not entirely absent from twelve metropolitan newspapers in their coverage of 1982 House contests. Some 54 percent of relevant items in each paper covered some sort of issue. That leaves almost half of the coverage with no reference whatsoever to issues, even before considering that issues rarely made the front page. Charles M. Tidmarch, Lisa J. Hyman, and Jill E. Sorkin, "Press Issue Agendas in the 1982 Congressional and Gubernatorial Election Campaigns," *Journal of Politics*, vol. 46 (November 1984), p. 1231.

cent.[11] And the coverage of incumbents is generally more favorable in its tone.[12] Since the media also bypass the issues, which challengers see as their strength, and representatives can communicate directly with voters at government expense, whereas challengers must use costly radio and television advertising, the information available to voters, insofar as it refers to House campaigns at all, slants toward the incumbent.

## Media Strategy and Publicity

What conditions encourage this pattern of favorable coverage for incumbents? In part, it is caused by the weak campaigns of many of the candidates challenging them. Challengers usually lack resources to create news events. "No amount of journalistic enterprise . . . by eager reporters compensates for the dead weight of invisibility that flows naturally from a lack of funds—to hire managers, schedule media events, and buy ads that help certify a contender's political legitimacy."[13] Even when challengers are strong and visible, newsworthiness favors incumbents, not because journalists spend less time following challengers or know less about them, but because challengers are presumed less authoritative and are then less able to make news. A story about an incumbent as an officeholder (announcing grants, commenting on a presidential speech) need not have a comment from the challenger in order to be balanced; but most stories about challengers focus on their candidacies, and responses from incumbents are usually solicited.

The most celebrated reason for the incumbent's edge has been the possible cooperation, if not collaboration, of local reporters and the representative—Bagdikian's "partners in progaganda." But charges of collusion must be considered overstatements. A very small percentage of press releases ever gets reprinted, and relatively few form the basis for stories.[14] In fact, so few releases are used, one might ask whether their production is a waste of time. Perhaps, but it is interesting to turn the observation around and ask not how many press releases result in stories, but how many stories

11. Peter Clarke and Susan H. Evans, *Covering Campaigns: Journalism in Congressional Elections* (Stanford University Press, 1983), p. 41.

12. Goldenberg and Traugott, *Campaigning for Congress*, table 8-5.

13. Clarke and Evans, *Covering Campaigns*, p. 32.

14. Leslie D. Polk, John Eddy, and Ann Andre, "Use of Congressional Publicity in a Wisconsin District," *Journalism Quarterly*, vol. 52 (Autumn 1975), pp. 543–46.

would not have been written without a press release as impetus? From this perspective, press secretaries write press releases in the hope of stimulating reporters to write stories or include their bosses in the context of another account. In the late 1970s Michael Robinson studied one "press aware [but] not press obsessed" member he dubbed "Congressman Press." In one year the congressman put out 144 press releases. The major daily in his district published 120 stories mentioning or featuring him that year. Of the stories in which he was featured either in the headline or the first paragraph, more than half were "essentially reworded releases. Given that there were fifty-two featured pieces in toto, on average, every other week Congressman Press was featured in a story virtually written in his own office." [15]

If major dailies sometimes rely on press releases as a main avenue of news about the local representative, such dependence becomes more common the smaller the newspaper. Smaller newspapers have limited funds to work with, fewer reporters, and are prone to boosterism. [16] Their reporting may approach sycophancy in its ardor. A 1986 preelection editorial in a small weekly paper in the rural Virginia district of the late Dan Daniel, a conservative Democrat, said,

Our first and only contact to date with challenger Frank Cole was over the telephone one morning when he called to threaten a lawsuit against us unless we stopped using Congressman Daniel's weekly newsletter, Capitol Comments.

We have used the newsletter for nearly 17 years. It is a service to readers who can glean from it the latest dealings in Washington and our representative's feelings on the issue.

Threatening lawsuits does not a voter sway. We were not impressed by such tactics and as is evident in the columns to the right ["Capitol Comments"], not intimidated either.

15. Michael J. Robinson, "Three Faces of Congressional Media," in Thomas E. Mann and Norman J. Ornstein, eds., *The New Congress* (Washington: American Enterprise Institute, 1981), p. 80.

16. The most complete study of the use of press releases in a political campaign, the 1973 race for New Jersey governor, showed that weeklies relied most on press releases for their campaign coverage and were much more likely to print them verbatim. Jan Pons Vermeer, *For Immediate Release: Candidate Press Releases in American Political Campaigns* (Westport, Conn.: Greenwood Press, 1982), especially chaps. 5, 7. On the boosterism of the community press, see Phillip J. Tichenor, George A. Donohue, and Clarice N. Olien, *Community Conflict and the Press* (Beverly Hills: Sage Publications, 1980).

We urge a resounding vote of confidence for our Congressman on Tuesday, November 4.[17]

As pleasant as it may be for incumbents to receive such support, it is not crucial to their campaign advantage. More important is that news stories about them are less the result of reporters' own initiatives than of newsmaking processes set in motion by the congressional office. And in this the local media are far from alone. Most news stories in any medium, local or national, emanate from routine processes instigated by the newsmaker—press conferences, releases, official proceedings—rather than enterprise methods such as interviews, spontaneous events, and independent research.[18] Reporters are constantly overworked and must find ways to manage their load. House members and House campaigns compete with other beats; local reporters assigned to them spend on average only 15 percent of their time on House campaigns.[19] With such limits on self-starting, reporters must rely on members to tell them when they are about to make news.

## Publicity and Voters' Decisions

All these advantages for House members would not matter if they did not bias coverage and inevitably affect voters' evaluations of the candidates. But audiences do not passively absorb news content, do they? Instead, they control whether and how much they learn from the media. They can choose not to read newspapers or watch television news. When they do make contact with news, they interpret it according to their own frameworks, making them resistant to persuasion.[20] And since most people pay

17. Farmville, Virginia, Herald, October 29, 1986. My thanks to Betty Dunkum for bringing this editorial to my attention.

18. The terms and the evidence first appeared in Leon V. Sigal, Reporters and Officials: The Organization and Politics of Newsmaking (Lexington, Mass.: D. C. Heath, 1973), chap. 6. For two recent replications of Sigal's work, see Jane Brown and others, "Invisible Power: Newspaper News Sources and the Limits of Diversity," Journalism Quarterly, vol. 64 (Spring 1987), pp. 45–54; and Dan Berkowitz, "TV News Sources and News Channels: A Study in Agenda-Building," Journalism Quarterly, vol. 64 (Summer-Autumn 1987), pp. 508–13.

19. Clarke and Evans, Covering Campaigns, p. 19.

20. The locus classicus is Joseph Klapper, The Effects of Mass Communication (Free Press, 1960). Recent restatements of the media effects that modify Klapper's notion of limited effects include Doris A. Graber, Processing the News (Longman, 1984); and Shanto Iyengar and Donald R. Kinder, News That Matters (University of Chicago Press, 1987).

attention to the news largely to reassure themselves that nothing new has happened that might influence their lives, they pay scant attention to most of what they are ostensibly reading or watching.[21]

Still, the media do provide the most basic information about candidates' experience and ideas. And by highlighting certain issues, they identify the criteria and standards by which political participants will be understood and judged. Audiences may more or less easily resist direct persuasion but not seemingly objective statements of fact. If the news begins to emphasize, say, inadequate U.S. weapons systems and the threat of certain foreign governments, politicians will increasingly be judged by their positions on defense spending, whether or not they were involved in the original stories. During presidential primaries, television and newspapers may present little information beyond their assessment of a candidate's viability, but voters' perceptions of viability narrow the plausible choices.[22] By stressing the so-called fact of Gary Hart's "surprisingly strong second-place finish," in the 1984 Iowa caucus—his 16.5 percent was far behind Walter Mondale's 49 percent and just barely ahead of George McGovern in third place—the media made Hart a viable candidate. He suddenly replaced John Glenn as Mondale's key rival and was able to win the New Hampshire primary the following week. By suggesting what political matters the audience should think about, then, the news indirectly but powerfully shapes political attitudes, assessments, and decisions.

Incumbents' greater publicity does not go unnoticed by voters. Since 1978 the biennial National Election Study has asked constituents whether they recalled having encountered, in the broadest sense of the word, either the House incumbent or the challenger. More than half of the respondents remember encountering their representative in print or on radio or television, and they recall seeing or hearing about incumbents at least twice as often as challengers, no matter what the context (table 5-1). This advantage of incumbency is important. The more encounters voters can recall, the more likely they are to remember the candidate, see him or her as attentive, and report something they like. Any single contact increases their recognition of either challenger or incumbent; but the incumbent

21. One study estimates that two-thirds of newspaper stories are not read past a possible glance at the headline or lead paragraph. Even with television, viewers' attention waxes and wanes through the broadcast. Graber, *Processing the News*, p. 82; and Mark R. Levy and John P. Robinson, *The Main Source: Learning from Television News* (Beverly Hills: Sage Publications, 1986).

22. See, for example, Henry E. Brady and Richard Johnston, "What's the Primary Message: Horse Race or Issue Journalism?" in Gary R. Orren and Nelson W. Polsby, eds., *Media and Momentum: The New Hampshire Primary and Nomination Politics* (Chatham, N.J.: Chatham House, 1987), pp. 127–86.

TABLE 5-1. Constituent Encounters with Incumbents Running for Reelection and with Challengers

Percent

| Type of Encounter | Incumbents | Challengers |
|---|---|---|
| Met personally | 12.5 | 3.3 |
| At meeting where candidate spoke | 11.2 | 1.8 |
| Talked with staff | 9.6 | 1.2 |
| Received mail | 56.1 | 12.0 |
| Read about in newspaper or magazine | 50.3 | 21.0 |
| Heard on radio | 26.1 | 8.0 |
| Saw on television | 51.0 | 19.3 |
| Other contact | 5.3 | 2.5 |
| Indirect contact | 27.1 | 8.6 |

SOURCE: 1986 National Election Study, Center for Political Studies. Study covered 1,990 respondents from districts where an incumbent ran for reelection, whether or not there was a challenger, and 1,456 respondents living in districts where an incumbent ran for reelection and faced a major-party opponent.

starts and finishes at a higher level than the challenger. It has been estimated that the probability of recognizing the challenger's name without remembering any encounters is less than one in three; the chance of recognizing the incumbent's name under those circumstances is twice as high.[23]

So, despite their inattentiveness voters apparently do learn from the media, and they remember more messages from incumbents than from challengers. Yet, does this mean that the messages themselves are responsible for the advantage of incumbency? After all, if these findings rely only on recollections, voters may think they remember having seen the incumbent on television only because they recognize the name, not the other way around.[24] Several studies investigating the effect that particular information about candidates has on voter evaluations have found that news audiences learn important new information about House members when it is provided and that this knowledge can help shape assessments of candidates.[25] However, no matter which medium is involved, the amount of

23. Gary C. Jacobson, *The Politics of Congressional Elections*, 2d ed. (Little, Brown, 1987), tables 5-9, 5-10.

24. On the problems of rationalization in the NES studies of congressional elections, see Robert B. Eubank, "Incumbent Effects on Individual-Level Voting Behavior in Congressional Elections: A Decade of Exaggeration," *Journal of Politics*, vol. 47 (August 1985), pp. 958–67.

25. Iyengar and Kinder, *News That Matters*, pp. 99–105; Stephanie Greco Larson, "Information Exposure and Learning about Congressional Voting," paper presented at the Midwest Political Science Association meeting, April 1987, especially tables 1 and 3; Larson, "Does Learning about a Congressman's Voting Affect Evaluations of Him despite a Successful Home Style?" paper presented at the American Political Science Association meeting, September 1987; and Albert D. Cover and Bruce S. Brumberg, "Baby Books and Ballots: The Impact of Congressional

learning is not great and the effects are short-lived. Press secretaries, then, are probably right that they must constantly reinforce name recognition. But clearly an incumbent's advantage does not depend on either the voters' unwillingness to pay attention or their chance to get information from the news. If voters are unaware of who their representatives are and what they stand for, the cause is partly that news organizations report too little about their activities and ideas.

Such neglect is not entirely the organizations' fault. When television markets or newspaper circulation areas do not coincide with congressional districts, as they rarely do, information flowing from member to media outlet to voter is limited at the first stage. Since fuller and more thorough coverage of House races occurs in high-overlap districts, these districts show constituents with better recognition of both incumbents and challengers, more who recall seeing the candidates on television, and ultimately a lower vote for the incumbent. Such was the case, at least, in the 1980 election. Moreover, high overlap boosts the encounters and recognition of the challengers more than those of the incumbents; the incumbents' vote totals are reduced, over and above the effects of campaign spending.[26]

How then do constituents decide between incumbents and challengers? The most important consideration is still partisanship. Although split-ticket defections have increased dramatically in the past thirty years, more than two-thirds of the votes cast in House elections are along party lines.[27] Since elections are won by building coalitions, however, differences in voters' awareness and evaluations of the candidates play a critical role in decisions at the polls.

The more familiar voters are with a candidate, the more likely they are to vote for him or her, and the more likely they are to cross party lines to do so. Familiarity is largely a surrogate for what voters report that they like or dislike about the two candidates, and the evaluations are more numerous and more favorable for the incumbent than for the challenger. The more voters see incumbents on television or read about them, the higher the rating they give them and the likelier that they will vote for them. Yet for candidates to try to win reelection through press coverage is a risky

Mail on Constituent Opinion," *American Political Science Review*, vol. 76 (June 1982), pp. 347–59.

26. James E. Campbell, John R. Alford, and Keith Henry, "Television Markets and Congressional Elections," *Legislative Studies Quarterly*, vol. 9 (November 1984), pp. 665–78.

27. Jacobson, *Politics of Congressional Elections*, 2d ed., table 5.1; and Barbara Hinckley, *Congressional Elections* (Washington: CQ Press, 1981), table 4-5.

strategy: publicity increases the number of things that voters say they like about incumbents, but it also increases the number of things they dislike. This disadvantage is especially critical since unfavorable information is often more vivid and unusual and may have a greater impact than favorable information.[28] Publicity's potential for damaging incumbents shows up best in one comparison of voters in districts where incumbents lost with those where they won.[29] In both sets of districts, virtually identical proportions of voters found something they liked about the incumbents who won and those who lost. The dramatic difference lay in that twice as many voters made negative comments about incumbents who had lost. What distinguishes winning incumbents from losing ones, in short, is not the positive appeal of their performances; it is that constituents have a reason to vote against them.

Since what voters dislike is a result of increased publicity, too much publicity in certain outlets is not a good thing. In fact, the less there is, the more the members themselves can use friendly weekly papers, newsletters, targeted mail, and the like to control the content. Put another way, even if the press does not give the member much coverage, this benign neglect ends up working to the incumbent's benefit. The irony of media strategies in the House is that more is not necessarily better.

## Less Is Not More
## for the Voters

To return to our paradox: Why do House members seeking reelection spend so much time and effort aggressively seeking publicity back home in as many outlets as possible when no news is pretty good news? One clue is provided by another campaign activity: spending. The more incumbents spend on their reelection races, the worse they apparently do at the polls.[30] But this does not imply that incumbents do worse *because* they spend more. Their expenditures go up in response to well-financed, politically experienced challengers who can buy enough visibility to provide a strong alternative. Since fundraising is irksome, incumbents would presumably prefer to spend nothing on reelection. But to avoid defeat by well-funded

28. Richard R. Lau, "Two Explanations for Negativity Effects in Political Behavior," *American Journal of Political Science*, vol. 29 (February 1985), pp. 119–38.

29. Jacobson, *Politics of Congressional Elections*, 2d ed., table 5.18.

30. Gary C. Jacobson, "The Effects of Campaign Spending in Congressional Elections," *American Political Science Review*, vol. 72 (June 1978), pp. 469–91.

challengers, they must react to, or better, preempt a campaign. Consequently, they raise and spend money on a regular basis.[31]

Incumbents use media the way they use money. All things being equal, gaining exposure through newspapers and television, like spending campaign funds, provides few unalloyed gains, but failing to get publicity could be highly damaging. They cannot then discourage campaign contributions or reporters' attention even though each additional dollar and bit of news coverage is more valuable for the challenger than the incumbent.

Incumbents engage in reactive exposure. They work to receive no less favorable a press than whatever the challengers receive. But if a strong opponent emerges, incumbents must be able to marshal high-profile initiatives, and they can do that only if local outlets are willing to cover them. They therefore have to maintain regular contacts with local journalists and accumulate chits they can cash. If reporters are provided with news on otherwise slow days, they will be more inclined to return the favor down the road—recall the press secretaries' arguments that the long-term relationship with the local news outlets is far more important than any single splash in the headlines.

Incumbents also engage in exposure that will dissuade otherwise daunting challengers from running, and what discourages strong challengers is not that incumbents have done everything right but that they have not done anything wrong.[32] So the volume of coverage is less crucial to incumbents than avoiding controversy that could provide an opening for a challenger. That is why most members' press releases and newsletters focus on blandly reassuring news: taking a position supported by most constituents, claiming credit for providing noncontroversial local benefits, announcing visits to the district, congressional art contests, candidacies to military academies. House members steer away from conflict and rely on ambiguity, whether in the communications they control or those disseminated by the news outlets. Thus their most widely distributed material, the postal patron newsletter, offers generalized "shared concern" but proposes few specific remedies.[33] For constituents with intense enough opinions to write the members, targeted mail can be used to reply—that way, for example,

31. See Ragsdale and Cook, "Representatives' Actions and Challengers' Reactions," p. 69.

32. See Jon R. Bond, Cary Covington, and Richard Fleisher, "Explaining Challenger Quality in Congressional Elections," *Journal of Politics*, vol. 47 (May 1985), pp. 510–29; and Ragsdale and Cook, "Representatives' Actions and Challengers' Reactions."

33. Diana Evans Yiannakis, "House Members' Communication Styles: Newsletters and Press Releases," *Journal of Politics*, vol. 44 (November 1982), table 1; and Paul Bradford Raymond, "Shaping the News: An Analysis of House Candidates' Campaign Communications," in Vermeer, ed., *Campaigns in the News*, pp. 13–29.

environmentally conscious constituents who are informed about a member's vote for new national wilderness areas need not be told about concurrent support for relaxing auto fleet mileage standards, an announcement that has been sent to all car dealers in the district. Members do go beyond banal, controversy-free communication, of course, but this narrowcasting makes it increasingly likely that they can approach being all things to all people.

Local newspapers, radio, and television rarely improve the quality of this communication. House members generally get favorable publicity; they, more than local journalists, decide when they will make news. If reporters come up with something potentially embarrassing, the necessity to maintain contact with a valued news source can easily outweigh the desire for a scoop. Without a respected challenger to suggest alternative issues and views, incumbents may never get much press, but what they do get tends to be on their own terms.

Sometimes they admit as much. A student of mine researching a paper wrote his representative, Barney Frank, asking how much reelection concerns shape what he does in Washington and back in his Massachusetts district. He received an unusually thoughtful and revealing reply that said in part,

> In general, I believe that my votes in Washington are based mostly on my view of what is good public policy, and not greatly on what I think my reelection requires. Where reelection comes in is not in how I decide what to do, but in how I decide which of my activities to give the most publicity to. That is, I may vote on several bills during a week, make several speeches, appear at several committee meetings, etc. If the press chooses to focus on any of those, the press has the right to do that. On the other hand, it is up to me to decide which of my activities I will give particular attention to, and in making those choices, obviously I am influenced heavily by what I think will most help my reelection.[34]

If House members are partly responsible for the dearth of information that voters could use to judge them, the news media are equally guilty. As Frank suggested, many public activities in which representatives participate could become news. But since local journalists are more reactive than aggressive, members can decide which stories get publicity.

34. Letter from Barney Frank to Matthew Fair, November 23, 1987. My thanks to Fair for allowing it to be quoted.

There need be nothing conspiratorial about this bias. The favorable content in the news comes directly from the seemingly neutral application of the key rules of newsworthiness—go where news is expected to happen and depend on authoritative sources to make it. But the result may be coverage that implicitly supports the status quo, much like the editorial page emphasis of newspapers, which is also biased toward incumbents.[35] House offices pursue their goals rationally, and journalists' rational attempts to manage the work load provoke a symbiosis allowing members to gain good copy at the same time that reporters obtain their story. But such dovetailing of rational strategies proscribes the rational responses of voters. The information available to voters on candidates is simply too sparse to allow them to cast informed ballots. Few members' records are scrutinized in the media. It is no wonder that voters are not more vigilant.

35. Clarke and Evans, *Covering Campaigns*, chap. 5.

# 6

# Setting the Congressional Agenda

WHEN HOUSE MEMBERS turn from focusing on their districts to taking account of national issues that interest them, it becomes the business of their press secretaries to help make sure that these issues become concerns for the national legislature. This means that press secretaries' interests turn toward the national media. What the newsmagazines, newspapers of record, and broadcast networks can help to do is to set the congressional agenda—the unwritten but influential list of problems that are generally considered to be important and worth some sort of action—and, not coincidentally, to boost a member's career in the process.

Helping to determine which issues Congress will consider carries clout in Washington. According to veterans of presidencies from Kennedy to Carter, most White House initiatives originate in Congress, which is an incubator of proposals and ideas.[1] Enterprising members seek out problems (or hear about them from their constituents) and use their staffs to study responses, introduce bills, and hold hearings—providing bureaucrats, lobbyists, and congressional colleagues with opportunities to find alternative solutions.

But the process of determining policy is not linear; it does not run straight from Congress to president or president to Congress, let alone from recognition of a problem to specification of a remedy. After all, policymakers are not only reacting to one another; they are anticipating each others' responses and often trying to be first to get their own proposals before the public. Likewise, responses may be floating separately from particular

1. Paul C. Light, *The President's Agenda: Domestic Policy Choice from Kennedy to Carter (with Notes on Ronald Reagan)* (Johns Hopkins University Press, 1982), pp. 89–90.

problems; instead of being created once the problem is noted, they may latch on to an issue after they have already been devised. [2]

Setting an agenda is especially valuable as a form of persuasion. It determines both what issues will be addressed or neglected and how they will be treated. Almost thirty years ago E. E. Schattschneider commented that political conflict is not "an intercollegiate debate in which the opponents agree in advance on a definition of the issues," but a conflict over which conflicts will be fought. [3] Once the terms of debate are set, the debate itself may be moot. In the dispute over abortion, for example, antiabortionists proclaim themselves "pro-life," while those favoring a woman's right to an abortion term themselves "pro-choice." Since most people are, in the abstract, in favor of both life and choice, the abortion debate may be fixed by the ultimate terminology—in Schattschneider's language, the definition of alternatives that prevails. [4] "[It] looks like an argument about what the argument is about, but politicians are not as confused as they seem to be." [5]

Yet the agenda, for all its power, does not guarantee any particular result. Raising an issue's prominence, often through exploiting one aspect of it, is necessary but not sufficient to enact a member's proposal. A case study I report here, on the 1985 attempt to renew the Federal Supplemental Compensation (FSC) program, illustrates the advantages and potential pitfalls of influencing policy by agenda setting. To pressure politicians who would have preferred to do nothing, FSC's proponents had to resort to calling attention to the program in a way to which the media would respond. A particular image of the problem became widespread in the news, but it was resolvable by responses different from the solution originally set forth. The pitfall for House members is that media strategies can work to call attention to their issues without ensuring the successes they seek.

2. Examples are not hard to find. One of the more bizarre was the activity in the mid-1980s among interest groups trying to increase funding for eradication of certain insects; with the AIDS epidemic looming, they pushed the erroneous claim that insects were capable of spreading the virus. The story is told in Katie Leishman, "AIDS and Insects," *Atlantic Monthly*, September 1987, pp. 56–72.

3. E. E. Schattschneider, *The Semisovereign People: A Realist's View of Democracy in America* (Holt, Rinehart & Winston, 1960), p. 68.

4. That is, to the extent that one set of terms can and will prevail. This ambivalence may be one reason for the patchwork character of abortion (and much other) legislation. On the reasons for the incoherence of public policy, see Murray Edelman, *Constructing the Political Spectacle* (University of Chicago Press, 1988).

5. Schattschneider, *Semisovereign People*, pp. 70–71.

## The Media and
## the Agenda

How is it that matters take their place on the policy agenda as problems to be grappled with? How are such problems distinguished from conditions that must be merely endured? Who or what defines the alternatives in the practice of legislating for and governing the nation? Those who have examined the process admit that it is somewhat mysterious. The essential first step is defining problems worthy of public consideration. In policy areas that are already prominent, empirical measures may be most influential. The state of the economy can be gauged from inflation rates or leading economic indicators; airplane safety can be determined by tracing how and under what circumstances fatal crashes occur. But most topics are less constantly visible, and require what John Kingdon terms "focusing events, crises and symbols." Ocean oil spills are not rare; they occur every day. Concern about them shows up on the political agenda only after disasters that are often attributed to human error. And at the beginning of the summer of 1989, environmentalists were in the anomalous situation of hoping for another hot summer so that pressure for legislation to combat the greenhouse effect would not wane.[6]

Yet how do issues attain, maintain, or lose prominence before the public? How do more occurrences become focusing events or symbols? One major factor is the media. Kingdon grants that the media might be important by allowing communication among policymakers, by magnifying (but not originating) issues, and by influencing public opinion, but that otherwise they have little independent effect on setting agendas.[7] And indeed, since reporters must wait for newsworthy happenings, their role in setting agendas is fundamentally unlike the roles of other participants. But they do more than merely reflect events. Because they are selective, they necessarily focus attention on particular newsmakers and particular stories, in effect helping to shape national priorities. Because newsmaking entails constant but implicit negotiations between sources and journalists, problems that reach the policy agenda through the news may depend not only on their connection with congressional sources but with media standards for quality news.

The assistance that the news media provide does not, however, occur

6. William Booth, "Environmentalists Praying for Another Hot Summer," *Berkshire Eagle*, June 25, 1989, p. A15.

7. John W. Kingdon, *Agendas, Alternatives, and Public Policies* (Little, Brown, 1984), p. 62.

without cost. Stories and editorials help define problems, link problems and alternatives, and either influence or, perhaps more likely, represent national moods. The trade-off is that for legislators and the issues that concern them to receive coverage, they may have to choose issues that fit reporters' requisites—fresh, clear-cut, easily synopsized, affecting as large a portion of the news audience as possible, and packaged with reforms that seem able to resolve the problems.

What can the media really accomplish? Certainly they may increase public awareness of an issue and mobilize opinion, especially for those matters that many Americans do not directly encounter.[8] This influence on Congress is largely indirect; the news molds public opinion, which pressures otherwise reluctant politicians. Thus President Reagan appealed to the public to support the 1981 tax cut, which mobilized constituents to write members who then became more willing to go along.

Yet while Reagan's use of the media to legislate is the most famous example in recent American politics, it is not the only or even the most important incidence of the way making news can help make laws. Stephen Hess has assumed that "Trying to use the media to get legislation through Congress is a Rube Goldberg design based on (A) legislator influencing (B) reporter to get information into (C) news outlet so as to convince (D) voters who will then put pressure on (E) other legislators. Given all of the problems inherent in successfully maneuvering through the maze, no wonder that legislative strategies are usually variations of (A) legislator asking (E) other legislators for their support."[9] But other legislators have to be receptive to such pleas, and their amenability to persuasion could be a product of press coverage of the issue—regardless of whether the coverage actually mobilizes public opinion.

Coverage can increase the prominence of a problem, and at the very least, visibility certifies importance. The press secretary to a Midwestern Republican who has pursued a pet issue noted some dividends from such attention: "Take the reform of the tobacco program. It's fun getting in the North Carolina media just for the hell of it. . . . But if it's in the *Post*, the boss's colleagues will read it and take these things seriously. That's really

8. See, for example, Lutz Erbring, Edie N. Goldenberg, and Arthur H. Miller, "Front-Page News and Real-World Cues: A New Look at Agenda-Setting by the Media," *American Journal of Political Science*, vol. 24 (February 1980), pp. 16–49; Benjamin I. Page, Robert Y. Shapiro, and Glenn R. Dempsey, "What Moves Public Opinion?" *American Political Science Review*, vol. 81 (March 1987), pp. 23–43; and Shanto Iyengar and Donald R. Kinder, *News That Matters: Television and American Opinion* (University of Chicago Press, 1987).

9. Stephen Hess, *The Ultimate Insiders: U.S. Senators in the National Media* (Brookings, 1986), p. 103.

where I *do* become part of the legislative process." Members of Congress and their staffs are part of the audience for national news: it is the way they discover what the rest of the country is finding out.[10] And while the media lag behind other cues, such as voters, committee leaders, or party colleagues, members themselves estimate the news to be about as influential as presidents and bureaucrats.[11]

But prominence does not merely call members' attention to an issue; it alters the way they respond to it. Members of Congress gravitate toward issues that offer the best chance of a payoff at a low cost, such as those marked by high national interest and low conflict among interest groups. Increased funding for medical research, for instance, makes virtually no one unhappy; the same has been true of aid to Israel, at least until the recent Palestinian uprising. At the other extreme, members shun issues marked by entrenched interests and low prominence—efforts to deregulate the trucking industry or to establish a coherent national industrial policy— where a legislator can only make enemies. But one way to place an issue on the congressional agenda, even when it generates high conflict, is to improve its visibility. This does not require mobilizing public opinion. Consider the example of consumer affairs:

> [T]he transfer of consumer politics to a wider public arena . . . is not primarily accomplished by lowering the information and organizational costs that inhibit collective action on a broad front; those costs remain formidable, and the "potential group" largely unorganized. What happens, rather, is that consumer affairs comes to be perceived as *politically* relevant by legislators; citizens with low incentives to consumer activism may nonetheless deem such issues relevant to their *vote.*[12]

Improved visibility itself causes members to perceive an increased cost for inaction. If elected officials are worried about angry reactions from constituents, they may feel they must deal with the problem or run the risk of being blamed for having done nothing.

10. See John W. Kingdon, *Congressmen's Voting Decisions,* 2d ed. (Harper and Row, 1981), chap. 8; and Michael J. Robinson and Maura E. Clancey, "King of the Hill," *Washington Journalism Review,* vol. 5 (July–August 1983), pp. 46–49.

11. Unpublished data from a survey of ninety-nine members of Congress ranking a number of indicators. My thanks to John Sullivan for providing me with the results.

12. David E. Price, "Policy Making in Congressional Committees: The Impact of 'Environmental' Factors," *American Political Science Review,* vol. 72 (June 1978), p. 563, note 51.

The news can also affect how problems will be understood. The public's basic understanding of a particular policy can be set by the initial story, which tends to be echoed (or rebutted) in later treatments by officials and reporters. "The way the press frames the issue is as important as whether or not it is covered at all. If the press characterizes a policy option one way early on in the decision-making process, it is very difficult for officials to turn that image around to their preferred perspective."[13] Savvy members of Congress can influence the debate and the outcome if they can interest journalists not only in a particular issue but in their reading of alternative approaches to dealing with it. "You're trying to influence the debate on the subject," commented Representative Les Aspin. "You're trying to anticipate where the story is going, but you're also trying to push the story in a certain way."[14]

In this process of framing an issue the press can help define which outsiders will be involved. Iron triangles of congressional committees, executive agencies, and interest groups all scratching each others' backs and foreclosing all other options for resolving a given problem have been succeeded if not replaced by so-called issue networks, more fluid connections of people concerned about particular policies.[15] Members of such networks talk about new developments and ideas, and the ideas spread as if Washington were an information grid. But shifts in the framing of issues will motivate others to promote their own concerns and enter into the game of governance. If drunk driving, for instance, were to become identified as a problem of inadequate transportation rather than one of alcohol abuse, the participants would not look the same.[16] An issue network can be held together by continuing press attention and willingness to communicate within the network in Washington.

Finally, the news plays gatekeeper by implicitly deciding which occurrences will become focusing events that will provoke congressional response. In effect, they construct the public reality that is distinct from the

13. Martin Linsky, Impact: How the Press Affects Federal Policymaking (Norton, 1986), p. 94.

14. Quoted in Katherine Winton Evans, "The News Maker: A Capitol Hill Pro Reveals His Secrets," Washington Journalism Review, vol. 3 (June 1981), p. 29.

15. Hugh Heclo, "Issue Networks and the Executive Establishment," in Anthony King, ed., The New American Political System (Washington: American Enterprise Institute, 1978), especially pp. 102–06. See also Thomas L. Gais, Mark A. Peterson, and Jack L. Walker, "Interest Groups, Iron Triangles and Representative Institutions in American National Government," British Journal of Political Science, vol. 14 (April 1984), pp. 161–85.

16. The example comes from Joseph R. Gusfield, The Culture of Public Problems: Drinking-Driving and the Symbolic Order (University of Chicago Press, 1981).

private worlds we otherwise inhabit, and they provide the "resources for discourse in public matters."[17] This is a key contribution to agenda setting, since "one dimension of power can be construed as the ability to have one's account become the perceived reality of others. Put slightly differently, a crucial dimension of power is the ability to create public events."[18]

Again, this is not to say that the press determines what issues Congress will take up. Many decisions have gone unreported when hidden in committee meetings or buried in a budget. But many might also not have been reached without the media's presence and involvement. Using the press to raise an issue to the policy agenda not only changes the issues that will be considered but implicitly persuades. As one press aide noted, "Define the political landscape to include your goals and then it's easier to respond to that landscape." And of course, getting mentioned in the New York Times or the Washington Post or on network television can enable members to become authoritative sources and to link media strategy and legislative strategy, which can allow them and their staffs to shape good public policy and advance a career at the same time.

Relatively few House press secretaries emphasized this link. Of the forty I interviewed, only fifteen—eight working for Democrats, seven for Republicans—made some spontaneous reference to the usefulness of news coverage in the legislative process. But press secretaries work nearly full-time to service the local press, which may undercut efforts to develop a concerted national media strategy. Besides, some members may be badly placed to gain national attention—freshman representatives or those on pork barrel committees such as Public Works or Merchant Marine. In some offices, legislative strategies are kept on a separate track from media strategies. This perspective was summarized by the press secretary to a moderate Southern Democrat: "He will pass textile legislation whether people know about it or not. We just get the word out and get him re-elected so he can come back and pass more legislation in the next session." Nevertheless, press secretaries do aim their journalistic skills at national reporters. To a significant number of House members in a political system

17. Harvey Molotch and Marilyn Lester, "News as Purposive Behavior: On the Strategic Use of Routine Events, Accidents and Scandals," American Sociological Review, vol. 39 (February 1974), p. 103. See also Gaye Tuchman, Making News: A Study in the Construction of Reality (Free Press, 1978).

18. Harvey Molotch and Marilyn Lester, "Accidental News: The Great Oil Spill as Local Occurrence and National Event," American Journal of Sociology, vol. 81 (September 1975), p. 237.

approaching an organized anarchy, the media constitute an important avenue of legislative work.


## Choosing an Issue

In their official capacity, all members of Congress are called upon to voice their concerns about a wide variety of domestic and foreign matters on which they deliberate. But their media strategies focus on a far more limited range. A shotgun approach of spotlighting different issues every day might work with local news outlets—for them the member's involvement itself is newsworthy—but credibility in the eyes of national reporters rests on leadership status, committee assignment, and the type of district represented.

Members gravitate toward issues that reporters would consider natural for them, most typically the ones covered by their committees. Since legislators receive assignments they are interested in, this emphasis is easy for them to accept. Subcommittee chairs, in particular, are legitimized as sources. They can hold hearings that will give reporters a news peg—an opportunity to change an ongoing condition into a spot report—and they can use the additional staff of the subcommittee to boost their press operations.

Even those who are not leaders can push an issue. If it has no home within the committee system, they can launch an informal caucus and can use the initiative to indicate their mastery of the problem's intricacies. One aide commented that his boss had helped found a task force to underscore the importance of technological retooling for aging industries. "We constantly get the word out of the agenda of that task force. It adds legitimacy to the agenda if [newspapers] pick it up and put it in the business section. . . . It's setting a legislative climate for fostering innovation, making sure that bills come before the House."

Any member may also commission investigations from the General Accounting Office, the congressional investigative and auditing agency, or the Congressional Research Service, the research branch of the Library of Congress, and release their findings through the press, often on an otherwise slow news day. For example, the findings of a GAO report commissioned by freshman Representative David Skaggs of Colorado on safety violations at the Rocky Flats nuclear weapons plant appeared on the front page of the *New York Times* on October 27, 1988, after the close of the One-hundredth Congress.

Finally, when more senior or more powerful members of a committee are not interested in becoming an authoritative source, the vacuum can be filled by entrepreneurial junior members. According to a press aide for a junior Western Democrat on Ways and Means, "I haven't been comfortable with making Medicare an issue, but if we get on the Health subcommittee, you've got legitimacy and you can push the issue. It's surprising, but a lot of people *don't* push, so it can happen that aggressive press operations *can* get attention. . . . It's much easier to get press if the guys I schmooze with see a direct correlation of an issue with his position. It's not much but it's enough."

Reporters' tendencies to ask most members about a limited range of subjects provide an incentive for members to specialize. A legislator can rarely stand out as a generalist when there are 434 competitors for the same spot. The best way to stand out is to emphasize one subject of continuing interest so that when it gets hot, reporters will turn to the authority. Several press secretaries cautioned against tactics that look no further than the moment, mentioning Donald Albosta as one who got too involved in 1983 with a flash-in-the-pan issue—whether the Reagan campaign had purloined the debate briefing papers of President Carter. When that sensation vanished from the news, so did Albosta.

How do members and their staffs choose matters of continuing interest? They must find an issue, or a different viewpoint or constituency on that issue, that is not already adequately spoken for by someone who would have easier access to reporters—a representative higher in the House hierarchy or a senator. Then they must choose what one press aide described as "nothing that will make a lot of enemies." Not surprisingly, publicity opportunities must be bypassed if they might antagonize the leaders of one's party or one's committee. As the press aide to an ambitious Democratic congresswoman put it, "The powerhouses have been around longer than she has, and she has competition from them. She's not going to hold a news conference about toxic waste unless [Jim] Florio is there with her or signs off on her. The same for [John] Dingell—on the diversion bill, they were on different sides. She could have lambasted him in the press but didn't; it would have been suicidal."

Neither of these choices differs from those that legislators would make if they were unconcerned about national publicity. But other possibilities rely more on the journalistic judgment that press secretaries are likely to bring to a House office. One is to follow the already hot topics to see if they could lead to any special bailiwick. Subject matters in the news, even when they are considered newsworthy in and of themselves, have an almost natural rise and decline.[19] A press aide can then decide whether the story is continuing to develop, whether it can be prolonged, and where it could be urged to go. As Les Aspin, drawing a parallel to journalistic enterprise, said,

> If a congressman [is] to get on the wires or in the *New York Times* or *Washington Post*, he's got to do something very different, put out something that wasn't there before. . . . You can't take what's in the headlines today and do a report on that because by the time the reporting is finished, the story will have moved on. You've got to be able to anticipate where that story's going two weeks ahead. Editors do it all the time. They say, "Where's this story going?" Then they assign somebody to go out and write it.[20]

House members and staffers can try to anticipate journalists' responses by asking themselves whether a problem is interesting, affects a large number of people or touches crucial cultural values, and has a straightforward solution.

Such an approach is useful with proposals that have gone nowhere through inside channels, even though they would seem to be politically popular to champion (or, at the very least, politically unpopular to oppose). Championing such issues is sometimes more attractive precisely because they are not subjects of debate on the floor or in committee. Washington insiders regularly ask themselves if they want the policy (if the bill is enacted) or the political issue (if the bill is defeated). House Republicans, denied the working majority they enjoyed in the Ninety-seventh Congress by their 1982 losses, ended up calling attention to bottled-up legislation for short-term political gain as part of, at best, a very long-term legislative strategy. Under these circumstances, short news bites are more than adequate. As the press secretary to a Republican leader noted,

> Take the constitutional amendment to balance the budget—we know it'll never pass out of committee or on the floor—you don't want to deal in substance. You're not in the kind of territory where you want to edu-

19. G. Ray Funkhouser, "The Issues of the Sixties: An Exploratory Study in the Dynamics of Public Opinion," *Public Opinion Quarterly*, vol. 37 (Spring 1973), pp. 62–75.
20. Quoted in Evans, "News Maker," p. 28.

cate or inform. You want to excite them, you want to deal on an emotional plane. Then TV is great—all you need to do is get a fifteen-second message across. If the legislative means to an end is procedural, like a motion on the floor, then TV doesn't do much at all, because you can't translate procedural matters into television.

This comment should not suggest that television news cannot move legislation along. The same press aide had earlier mentioned pressuring members who wanted to avoid taking risks. He referred to an anticrime bill that contained conservative sections on preventive detention and mandatory sentencing and that passed in the closing days of the Ninety-eighth Congress: "We can create an image that crime is bad and that Congress can do something about it. The members from marginal constituencies can fear what the camera can do for them, the impact and the image it has with his or her constituency. Very few people have a notion of what the crime bill had in it, but it was an anticrime bill."

Setting the agenda by publicizing this or that problem is a slow process, however. Press releases and informal contacts with reporters are designed less to get immediate attention than to let it be known that a member is interested in a particular subject. One press assistant termed the activity "looking around and seeing [who else is] interested." Strategically placed correspondents or editors may have a personal interest that meshes with the member's concern—one press aide, seeking to call attention to the restrictive immigration laws on Amerasian children fathered by servicemen during the Vietnam War, found someone at "CBS Morning News" who had done a Vietnam series and was interested in this follow-up. Op-ed pieces by a member (or by a staffer under the member's byline) can also be offered. Local media outside the member's own district can provide opportunities to suggest to a colleague's constituents that they write their representative. And ideas may be reinforced because colleagues often pay close attention to news in their hometown papers. A press secretary to a four-term Eastern Democrat said, "You try to ascertain which media are most important to [other members of Congress]. . . . Papers call from other members' districts, but we talked to them because [X] can talk to members on the floor, and more effectively if the same points [X] makes on the floor [X] makes in the local paper."

Such agenda setting can take on a life of its own. Public prominence makes a member's reactions potentially newsworthy in and of themselves and may put further pressure on Washington to get something done. The press secretary to a class-of-1974 Democrat described (not without some hyperbole) the dynamic:

> If I leak a story like the story in the *New York Times* on asbestos and the name [Y] is attached, what happens is an immediate phenomenal reaction. The calls come cascading in, and the name [Y] and asbestos in schools are intertwined. Suddenly, he's nationally known because of asbestos compensation and asbestos in schools. Then other members are calling [Y] asking about the report, asking for more information, asking if the bill is really important. Then he can introduce a bill. He kicks the tail of the administration, and he gets lots of cosponsors who go out and get hits themselves.

Of course, such snowballing is not unstoppable—the decision may be sidetracked by another problem that crops up; reporters have short attention spans when a story becomes old; the problem can be defused by a solution different from the one championed by the member. Setting the agenda may be the necessary first step, but it does not guarantee a single political response. The outside strategy may have to be succeeded by an inside strategy, and that may be a difficult balancing act to bring off convincingly.

## Party Leaders and the Agenda

Using publicity to set an agenda may be strongest exactly where one would not have expected it: among the party leadership. Studies in the early 1980s showed how backbenchers used the press to promote their issues and advance their careers, but the studies overlooked the ways committee and party leaders also used publicity. The omission is not strange; most observers might find such outside strategies superfluous. After all, the leaders of the majority are the ones who set the House agenda. They decide which issues will be considered when, and which alternatives will be offered in what order. This way of scheduling implicitly persuades members en masse and is more efficient and less politically costly than using one-on-one sanctions and rewards.[21]

21. Barbara Sinclair, in *Majority Leadership in the U.S. House* (Johns Hopkins University Press, 1983), points out that the only coercive approach taken by the majority leadership under

Minority leaders, however, have long been compelled to assert their priorities in public. Little more than consultants in agenda setting, they have three strategic choices: working behind the scenes to achieve a compromise on the matters to be taken up, going public with their alternatives on the issues selected by the majority party, or using their access to the media and whatever access they have to the legislative process to address issues that they think have been bypassed. Minority leaders can use publicity, then, to pressure the majority into action or to take politically advantageous positions. Because Republicans have been in the minority in the House since 1954, their leaders have become accustomed to using the press if they are to have any real say in the issues and alternatives under consideration. Although the press treated the election of Newt Gingrich as Minority Whip in March 1989 as an extraordinary occurrence, given his aggressiveness, his abrasive personality, and his lack of inside experience, he is merely the latest exemplar of a high-profile tradition that goes back at least to the two Republican congressional leaders of the early 1960s, Senator Everett Dirksen and Representative Charles Halleck, whose strategy became known as the "Ev and Charlie Show." [22]

Now party leaders in both the majority and the minority routinely use the media to set the political agenda. The Democratic leadership's discovery of the agenda-setting power of the press occurred almost accidentally when the party lost both the White House and Senate in 1980, unexpectedly making Speaker Tip O'Neill the so-called highest-ranking Democrat in Washington. Undercut by conservative majorities on committees and on the floor, the Speaker's parliamentary powers at first proved ineffective, forcing him to adopt a more public strategy devised by his new press secretary, Christopher Matthews. Through his masterly performance, O'Neill transformed the office of Speaker into a high-profile post wielding its influence through the press. The Democratic leadership now meets with re-

---

Speaker O'Neill was scheduling, which coerced all the members together. She termed it the single most important power of leaders. Since then leaders have taken increasing advantage of multiple referral of bills to several committees and complex rules for the floor decisions to shape final outcomes. See Stanley Bach and Steven S. Smith, *Managing Uncertainty in the House of Representatives: Adaptation and Innovation in Special Rules* (Brookings, 1988).

22. In general, see Charles O. Jones, *The Minority Party in Congress* (Little, Brown, 1970). Gingrich's narrow (89–87) election over the more behind-the-scenes Edward Madigan was taken to indicate his colleagues' endorsement of an aggressively public partisanship, but Madigan was handicapped by his moderate politics and because he came from the same state as Minority Leader Robert Michel. What Gingrich's choice does suggest is that playing little else except the outside game—even when that may ruffle the feathers of colleagues—no longer disqualifies members from being selected a party leader.

porters every day in the Speaker's offices.[23] In some of the most recent of these "Speaker's briefings," not only would Jim Wright field questions from the reporters clustered around his desk, but Majority Leader Thomas Foley, Majority Whip Tony Coelho, and Chief Deputy Majority Whip David Bonior were also present to huddle with small groups of reporters afterward. By formal and informal channels, by announcing a position, or by reacting to reporters' questions, leaders now alert colleagues and others in Washington about the same issues and alternatives that they will help to channel and shape in the formal legislative process down the road.

In some, albeit rare, instances the majority leadership's formal power to schedule may be useless if its agenda does not correspond with the agenda implicitly emphasized by the networks or the newspapers of record. Early in 1989, for example, a pay raise for federal officials (including legislators themselves) was to have automatically taken effect if Congress did not vote it down by a set date. The House Democratic leadership, anticipating that members would find it politically impossible to support the raise publicly, refused to schedule a vote and planned to hold only pro forma sessions until the deadline passed. Republicans, however, took advantage of the one-minute speeches allowed at the beginning of each session to blast the Democratic delay. Attracted by a clear-cut debate and the drama of a deadline, the press provided massive coverage. Ultimately, the coverage—and polls showing popular disapproval of the pay hike—forced House leaders to schedule a vote, which overwhelmingly killed the raise. The leaders had let the press set the agenda. As Representative Michael Andrews reflected, "They should have gone out and sold it. . . . It hardened the perception that we were trying to get something we didn't deserve."[24]

More typically, the persuasion accorded by press attention complements leaders' scheduling power because publicity can reinforce the significance of an issue and present the leaders' own solutions. It can also reinforce the power inherent in formally scheduling a bill, because it can be used indirectly to pressure others, on and off Capitol Hill, to act or to desist from acting. Little wonder, then, that Barbara Sinclair, a political scientist who was a participant-observer in Wright's office when he was Majority Leader

23. A good overview of this shift is Alan Ehrenhalt, "Media, Power Shifts Dominate O'Neill's House," *Congressional Quarterly Weekly Report*, September 13, 1986, pp. 2131–38. Speakers' briefings are now so institutionalized that it became newsworthy in April 1989 when Speaker Wright, awaiting the decision of the House Committee on Standards of Conduct on some of his financial dealings, stopped holding them for a week.

24. Quoted in Janet Hook, "How the Pay-Raise Strategy Came Unraveled," *Congressional Quarterly Weekly Report*, February 11, 1989, p. 265.

and then Speaker, has written that in the future "congressional leaders are likely to combine newer media-based strategies with older insider strategies more frequently."[25]

## Selling the Issue:
## A Case Study

The possibilities and limitations of using publicity to set the congressional agenda come more clearly into focus with an action that accomplished some but not all of its goals: the 1985 attempt to renew an expiring unemployment compensation program. Federal Supplemental Compensation (FSC) was created during the 1982 recession when the unemployment rate was the highest it had been since World War II. The program provided at least eight and as many as fourteen additional weeks of federal benefits for those who had exhausted their basic twenty-six weeks of state unemployment benefits. When I signed on as congressional fellow in the office of Representative Don J. Pease in December 1984 to review his press operations and suggest possibilities for a more concerted media strategy, his preoccupation was the expiration of the FSC program on March 31, 1985.[26]

In 1984 Pease won his fifth term as the Democrat representing the Thirteenth District of Ohio, just west of Cleveland and centered on Lorain County, a steel region that had double-digit unemployment. In the wake of Ronald Reagan's reelection in 1984, the rising budget deficit, and an America that seemed to be turning to the right, Pease was skeptical of the chances for keeping FSC alive. Nor was he convinced that the program was the best it could be: its benefits were available regardless of the health of the local economy. Still, he concluded that promoting its renewal was essential, if only to keep the issue of unemployment before Congress and the public so that future consideration of job training legislation and continued support for retraining workers displaced by foreign competition would be made easier.

Unemployment was a problem that had not gone away. The economy was on an upswing nationally, but in many pockets the recovery had not

25. Barbara Sinclair, "Leadership Strategies in the Modern Congress," in Christopher J. Deering, ed., *Congressional Politics* (Homewood, Ill.: Dorsey Press, 1989), p. 153.

26. My thanks to Representative Pease and his staff for permission to recount this story. Of course, I bear responsibility for any errors of fact or interpretation. All unattributed quotations are from my notes or documents in my possession.

arrived. Although the unemployment rate had declined since 1982, it was still historically high, not even counting so-called discouraged workers, who had stopped looking for jobs, and those working part-time because they could not find full-time jobs, all of whom were excluded from Bureau of Labor Statistics calculations. Total employment may have increased, but many of the new jobs were in the service economy; not only did they pay less but they were less secure in the event of another downturn.

Expiration of FSC would mean that thousands of workers would be immediately dropped from public assistance and left with virtually no other source of government help. In the patchwork of unemployment insurance programs, the combined federal and state extended benefits program of assistance to the long-term unemployed went into effect only when it was triggered by the state unemployment rate. At the start of 1985 these benefits were in effect only in Alaska and Puerto Rico. Several ideas—such as substate triggers to reach workers in high-unemployment pockets in states that were otherwise ineligible—had been proposed. In the Ninety-eighth Congress Pease had introduced a bill with William Clinger of Pennsylvania to combine the FSC and extended benefits programs into a single program with less restrictive eligibility requirements. The proposal, however, was not high on the agenda of the Ways and Means Committee, whose primary concern at the start of the Ninety-ninth Congress was what (if anything) to do about tax reform. Any consideration of unemployment would have to begin with the impending expiration of FSC, but if the program were extended for even a short time, the committee might be pressured to consider the Pease-Clinger bill and other proposals.

Toward the end of 1984 Pease held a series of meetings with his staff to consider establishing a media strategy to keep the unemployment problem before the public. He was initially apprehensive about going public. He had been slowly gaining influence in the House through his membership on Ways and Means and by his position as a regional whip. In addition, as he reminded his staff, "I'm known for a commonsense approach, reasonableness, an unthreatening style; I'm concerned that quotable statements will infringe on that." And indeed, press accounts had described him as "hard-working and mild-mannered" or "the bespectacled Pease, who resembles a professor more than a crusader."[27] But Pease did have strengths that could support an outside strategy. In particular, his years as editor-publisher of the *Oberlin News-Tribune* had given him a knack for editori-

27. *Washington Weekly*, vol. 1, no. 10 (1984), p. 1; and *Akron Beacon-Journal*, August 21, 1984, p. C5.

alizing in what his staff called "Peasese"—clear language and short, punchy sentences and paragraphs. And unlike many members, he continued to write his own weekly columns and op-ed pieces. Thus a staff consensus emerged: an outside strategy indeed, but instead of relying on glib quotability, its core would be "facts and logic."

Unemployment was an appropriate issue for a media strategy. Not only was it germane to his district, but Pease had acquired considerable expertise on the subject from two terms on the subcommittee of Ways and Means that dealt with public assistance and unemployment compensation. He had also cochaired, with Clinger, a task force on unemployment insurance within the Northeast-Midwest Congressional Coalition, a Rust Belt caucus. Unemployment was a sporadically recurring problem likely to reappear on the political agenda. It was thus a way for Pease to get his name known so that he could promote related issues with which he was concerned. Moreover, the path was clear. There were no competing congressional authorities on unemployment. No one but Pease had both the position and the desire to pursue the issue: even members of the small Public Assistance Subcommittee had turned to other interests. Finally, a problem such as unemployment could be part of a manageable strategy because opportunities for publicity could be anticipated well in advance. If press releases were timed regularly, reporters would begin looking for them. One such opportunity would occur the first Friday of each month when the Bureau of Labor Statistics released the previous month's unemployment statistics. Another would come after the Commerce Department released the monthly trade deficit figures, when Pease could use his position on the Ways and Means Subcommittee on Trade to dramatize how many jobs were lost with each increase in the deficit.

### Setting the Strategy

At the beginning of 1985 the staff collaborated on an initial press release set to go out on January 9 when BLS would announce the December unemployment figures. Actually, two releases were prepared—one if the figures went up, one if they went down or stayed the same—and redrafted by Pease. The release asserted that the unemployment rate was stuck around 7 percent, a historically high level, and even that percentage was a low estimate, given the increasing duration of unemployment and the number of discouraged workers. I picked up the figures—up one-tenth of

1 percent—at the Labor Department on the way to Capitol Hill in the morning, called up the appropriate draft from the computer, filled in the gaps, and mimeographed the release. While the press secretary made her usual contact with the Washington reporters from Ohio papers, I took copies to the House and Senate press galleries and then dropped more off with reporters on the labor beat in various bureaus.

This activity produced mixed results. The national media ignored Pease's statements, but the Washington bureau chief for the *Cleveland Plain Dealer*, who had long suspected that the unemployment statistics were incomplete, was inspired to interview Pease on the telephone and write a story using the December figures as the peg. The story made the top of the front page.[28] But whether or not it stimulated publicity, the release drove home the message that Pease was working hard on unemployment issues. This reputation was furthered by his January 29 op-ed piece, written with Clinger, in the *Wall Street Journal* on the need to reform the patchwork unemployment system before, not during, an economic downturn. Following the Commerce Department's January 30 announcement of the record $88 million trade deficit in 1984, Pease's press release calculated that 2.2 million jobs were created overseas that would have otherwise been created in the United States, a detail picked up at the end of the *Washington Post*'s front-page trade deficit story. The story identified Pease as a "congressional trade specialist," which won, to his surprise, congratulations from several colleagues.

Still, the strategy would not have gone far had there been no vehicle to promote. In the Ninety-eighth Congress, Pease and Fortney "Pete" Stark had introduced a bill to renew FSC for eighteen months; it could easily be dusted off and reintroduced, which it was, on January 31, followed on February 7 by a reintroduction of the Pease-Clinger Bill to merge FSC and extended benefits.[29]

The Public Assistance Subcommittee was slow to react, however. First, Harold Ford had to be reelected chair and the composition of the subcommittee decided. Then hearings were delayed, presumably because Ford was deferring to Ways and Means Chair Dan Rostenkowski's unwillingness to waste time on legislation that he thought could not be passed. Many

28. Thomas Brazaitis, "Pease Sees Thorn in Rosy Unemployment Figures," *Cleveland Plain Dealer*, January 10, 1985, p. A1.

29. Stark also graciously agreed to switch the names on the resolution so that his came second. This may seem like a minor point, but a Pease-Stark Bill was more likely to buttress Pease's claim to being an authoritative source than a Stark-Pease Bill.

junior Democrats thought pushing a bill could make an important political point, possibly by passing the buck to the Republican Senate, which would have the distasteful choice of concurring with it or killing it. Rostenkowski disagreed. He saw no point in what he thought "an empty exercise."

Given doubts among both Democrats and Republicans about the value of FSC, merely holding hearings would not have ensured that the legislation would move out of subcommittee. But hearings were necessary to push the process to its next stage and to certify unemployment as an issue of continuing importance. While Rostenkowski considered hearings as the first step on a slippery slope, other party leaders might have been more amenable to them, if only to allow members to take credit for doing *something* to save unemployment benefits. At this stage, therefore, adopting an inside strategy still held possibilities. One afternoon as they rode a downward elevator in the Capitol, Pease and a key ally, Sander Levin, were speculating on whether Speaker O'Neill could be induced to intercede and mediate disagreements over how to handle the legislation. As a staffer recounted it, Pease said, "Well, why don't we go right back upstairs and make an appointment?" and pushed the "up" button to ascend to the Speaker's office. A few days later, O'Neill met with Pease, Levin, Ford, and Rostenkowski. When Pease suggested expediting hearings, O'Neill asked Rostenkowski if it could be done. Grumblingly and grudgingly, the chair of Ways and Means agreed.

Once the hearings were announced on February 12, Pease's staff sent a media kit to those reporters who had already received the unemployment and trade press releases and to others in Washington. In effect, Pease was attempting to reinvest his previous publicity to get back more, so the kit included the *Wall Street Journal* op-ed piece, the *Plain Dealer* front-page story, and a profile in the *Akron Beacon-Journal*, as well as previous press releases. In a cover letter Pease called attention to the upcoming hearings and reinforced two interlocked themes—the continuing importance of his issue and his accessibility to the press:

> I have been impressed by recent press coverage of the enduring problems of unemployment and underemployment in the United States. However, I've noted few official comments in any stories. That's not terribly surprising. After all, it's not always politically expedient, and the Reagan Administration has certainly tried to act as if unemployment will naturally take care of itself. . . . I have spoken out in the past on unemployment, and I intend to continue to do so, particularly as hear-

ings begin this week in the House on comprehensive reforms of unemployment assistance. I am available to any reporter who wishes to discuss unemployment and related matters, and I'd welcome any questions on these subjects.

## Hearings Inside, Press Conferences Outside

The hearings, which began on February 20, occasioned little attention from reporters. Held in an obscure basement meeting room in the Rayburn House Office Building, they had a small audience of labor lobbyists, staffers for other members of Congress, and a smattering of regional reporters for news outlets in the districts of members who were on the subcommittee or were slated to testify. Few witnesses were of any prominence. Indeed, the Reagan administration's desire to play down its opposition to extending FSC was indicated by the emissary it sent, a deputy assistant secretary of labor. Republican members of the subcommittee were absent; only the ranking minority member, Carroll Campbell, attended any of the hearings. But this very lack of competition from other representatives would reinforce Pease's role as spokesperson for unemployment issues.

The hearings ended on February 26. Rostenkowski apparently considered O'Neill's request satisfied. With no sign that the Ways and Means chair would encourage Ford to report out a bill, Pease's aides again turned to the outside strategy to keep FSC renewal moving. The press had now begun to contact Pease's office rather than the other way around. During the hearings a reporter from *Congressional Quarterly Weekly Report* wrote a two-page story on the expiration of the program, complete with a photograph of Pease and a quotation in boldface.[30] Another journalist, from the "MacNeil-Lehrer News Hour," suggested the possibility (never realized) of a broadcast comparing the plight of the farmers—then receiving extraordinary attention in the news—with that of unemployed workers.

But with the legislation stalled, attention to FSC would have petered out if a new publicity vehicle were not available. Fortunately, a coalition of labor organizations allied with religious and civil rights groups and known as the Full Employment Action Council (FEAC) was preparing its own report, one that would estimate much higher unemployment because it counted discouraged workers and those forced to work part-time. This

---

30. Janet Hook, "Expiration of Extra Jobless Aid Sparks Debate on Alternatives," *Congressional Quarterly Weekly Report*, March 2, 1985, pp. 402–03.

report was to be released on March 8, the same day as the BLS February unemployment figures. Having witnessed Pease's efforts, FEAC staff asked if he would introduce the report at a Capitol Hill press conference following the BLS presentation before the Joint Economic Committee. The effort made sense from both sides: the FEAC needed to legitimize their report in Congress, and Pease needed new data to emphasize the persistence of seriously high rates of unemployment.

Still, seeking further publicity meant challenging Rostenkowski's opposition to the proposal. By now, however, Pease was ready to move, even if he did range beyond his usual quiet methods. In a staff meeting held to decide whether to accept FEAC's invitation, he concluded,

> I'm not eager to criticize the Democratic leadership but this can accomplish the same purposes. We must sound the alarm: it's March 8; the program expires in twenty-three days; the House is not in session for thirteen days; the decision is to be made by the House leadership within the next few days. . . . If the leadership is going to make the right decision, people must be in contact with O'Neill, Rostenkowski, and the like. . . . Otherwise, all the pressure will be off until the next recession.

Pease agreed to hold the press conference, and both his office and the FEAC sent out media advisories, but reporters only stopped at the Joint Economic Committee hearings and few showed up at the conference (Pease gamely termed the conference a "good exercise"). The FEAC report was, however, finally noticed in a few short paragraphs in *Congressional Quarterly*, which picked up his quip that "Workers are moving from the assembly line to the burger line," a one-liner drafted to dramatize the shift from manufacturing to service jobs. And with the March 31 deadline approaching, reporters had begun to pay at least passing attention to the demise of FSC and the prospect that some 325,000 unemployed workers would be kicked off the public rolls.[31] Such a story made better news than the complexities of the statistics that estimated the extent of unemployment. It was clear-cut, dramatic, and the direction of the action could be anticipated early enough for reporters to be in the right place at the right time.

31. For example, the *New York Times* business section gave a couple of paragraphs in a "Washington Watch" section starting, "Despite a big push now under way in Congress, chances are not considered bright for extending a Federal unemployment benefits program for the long-term jobless beyond its March 31 expiration." The source for this was Senator John Heinz. Clyde H. Farnsworth, "Washington Watch," *New York Times*, March 4, 1985, p. D2.

## Using the Deadline

The expiration of FSC began to seem the only news peg that could call attention to unemployment. Pease agreed that it had to be exploited. FEAC also decided to push the outside strategy one step further. Taking a page from the farmers who were then pouring into Washington, it invited unemployed workers from across the country to rally on the morning of March 20 and to lobby members in the afternoon. On March 14 Pease, joined by Sander Levin, sent a letter to House colleagues that proclaimed in inch-high capital letters, "325,000 UNEMPLOYED WORKERS WILL LOSE THEIR BENEFITS MARCH 31." The letter announced the rally, which would "call attention to the imminent demise of FSC," and invited the members to "*Please* join us in urging the majority and minority leadership, and the President, to expedite extension of FSC."

Although Pease had decided to pressure the leadership, there were pitfalls. One day in early March when members of his staff skimmed the newswires, they were surprised to find him mentioned in investigative reporter Jack Anderson's column that was set to run the next day. Initial pleasure at seeing Anderson decry the forthcoming FSC cutoff and praise Pease's labor to save the program turned to dismay when the columnist blamed Majority Leader Jim Wright for dragging his feet on the issue. I had been the source for an Anderson staff member on some of the FSC information, but no one in the office had ever considered Wright an obstacle.[32] The publication of such an accusation, especially if it appeared that Pease's office was the source, could compromise working relations with the leadership. Fortunately, the next day's *Washington Post* ran the column without any references to FSC at all.

As the March 20 rally approached, there was some movement among the party leadership, which suggested that applying both inside and outside pressure was paying off. Shortly before the rally, Levin's office received a call from one of O'Neill's aides: "Rostenkowski's unwilling to support a bill that will not get anywhere. He's the prototypical legislator. But you should know that O'Neill doesn't feel that way." In effect, the Speaker was indicating his readiness to pressure Rostenkowski. To join in the outside strategy was one possibility, and since President Reagan had not yet committed

---

32. Anderson got the information in an almost accidental way. One of his assistants had telephoned me to ask about another topic I was working on—legislative responses to the industrial accident in Bhopal, India. I was slow to return the call because of my work on unemployment. When she called again, I apologized and explained what had delayed me. Intrigued, she asked for details. I forgot all about it until the Anderson piece surfaced on the wires.

himself, O'Neill was prepared to send a letter asking where he stood. The Speaker's aide asked Levin's and Pease's staffs to submit a draft to him as quickly as possible.

The letter was a perfect way to placate those such as Rostenkowski who wished to avoid passing a law just to incur a veto. It first addressed the deadline: "In 11 days, the Federal Supplemental Compensation program will expire. . . . Unless you and the Congress can agree on terms for extending FSC, over a quarter million people will be instantaneously cut off." However, echoing Rostenkowski the letter concluded, "I am prepared to bring legislation extending FSC to the floor of the House, but it should not be an empty exercise. . . . Mr. President, where do you stand?" Regardless of how Reagan responded, the publicity would call attention to the expiration and protect those favoring renewal from being accused of advocating an irresponsible political act. As luck would have it, Reagan was readying for a rare press conference on the evening of March 21; O'Neill was scheduled to release his letter that morning.

In the meantime, though, the unemployed workers would come to Washington. FEAC asked a number of representatives and senators to speak at the rally on the steps of the Labor Department. Pease accepted the invitation. Remembering his quip about workers staying employed only by transferring "from the assembly line to the burger line," one staff member suggested, possibly tongue in cheek, that Pease show up with a spatula. The idea took off. For one thing, television cameras might be present, and the visual symbolism might make a good news clip. No one was sure if the normally staid Pease could bring it off, but everyone agreed it was worth a try. The day of the rally, the press secretary brought a spatula from home, and Pease set out for the Labor Department. The crowd was small, but it was spirited and compact enough to give the impression that it was larger. When his turn came up, Pease vigorously deplored official Washington's callousness toward unemployed workers: "If you want to know the truth, the Reagan administration acts as if you don't even exist." Then, raising the spatula in his right hand, he shouted, "Do you know what this is? *This* is a burger flipper. *This* is the Reagan administration's answer to unemployment. And *you* can flip burgers all day, and *your spouse* can flip burgers all day, and you *still* won't get above the poverty line!" As far as the staff could tell, the idea had seemed to work. Television cameras whirred as the representative wielded the spatula. A Baltimore *Sun* reporter who had been at the rally phoned for further details, as did a reporter from a medium-sized Pennsylvania paper who had taken the story from the wires and cited Pease's earlier comments in *Congressional Quarterly*.

The network evening news programs ignored the story, however, and the next morning neither the *New York Times* nor the *Washington Post* mentioned it. The staff's one consolation was a color photograph in the Baltimore *Sun*, although the caption neglected to explain why Pease was waving the spatula. The regional wires had noted his logic, but most news organizations had paid far less attention to the unemployed workers' rally than they had to the farmers' protest several weeks before. That would begin to change; the same morning in his daily Speaker's briefing, O'Neill released the letter to the president.

### Bringing in the Big Guns

O'Neill read the letter, updated to invite the president to state his position on "any variety of extension that you could support," and added, "I hope that some media person will ask the president about FSC tonight." This attempt to set the journalists' agenda met with resistance, however. Reporters were more interested in asking O'Neill about the MX missile— in particular, the controversy over Les Aspin, the new chair of the Armed Services Committee, who was beginning to support additions to the missile force. I counted five questions on MX before the Speaker steered the discussion back to FSC and Reagan's responsibility: "It's my understanding that the Senate won't take it up. It's my understanding that the president is locked in concrete. I'm appealing to his decency. Hundreds of thousands of people will be without benefits. Here is a window for compromise." When a reporter asked, "If it was so important, why have you waited?" O'Neill replied, "I was waiting for a signal from the president."

O'Neill's letter got the action that the unemployed workers' rally could not. For the first time a reporter from the *New York Times* contacted Pease's office about the status of FSC. And in his press conference Reagan did have to address the issue. Like O'Neill's letter, the question for the president used the peg of the deadline and the prospect of 340,000 Americans losing unemployment benefits: "Are you going to let this happen or do you plan to take some action to extend the program?" Reagan's response was, in part, "We believe that it is time. It has been extended, you know, for quite some time through the emergency of the recession." After noting that 300,000 people were going back to work and emphasizing the need for job training, he concluded, "we don't believe that we should continue with this program indefinitely."[33]

33. The transcript of the press conference is in *Congressional Quarterly Weekly Report*, March 30, 1985, p. 596.

The answer was imprecise; nobody was favoring an indefinite renewal of FSC. But the tone was clear. Even a solution, mentioned by O'Neill, to allow those on the rolls before March 31 to receive the full amount to which they were entitled—a "wind-down" of FSC rather than an abrupt termination—could be vetoed. Nothing in Reagan's answer was likely to push Rostenkowski to schedule markups.

Still, there was some good news. FSC had become newsworthy. More reporters from national outlets such as CBS radio and local outlets outside Ohio were calling Pease's office. An op-ed piece by the representative on "the new unemployment" that had been turned down by the *Washington Post* was now slated by the *Los Angeles Times* for its Sunday "Outlook" section. And on another front, Representative James Oberstar had been lining up support to force a Democratic Caucus meeting on FSC; Rostenkowski was informed on Friday that the fifty signatures required were in hand. Pease told his staff that he had requested Rostenkowski to "hang loose," suggesting that there might be substantial support in the caucus for a program that was less costly than the eighteen-month extension originally proposed.

The following Monday Speaker O'Neill, Majority Leader Jim Wright, Majority Whip Thomas Foley, Caucus Chair Richard Gephardt, and several members from high-unemployment districts (Pease, Levin, Oberstar, and John Murtha) attended a meeting to consider options and strategies. Rostenkowski was notable by his absence. The caucus was expected to support renewal for six months or less, with an expression of commitment to some sort of reform by the end of that period. A six-month extension was deemed possible only with a reduction of the number of benefit weeks available. Otherwise, two months was probably the maximum, given fiscal constraints. Pease was willing to accept these limitations if they were linked to consideration of his bill to reform and combine FSC and extended benefits. But for any of this to occur, the subcommittee and committee had to act, and time was running out.

The outside strategy had not yet run its course: Pease's op-ed piece appeared in the *Los Angeles Times* on March 24, and he accepted an invitation to be a guest on a C-SPAN call-in show on March 27. But with the Republican Senate awaiting House action before doing anything of its own, it was time to change tactics. The unemployment issue now became painted as the first confrontation in the Ninety-ninth Congress between the Democrat-controlled House and President Reagan over "fairness." On March 27 the Democratic Caucus meeting called by Oberstar urged Ways and Means to report out a bill that would extend FSC for three months.

During that time, Congress would overhaul the FSC and extended benefits programs to target them at areas with high unemployment, preferably using substate triggers. Although some influential Republicans, such as Minority Leader Robert Michel and Silvio Conte, ranking minority member of the House Appropriations Committee, were on record as favoring an extension of FSC, Democratic leaders specified that the issue would show that, in Gephardt's words, "As Democrats, we need to clearly articulate to the country our priorities as opposed to the President."[34] Now that the unemployment issue was on the agenda, partisan position taking was de rigueur.

This shift in tactics was not without its costs. When his staff opened the *Washington Post* the next morning, they were chagrined to find that Oberstar and Gephardt had held a press conference after the caucus that had received prominent treatment, complete with a photo of the two, but no mention of Pease or his proposal. Although Pease was not shut out of the *New York Times* account, his squatter's rights to the issue had expired, and his role as its chief spokesperson was being challenged.[35] Bringing in allies is a sign that an issue is becoming prominent, but allies can also dilute the power of the authoritative source.

### Inside Ways and Means

The pressure of publicity was ultimately successful in persuading Rostenkowski to accede to the requests of party leaders and caucuses. Late on March 27 a legislative schedule was assembled. The subcommittee would mark up a proposal the next day; the full Ways and Means Committee would vote on it the following Tuesday, April 2. Under an accelerated timetable, it would report a proposal to the floor before the scheduled Easter recess was to begin on April 5 and in time to get the checks to the unemployed the second week of the month. That afternoon, committee staff met with aides of the majority members. One committee staff member noted the importance of the outside strategy: "Events have overtaken [Rostenkowski]. Many events have occurred outside the committee to really push this." He added that solving the cutoff problem by a phaseout in place would not satisfy the House leadership or the Democratic Caucus, but

34. Quoted in Jonathan Fuerbringer, "Democrats Push for Extension of Jobless Benefits," *New York Times*, March 28, 1985, p. A25.

35. Compare Fuerbringer, "Democrats Push for Extension," with Helen Dewar, "Democrats Ask Renewal of Job Aid, President Opposes Long-Term Payments," *Washington Post*, March 28, 1985, p. A3.

Robert Packwood, chair of the Senate Finance Committee, had told Rostenkowski such a proposal would be "all I could live with and the White House could live with." If the House committee passed a more ambitious measure, some Republicans threatened to invoke a three-day delay for allowing expression of dissenting views that would push action past the recess unless the rule was suspended by a two-thirds majority. Even if the bill passed both houses, the president might veto it while Congress was in recess. A three-month extension was now the most that could be hoped for, and none of the conditions made it propitious to consider reform. As a committee staffer put it, "The substate trigger takes the back seat to reform which takes the back seat to the sheer expiration of FSC."

The impending expiration had raised the issue to the agenda without dictating a given response. Moreover, support in the subcommittee was uncertain. When the Democratic members caucused before the subcommittee markup on March 28, Pease found only two sure votes—his and Stark's—for an extension. Ford would vote with the majority. Barbara Kennelly was noncommittal. Robert Matsui saw it as "a program patched together late at night." Neither Kennelly nor Matsui thought that extension would improve chances for the reforms or job training provisions they both supported.

When the subcommittee was called to order, the possibility of an extension beyond a phaseout-in-place seemed dim. Had the only question been safeguarding the benefits of those already on the rolls, the outcome in subcommittee might have turned out differently, particularly since Campbell held the proxies of his two absent Republican colleagues. But through a tactical error Campbell changed the alignments by altering the image of what they were voting on. He said noncommittally that he would be inclined to support reform "rather shortly" but "wouldn't burden the Senate in the last hours." Raising the partisan stakes, he then said anything beyond a phaseout would simply be vetoed by the president. Matsui exploded. Angered by Reagan's recent defiant Clint Eastwood tone toward Congress, he stormed at Campbell, "Maybe we could have a little fun here if we want. Let him veto something we pass. We could always tell Reagan to make our day." Sensing the opportunity if not the necessity for a compromise among the majority, Ford called a recess. When the members returned, they approved, on a party-line vote, a three-month extension of FSC that cut the number of weeks of eligibility. The Pease-Clinger reforms were not included in the bill, but they were approved as a separate bill to be considered by full committee later.

Pease's office continued to receive calls from newspapers asking for updates on the status of FSC. Saturday's *Los Angeles Times* ran a front page article focusing on "a growing army of jobless persons who are falling outside the safety net of government unemployment compensation," with references to the Washington rally and Pease's fight.[36] But by now, Pease had stepped back from the outside strategy. Though the FEAC had arranged a press conference with leaders of the National Unemployment Network, he decided to pass up the opportunity and instead attempt to use inside tactics to get some form of extension passed and keep the Pease-Clinger reform alive. Rostenkowski's support was still doubtful as long as Packwood would not go beyond supporting a phaseout, and any opposition from Rostenkowski might provide cover for other Democrats. But the extent of Republican support was unclear, since many hailed from districts still hard hit by high unemployment.[37]

When the full Ways and Means Committee met on April 2, Ford introduced the proposal to extend FSC for three months. Campbell promptly presented an amendment to eliminate the extension in favor of a phaseout in place, arguing that to support anything except his amendment would result in stalemate or in veto, and either could deny further benefits from reaching those already on the rolls. In one stroke he turned the deadline against Pease and, by implying that the Reagan administration was opposed to any extension, even a phaseout in place, took the high moral ground. Although the first Democrats to speak urged that the amendment be defeated, the ranking minority member, John Duncan, responded simply: "To vote against the Campbell amendment is to vote against any relief." Conservative Democrats agreed, and Rostenkowski, last to speak, went with Campbell: "It's a question of getting a bill signed or a subcommittee extending false hope. . . . This committee ought to do what's doable."

Realizing that the game was up, Ford proposed to extend FSC for thirty days, but the motion was voted down 19–17. Campbell's amendment was then adopted 20–16. Eight Democrats voted for the phaseout in place; only one Republican, Richard Schulze of Pennsylvania, voted against it. Some staff argued against reporting this bill to the floor, anticipating that the drama of workers being thrown off the rolls at once would attract more

36. Lee May, "325,000 Jobless Facing End of Extended Benefits," *Los Angeles Times*, March 30, 1985, p. 1.

37. Despite Packwood's opposition, Senate defeat of an extension was not inevitable. Majority Leader Robert Dole had to suspend Senate business on March 27 to prevent Arlen Specter and Carl Levin from clogging the progress of unrelated legislation by tacking on a floor amendment that would have extended FSC for six months.

attention and do more in the long run to reassert unemployment as a worthy issue. But in the spotlight, facing the deadline, and wishing to do something, the committee voted unanimously to send the amended bill to the House floor. Late that afternoon, the House approved the phaseout by a unanimous voice vote; the Senate followed suit the next day after defeating efforts at extension and reform, with Packwood using the same arguments as Campbell. Reagan signed the bill into law on Good Friday, April 5.

After the Ways and Means vote, Pease wearily mused, "It was amazing to get seventeen members against the chairman. . . . It went farther than I ever thought it would without our efforts. Our reputation, for what it's worth, is enhanced. There's some pleasure in that." But with the end of the FSC battle, unemployment became old news, and reporters went on to other things. A few stories appeared just after the phaseout vote, but after that joblessness was mentioned only when BLS released the monthly statistics.

Enacting the phaseout was also the end of the Ninety-ninth Congress's concern for unemployment insurance, though Pease did win a victory in 1986 in the renewal of trade adjustment assistance. His legislative director had hoped that Campbell would be willing to join a bipartisan proposal to reform the mechanism of providing extended benefits, but nothing came of it before Campbell began running for governor of South Carolina. As Pease suspected, once the FSC issue was off the agenda, pressure to reform the unemployment insurance program was off as well.

## Congressional Agendas and Media Agendas

Turning to the press to promote an issue has become more attractive as setting an agenda in Washington has become more complex. The spotlight not only draws attention but also obliges politicians to respond in some way. Thus in the case of FSC, publicity helped an issue shoulder onto the agenda when powerful House members would have preferred that nothing be done.

Media strategies to promote one issue also make members more effective in selling other issues and accomplishing other legislative tasks. Pease used his office's systematic contact with reporters to link his name to one issue; he could emerge as spokesperson on other problems. Whatever reputation he had built could only help in taking further advantage of media attention and making use of inside opportunities.[38] After all, what members do to attract attention so they can set an issue on the agenda is not fundamentally different from what they do to create a reputation within the House. It requires surveying the opportunities within their committees, noting the appropriate niches, and developing an expertise that will win respect in Washington and votes back home. The inside rules play well in winning outside publicity.

But for setting an agenda, only some problems and positions are newsworthy and therefore useful. Pease's success was partial, and his difficulty in calling attention to unemployment shows how political entrepreneurs must adapt to the needs of the press. Because unemployment rates had become old news by 1985, reporters often did not respond to his determined publicity efforts until he took advantage of the drama inherent in the approaching expiration of the FSC program. But his emphasis on this news peg undercut his earlier emphasis on the true gravity of the situation and his concern that workers would be recycled into insecure service jobs. More important, raising the question of what to do about those who were about to lose their benefits may have placed the issue on the political agenda, but it invited remedies Pease found less effective than his own. Successfully setting an agenda through a press strategy does not guarantee that favored solutions will become the frontrunners.

Of course, the failure to get FSC renewed was shaped by the wake of Reagan's reelection victory, fiscal constraints that discouraged new spending, the lack of an agreed-upon, readily available alternative to a phaseout, the partisan division of Congress into a Democratic House and a Republican Senate, and the presence of other, seemingly more tractable, national problems. These factors probably affected the final legislative product more than media strategy or coverage. But such influences came into play only after the press had emphasized the imminence of the expiration and implicitly pressured Congress to respond.

The journey of FSC legislation in 1985 provides one model of how to

38. Successive editions of Alan Ehrenhalt's *Politics in America*, a guide to Congress, show some effects of reputation building. In 1983 the guide noted that Pease had been "more successful at articulating his ideas than at persuading colleagues to accept them." By 1985 he had become a spokesperson, "a soft-spoken intellectual with a scholar's appetite for detail, and he would not strike anybody at first glance as labor's man on Ways and Means. . . . He has done his best to promote the AFL-CIO point of view, and he has won some victories." By 1987, following his close involvement in tax reform and trade legislation, he was judged a "key player on two major national issues." See Alan Ehrenhalt, ed., *Politics in America 1984* (Washington: CQ Press, 1983), p. 1199; Ehrenhalt, ed., *Politics in America 1986* (Washington: CQ Press, 1985), p. 1219; and Ehrenhalt, ed., *Politics in America: The 100th Congress* (Washington: CQ Press, 1987), p. 1195.

build a legislative strategy. Press strategies call attention to the importance of an issue, to a member's position on the issue, and to his or her qualifications to address the issue, but they will fall short of success unless some kind of institutional action—subcommittee hearings, markups, floor resolutions—provides a peg for further coverage. If institutional action grinds to a halt, sponsors may have to keep the momentum going by enlisting the support of colleagues or others who can attract attention without threatening the member's reputation for being the authoritative source. Such attention can force further institutional actions that will confirm the newsworthiness of the topic, and so on.

But this cycle relies on the news media's willingness to report on the issue, and that assistance comes with a price: the issue has to satisfy journalistic criteria of importance and interest. Problems that are complex, have no distinct sides, seem to affect few people, or lack an easily grasped "there oughta be a law" solution are harder to promote. Legislators who wish to weld media strategies to legislative strategies may either have to find matters that meet journalists' standards or package difficult issues and proposed policies in such a way that they seem simpler and more clear-cut than they are.

# Enacting Legislation

In November 1961 when Speaker Sam Rayburn died, Majority Leader John McCormack was clearly heir apparent. That meant the real leadership battle was over who would succeed McCormack—Carl Albert or Richard Bolling. Bolling ultimately withdrew, but not before demonstrating to many that the outside strategy of using publicity to influence decisions in the House was less effective than Albert's inside strategy. For contemporaries the contest between Albert and Bolling made a useful case study because each competitor used his resources well: "The man who held the better cards made no more mistakes than his opponent, and, in the end, he won."[1]

Albert's inside strategy was the customary one at the time. He spoke behind the scenes with colleagues and usually received their support because of friendship and past favors. He avoided publicity and the threat he thought it posed for smoothing over differences.

I never once threw knives or wrote mean things, although plenty of knives got thrown at me. I never once got on television. The sum total of my national publicity was a release when I got into the race and a release when I got up to Washington saying I thought I had enough votes to win. I refused to go on television although I was invited to go on most of the news and panel shows. I never mentioned Bolling's name at all. I never mentioned issues or anything.[2]

1. Nelson W. Polsby, "Two Strategies of Influence: Choosing a Majority Leader, 1962," in Robert L. Peabody and Nelson W. Polsby, eds., *New Perspectives on the House of Representatives*, 2d ed. (Chicago: Rand McNally, 1969), p. 331.
2. Quoted in Polsby, "Two Strategies," p. 337.

Lacking Albert's popularity, Bolling countered by publicly highlighting their ideological differences, trying to influence colleagues through people outside the House who had their ears. He also hoped to use his many press contacts, who regarded him, in the words of one reporter, as "a good news source and popular among newsmen . . . [and] even more popular when he was moved to [the Rules Committee] as Rayburn's obvious protégé."[3]

Bolling's candidacy was uphill, but it was by no means doomed to failure. Even at the height of legislators' dependence on an inside strategy, working with the press to get something done in Congress was far from unheard of.[4] Albert's approach paid off mostly because the decision was more procedural than substantive and because House members, casting a secret ballot, were safe from outside surveillance. "Outside strategies are favored, presumably, when these conditions are reversed."[5]

Of course, such conditions are typically reversed in the 1980s. In fact, because virtually all steps in the legislative process have been opened to press scrutiny and because of the politically charged character of most decisions, conditions favoring an inside strategy are now rarely met. In addition, the dispersion of power in the House, the complex system of overlapping committees and subcommittees, and the labyrinthine journey that bills must take on Capitol Hill make one-on-one bargaining difficult—it is unclear exactly with whom one should bargain. As Representative Thomas Downey, an influential class-of-1974 member, has said, "Not getting publicity limits your effectiveness. . . . I can't think of someone around here who's effective just by being on the inside."[6]

## Can Complementarity Work?

Does this mean that an outside strategy is now *the* way of getting something done in Congress and in Washington? Nonmembers seeking to influence Congress seem to think so. As power became dispersed on Capitol Hill in the 1970s, would-be leaders outside Congress had more to keep track of, more people to deal with, and more potential obstacles. Decision-

3. Quoted in Polsby, "Two Strategies," p. 348, note 2.

4. Ralph K. Huitt, "The Outsider in the Senate: An Alternative Role," *American Political Science Review*, vol. 55 (September 1961), pp. 566–75; and John E. Owens, "Extreme Advocacy Leadership in the Pre-Reform House: Wright Patman and the House Banking and Currency Committee," *British Journal of Political Science*, vol. 15 (April 1985), pp. 187–206.

5. Polsby, "Two Strategies," p. 356.

6. Quoted in Burdett A. Loomis, *The New American Politician: Ambition, Entrepreneurship, and the Changing Face of Political Life* (Basic Books, 1988), p. 80.

making inside Congress became more collegial after earlier systems of czar rule by the Speaker and an emphasis on working through committees.[7] It is no longer easy to shape events on the Hill or move a bill along simply by contacting a few strategically placed people. Instead, persuading constituents to lobby their representatives or to write Congress en masse has become the accepted way to get things done. As James Baker, White House chief of staff under Ronald Reagan, said, "A, you've got to have a message, and B, you've got to be able to sell that message. . . . You've got to be able to sell it not just to the public but also on the Hill. But the key to selling it on the Hill is to sell it publicly."[8]

Presidents have increasingly appealed to the public for support. Even before Ronald Reagan, going public had largely supplanted the bargaining that was once the key to executive power.[9] Rather than turn to an outside strategy only if other efforts have failed, contemporary presidents have begun with public appeals, resorting to backroom bargaining only to win swing votes. Interest groups and lobbies also deal with the media much more often than in the past, whether they proceed like citizens' groups, wooing reporters, or like corporate groups that simply buy advertisements. Either way they avoid the herculean task of lobbying all 535 members of Congress separately.[10]

The adequacy of using only an outside strategy depends on its goals. It may be enough merely to call attention to a problem that someone else has to take care of. The legislative process involves not only enactment of bills, but implementation of their provisions by the executive branch and oversight of the results by Congress. Through the media, which are often ready for stories of government mismanagement, Congress can call attention to practices within the executive branch that ignore public opinion or interpret congressional intent too freely.

Likewise, representatives may not always be interested in passing legislation. Some Republicans, most notably the outspoken members of the Conservative Opportunity Society (COS), have recently argued that setting

7. Steven S. Smith, "New Patterns of Decisionmaking in Congress," in John E. Chubb and Paul E. Peterson, eds., *The New Direction in American Politics* (Brookings, 1985).

8. Quoted in Mark Hertsgaard, *On Bended Knee: The Press and the Reagan Presidency* (Farrar Straus Giroux, 1988), p. 23.

9. Samuel Kernell, *Going Public: New Strategies of Presidential Leadership* (Washington: CQ Press, 1986). Richard Neustadt's latest afterwords in *Presidential Power: The Politics of Leadership from FDR to Carter* (John Wiley, 1980), the classic exposition of the primacy of bargaining, show resigned support for increasing use of television as a means of persuasion.

10. Kay Lehman Schlozman and John T. Tierney, *Organized Interests and American Democracy* (Harper and Row, 1986), pp. 170–82, especially tables 7.3 and 8.1.

forth a coherent agenda should be the goal. "This is very much a long-term strategy," said a press assistant to a freshman Republican active in COS. "We've been so long with the Republicans in the minority [that] it's easier to be in the minority [than govern] unless we can demonstrate that we could govern, come up with plans and alternatives rather than saying no." Others disagree; the press aide to a conservative Republican on the Appropriations Committee complained, "Some members are advocating philosophical goals through the national media, getting their message across. But they won't get a bill passed all session." But in an era in which parties are becoming polarized, Democrats and Republicans alike set forth issues with partisan truculence, largely for short-term political gain: either they will get the policy they want or they will have ready to hand an issue to run on in the next campaign. Tony Coelho, when chair of the House Democratic Congressional Campaign Committee, commented, "Politics should not control legislation, but we need to know the politics of the legislation. . . . Republicans are doing this marketing. We need to concentrate more on who delivers the message and how."[11]

Inside strategies have not been entirely displaced, however. Even in the 1981 debate over Reagan's severe budget cuts—the clearest case we have of a campaign to influence Congress by mobilizing public opinion—key votes were won by trading favors. For a president to advocate a policy agenda and then invoke the specter of public disapproval if Congress fails to act has often been enough for some form of legislation to be drafted and passed; but resentment among legislators accustomed to bargaining and to being consulted may build and threaten the president's success. A classic case was the revolt of the House Republicans in 1986 when they were faced with the tax reform package that emerged from Ways and Means. When the adoption of rules necessary to consider the package was defeated because it received almost no Republican support, Reagan had to consult with members of his party in person to win them over. Presidents may also have to turn to bargaining to find agreement on the fine points of an agenda. Likewise, while interest groups report a sharp rise in their use of television and newspaper ads, they are also more active in almost all methods of influence, including direct contact and consultation.[12]

For those who want to be key legislators, the outside strategy can only go so far. The media may help set an agenda and increase the prominence of an issue, but the outside strategy is a blunt instrument. Enacting legis-

11. Quoted in Richard E. Cohen, "Taking the Very Long View, the Parties Begin Planning for 1992 House Elections," National Journal, April 13, 1985, p. 795.
12. Schlozman and Tierney, Organized Interests, p. 157.

lation still requires deliberation on the particulars of a bill and consultation and compromise to build a coalition. Contrary to speculation, however, being a show horse is not incompatible with being a work horse; no empirical investigation has been able to prove that seeking or receiving publicity precludes legislative labor.[13] Work horses can find publicity useful to advance their goals when inside strategies are impractical. Even after the agenda has been set, they can use the media to narrow the debate to consideration of a few alternatives and specification of their main components. One press secretary to a Republican on the House Judiciary Committee pointed out the benefits:

> One is packaging, communicating your idea. Any package has to have proper substance *and* attention getters *and* articulation of what you're doing. . . . If legislation is to go anywhere, it has to be understood. With immigration, we could see the education in the media; members knew pretty well what was going on. They were asking less often, "What are employer sanctions?" than "Why is [X] pushing this approach to employer sanctions?" It's a big oversight to neglect packaging.

Both leaders and backbenchers are increasingly called on to pursue inside and outside strategies simultaneously. Time routinely elevates members to power committees—Appropriations, Budget, Rules, or Ways and Means—or to leadership of a subcommittee.[14] Yet attaining a position of some influence does not make an outside strategy superfluous; and such a post may make it easier to attract attention. Members seek a good reputation among journalists, which can be translated into influence in Con-

13. The only published article to show empirical evidence of the divide is James L. Payne, "Show Horses and Work Horses in the United States House of Representatives," *Polity*, vol. 12 (Spring 1980), pp. 428–56, but Payne's findings are almost entirely a methodological artifact; see my "Show Horses in House Elections: The Advantages and Disadvantages of National Media Visibility," in Jan Pons Vermeer, ed., *Campaigns in the News: Mass Media and Congressional Elections* (Westport, Conn.: Greenwood Press, 1987), note 1. See also Laura I. Langbein and Lee Sigelman, "Show Horses, Work Horses, and Dead Horses," *American Politics Quarterly*, vol. 17, no. 1 (1989), pp. 80–95. Members may sometimes be show horses, increasing their public participation on reelection-oriented matters, and work horses at other times, emphasizing behind-the-scenes negotiation on policy-oriented concerns. See Richard L. Hall, "Participation and Purpose in Committee Decision Making," *American Political Science Review*, vol. 81 (March 1987), pp. 105–27.

14. For example, by 1982 all but one of the members first elected in 1974 sat on power committees or were subcommittee leaders (chairs or ranking minority members). Burdett A. Loomis, "Congressional Careers and Party Leadership in the Contemporary House of Representatives," *American Journal of Political Science*, vol. 28 (February 1984), table 1.

gress, which then leads to increased favorable coverage, and so forth. To be a major player in Washington, a person must now achieve two reputations, one among colleagues and the other among reporters, government officials, lobbyists, and the public. Little wonder that Christopher Matthews, Tip O'Neill's administrative assistant, could list the keys to success on Capitol Hill in clear order: "the right style so that a member can get attention when it matters, the right issues and the ability to get things done internally."[15]

There is, however, a tension between outside strategies and inside strategies that must be managed if legislation is to be enacted. An inside strategy demands pliability to allow bargaining and compromise, and as a result the legendary tacticians of Congress rarely took a clear position on an issue they were considering. This was one of the keys to Wilbur Mills's success as chair of the House Ways and Means Committee: "On many issues, Mills is inscrutable to the members: they don't know if he has a position or, if he does, what it is. . . . To [committee members] he is an extremely skillful leader who responds to them in such a way that his conclusions, drawn from their discussions, become their conclusions."[16] Mills may have been unusually crafty, but party leaders, for whom keeping peace in the family is more important than enacting a given program, and committee leaders, who must be perceived as fair by committee members to stay in their positions, may prefer to avoid the close identification with a particular stand that could impair effectiveness as an inside player.[17]

An outside strategy, because it must rely on the media, needs a clear-cut, possibly definitive position that severely limits flexibility. Backbenchers can win attention by being linked to a particular view on a particular issue. Leaders of parties and committees must often respond in kind to avoid losing the spotlight. If journalists see mostly disingenuous tentativeness, they will turn elsewhere. And members who defer to a colleague on a matter of mutual concern may alert reporters that there is another expert voice on the issue and may lose influence. Far from the fluidity and mutual deference that characterizes the inside strategy, an outside strategy fa-

15. Quoted in Richard E. Cohen and Burt Solomon, "Congress's Rising Stars," *National Journal*, January 24, 1987, p. 176.

16. John F. Manley, *The Politics of Finance: The House Committee on Ways and Means* (Little, Brown, 1970), pp. 108–09.

17. Barbara Sinclair, *Majority Leadership in the U.S. House* (Johns Hopkins University Press, 1983); and Glenn R. Parker, "The Selection of Committee Leaders in the House of Representatives," *American Politics Quarterly*, vol. 7 (January 1979), pp. 71–93.

vors members who stake out turf for themselves alone and defend it in no uncertain terms.

Moreover, calling attention to an issue is not the same as responding to it, particularly if the subject occasions divisiveness. When asked about the role of the media in legislative strategies, the press assistant to a three-term moderate Southern Democrat replied,

> It depends on the issue being considered. Like the idea for a network for missing children—get it associated with the person and it gets its own constituency right off the bat. If members are not aware whether it's a good thing to support, they can then see that it is. But with highly debated issues, like covert aid to Nicaragua, it doesn't help. There's a confusing debate on the floor and a confusing debate in the papers.

The problem becomes how to exploit media attention while avoiding the disadvantages. The press secretary to a Republican leader provided one option: "Before legislative action, you want exposure, you want to generate public attention and public interest. Then you get to actually legislating and putting the pieces of the puzzle together, and you *don't* want it; you've got everything cranked up and then a story in the *Post* can kill you. . . . Sometimes it becomes a matter of shutting off initiatives: don't go to the press and don't generate an initiative and they won't be there." Turning off the spigot is not always so easy, however; once journalists discover an issue, the trajectory of coverage often has a logic of its own that defies being turned away, let alone turned off.

Balance and adroitness in changing from one strategy to another and back must be the goal, especially for House leaders. To illustrate both the difficulties of this approach and how it can be brought off, I will take two examples, that of Les Aspin and of Dan Rostenkowski, from the Ninety-ninth Congress (1985-86). In each case the legislators became powerful by mastering the skills of both insider and outsider.

## The Outsider and the Inside Strategy

Les Aspin's career path to the House marked him as an outsider from the start. Instead of moving up through local politics, his political experience was largely in Washington. An economics professor, he had worked for Walter Heller, chair of the Council of Economic Advisers, under Robert McNamara in the Defense Department, and on the staff of Senator William Proxmire. Returning to Wisconsin to work on President Johnson's soon-to-be-abandoned reelection campaign, Aspin unsuccessfully ran in a 1968 statewide primary for treasurer, then moved to the state's southeastern corner to challenge an incumbent Republican whom he defeated in 1970.

When Aspin reached Washington, he asked for and got a seat on the Armed Services Committee, at the time composed almost entirely of hawkish porkbarrelers trying to augment military projects in their districts.[18] As a critic of armed services policies, he was quickly able to carve out a niche. Moreover, he cultivated the press with quotable comments, information, and exposés on mismanagement, cost overruns, and conflict of interest in the Pentagon, news he often embargoed for release on slow news days such as Mondays. As he later noted, his prime concern was to get "a good story in something that matters . . . the *Wall Street Journal*, the *New York Times*, the *Washington Post*. Not because that carries back home but because it establishes bona fides with the people who it's important to impress, the community that you're dealing with . . . the defense community, or the foreign policy community, or the economics community."[19]

In his first term Aspin received extraordinary publicity in national newspapers. The *Almanac of American Politics* wrote, "There is little question these days what member of the House consistently churns out the most headlines and solid news stories . . . a 34-year-old, second-term Democrat from Wisconsin named Les Aspin."[20] In 1972, his second year in office, he was among the five House members from outside the New York area

18. On Armed Services, see Lewis Anthony Dexter, "Congressmen and the Making of Military Policy," in Peabody and Polsby, eds., *New Perspectives*, 2d ed., pp. 175–94; R. Douglas Arnold, *Congress and the Bureaucracy: A Theory of Influence* (Yale University Press, 1979), chap. 6; and Bruce A. Ray, "The Responsiveness of the U.S. Congressional Armed Services Committees to Their Parent Bodies," *Legislative Studies Quarterly*, vol. 5 (November 1980), pp. 501–15. Armed Services is still generally the most conservative committee in the House; in 1985 its members in both parties supported the conservative coalition 75 percent of the time, compared with the chamber average of 56 percent. Norman J. Ornstein, Thomas E. Mann, and Michael J. Malbin, *Vital Statistics on Congress, 1987–88* (Washington: CQ Press, 1987), p. 212.

19. Quoted in Katherine Winton Evans, "The News Maker: A Capitol Hill Pro Reveals His Secrets," *Washington Journalism Review*, vol. 3 (June 1981), p. 32. Aspin also said he did not aim directly for television, which might follow up on the publicity he would receive in the *Post* or the *Times*.

20. Michael Barone, Grant Ujifusa, and Douglas Matthews, *The Almanac of American Politics 1974: The Senators, the Representatives—Their Records, States, and Districts*, 2d ed. (Boston: Gambit, 1973), p. 1095.

mentioned most often in the *New York Times*.[21] In 1973, 1975, 1976, and 1977 he was among the ten House members mentioned most in the *Times*.

Aspin's high visibility did not win friends among his more senior colleagues on Armed Services. The chair, the conservative autocrat F. Edward Hébert, publicly told him in 1973 to "put up or shut up." Aspin blandly replied, "It's a sign that the system is really opening up when the chairman gets into a dialogue with a very junior member."[22] But while building respect through his press operations, he was also working behind the scene. He had begun building legislative coalitions to complement his press preoccupation with waste and fraud in the Defense Department. In his first year in office he had offered a floor amendment to put a spending ceiling equivalent to 1971 appropriations on the committee's 1972 defense appropration bill. Though that attempt was defeated, a similar amendment in 1973, cutting $1.5 billion in Pentagon procurement appropriations, passed 242–163 when Aspin was able to assemble a coalition of fiscally conservative Republicans and Democratic critics of the Pentagon (the amendment, not surprisingly, was dropped in the House-Senate conference). After he helped eject Hébert as Armed Services chair in favor of the more affable Melvin Price in 1975, he devoted more attention to working up the ladder of seniority to become chair of the Armed Services Subcommittee on Military Personnel and Compensation in 1983 and to being involved in backroom politicking on the Budget Committee and on the nuclear freeze battle. Then in 1985, though only seventh in committee rank, he parlayed his image into election to chair of the Armed Services Committee, beating the second-ranking Democrat, Charles Bennett.

Aspin was now in a position to be an inside player par excellence. But the troubles he faced in the Ninety-ninth Congress nearly resulted in his ouster from the chair in 1987. Some saw his problems as those of a show horse personality trying to adapt unsuccessfully to life as a work horse.[23] And indeed, in crafting compromises Aspin did continue to work as a loner, just as media-conscious members must in order to control the spotlight, and he dismissed many of the personal connections that insider leaders have traditionally exploited. More importantly, however, he aban-

21. For the record, these five were, in descending order, Mills, McCloskey, Ashbrook, Albert, and Aspin. Further indications of the company Aspin kept were the 1973 rankings (Albert, Mills, Aspin, Patman, O'Neill) and the 1975 rankings (Udall, Albert, Ullman, Reuss, Aspin).

22. Quoted in Alan Ehrenhalt, ed., *Politics in America: Members of Congress in Washington and at Home* (Washington: CQ Press, 1983), p. 1643.

23. See Christopher J. Matthews, "The Old Breed Strikes Back," *New Republic*, March 2, 1987, pp. 21–23.

doned much of the public criticism of the defense establishment he had been known for, breaking one of the main rules of politics: "Dance with the one that brung ya." Yet he owed his victory in the Democratic Caucus at least in part to his skills as an outsider and the expectations that he would serve as a spokesperson for the more dovish Democratic majority on or off the floor on such issues as MX missile procurement or aid to Nicaraguan contras. Representative Bob Edgar, for example, had argued that Democrats "need a spokesman who can go face to face with the administration and the Senate. . . . People feel Les could do a better job of articulating defense issues, especially before TV and radio."[24]

In his eagerness to show that he could play the inside game, Aspin sought out the hawkish senior committee members deferentially and avoided the press and public statements altogether, even as reporters began to depict the debate on building additional MX missiles as an either-or, Congress-versus-president battle. Ignoring the media's framing of the debate, he stayed studiously uncommitted. In March 1985 he initially hoped to delay the MX vote until after the start of the Geneva arms control talks so as to remove President Reagan's argument that the missile was a bargaining chip in the negotiation, but the administration refused to play along. A few days later a leak after a closed meeting with House Democratic leaders revealed that Aspin had decided to support additional missiles but with a cap on the number to be deployed. He later explained that to preserve room for negotiation he had to avoid locking himself into a public position too early. His ultimate endorsement of $1.5 billion for twenty-one more MX missiles provoked a backlash among those who had supported his outside strategy. One MX opponent, Representative Les AuCoin, fumed, "Aspin has used the conspicuous position we have given him to blur the distinction between the parties. We can't attack Reagan for his support for first-strike weapons when the chairman of the House Armed Services Committee is wiring the deal for him. Frankly, it burns the hell out of us."[25] Even though Aspin achieved impressive results on such tough issues as reform of military pensions, what had been an advantage for inside players like Wilbur Mills—their unwillingness to commit themselves too early—had in the spotlight become a liability for him.

At the start of the One-hundredth Congress in January 1987, all com-

24. Quoted in Nadine Cohodas and Diane Granat, "House Seniority System Jolted; Price Dumped, Aspin Elected," *Congressional Quarterly Weekly Report*, January 5, 1985, p. 9.
25. Quoted in Andy Plattner, "To Les Aspin, MX Victory Brings Some Pain," *Congressional Quarterly Weekly Report*, March 30, 1985, p. 564.

mittee chairs came up for election by the House Democratic Caucus. Aspin's chief opposition for the Armed Services chair was Marvin Leath, who, in the words of Representative Barney Frank, "although very conservative, has won a lot of support within the caucus for being intellectually honest and consistent. . . . There's no problem figuring out who he is and where he is. . . . One of the problems people have with Les is that he hasn't been straightforward."[26] Aspin lost the initial vote of confidence, 130–124; but two weeks later he defeated three competitors after admitting—in person, in a contrite "Dear Colleague" letter, and most tellingly in a pleading interview in the *Washington Post* that appeared the morning of the second vote—that the rebuff had told him to change his style.

As he confessed in the *Washington Post*, he had not anticipated the problems he faced after years as a media-whiz loner. "An individual congressman, who's a specialist in the area, who knows how to think through a problem, who knows how to deal with the political thing, I think, can put together ad hoc solutions. . . . But you can't do that if you're committee chairman. . . . You're supposed to lead a permanent coalition." After the vote, he believed there were "a lot of things I need to do differently in . . . the way I deal with my colleagues on a one-to-one basis. I need to be more open, more up front. . . . The message is not that you have to toe the party line on issues. . . . What it does say is . . . you can't surprise people. You've got to be frank about what you're doing."[27] In short, seeking to play an inside role, Aspin could not easily balance it with the outside strategy that had brought him success. He had fourteen years of experience building temporary coalitions through the media, and his supporters expected him to continue.

Aspin's chastened tone presaged changed behavior. When he stood for reelection as chair in 1989, he had virtually no opposition. His activity in the One-hundredth Congress showed him a master of media strategy as played by a committee chair rather than by a backbencher: he became the key spokesperson for both the committee and for the Democratic majority. Most notably, instead of his 1985 coyness about the MX and the contras, he came out with well-publicized criticism of the B-1 bomber and of President Reagan's approach to arms control. Within the committee, he la-

26. Quoted in Janet Hook and Jacqueline Calmes, "Aspin May Face Challenge at Armed Services," *Congressional Quarterly Weekly Report*, July 12, 1986, p. 1565.

27. Quoted in Sidney Blumenthal, "Les Aspin at High Noon," *Washington Post*, January 22, 1987, p. B1; and quoted in Jacqueline Calmes, "Aspin Makes Comeback at Armed Services," *Congressional Quarterly Weekly Report*, January 24, 1987, p. 139.

bored to include even the staunchest prodefense members in the decision on the military spending bill and on whatever military reform issues on which they could find common ground. He worked with Democratic arch-hawk Samuel Stratton to respond toughly against the procurement excesses of the B-1 and to draft an amendment to implement competitive procurement for the stealth bomber. At the same time, he persuaded other hardliners that high spending on Reagan's strategic defense initiative could jeopardize conventional weapons programs. When Armed Services finished its work on the military spending bill, it was still past the targets of the Budget Committee, and Aspin was able to assuage doubts about its representativeness by artfully shaping a procedure to consider some 200 amendments on the floor.[28]

It may well be that after his close call, Aspin improved his skill at an inside strategy. But equally important, he now took greater care that the inside game be played in terms that fit his outside mass-mediated reputation so that the two would complement one another. Acceding to the chair of Armed Services was not a reason to drop the outside game but a commitment to reinvigorate it.

## The Insider and the Outside Strategy

Dan Rostenkowski was first elected to the House from a Chicago district in 1958—or perhaps one should say anointed, given that he was a protégé of Mayor Richard Daley. Rostenkowski was more interested in rising in the ranks of Chicago politics and in the House than in any particular set of policies. For him, as for most members of the prereform House, an appointment to the Ways and Means Committee was coveted not because of its jurisdiction over tax policy, but because it was perhaps the most influential committee and because its Democratic members controlled committee assignments. In the contexts in which Rostenkowski operated, whether Chicago machine politics, the leadership circles of Speaker John

28. Aspin decided to space out dovish and hawkish amendments to ensure that members concerned about looking lax could show otherwise: "The House doesn't want to go on one tack for too long. . . . If it hits a couple of votes going left, the boys are then looking to tack back and go to the right." Quoted in Linda Greenhouse, "A Military Bill Like None Other," *New York Times*, May 13, 1987, p. B12.

McCormack, or Ways and Means under Wilbur Mills's tutelage, publicity was best avoided until the political decisions had been made.[29]

Of course, when Rostenkowski became chair of Ways and Means in 1981, the position was hardly delimited by smoke-filled rooms: his predecessors, Mills and Al Ullman, had been among the most visible members of the House. But neither had used this visibility to abet legislative goals, and there was little reason to think that Rostenkowski would act differently. His chief objective, like Mills's, was to win, to assemble bills that would pass the House floor and become law. And his was the motto of all bargainers pursuing the inside strategy: "to do what is doable."

In the classic style of a Chicago ward politician, Rostenkowski succeeded in winning committee loyalty through including the subcommittee chairs and other members in decisions. By his third term as chair he had restored to the position much of the power that Mills's fall from grace and Ullman's vacillating leadership had compromised. But his reputation still suffered from the missteps of his first term as chair. His attempt to out-Reagan Reagan in 1981 with new packages of tax cuts was thought unseemly, and it was stopped by a coalition of Republicans and conservative Democrats. The next year, when tax increases seemed inevitable, his troops refused to send a bill to the Senate, so the chair ended up going to a House-Senate conference without a bill to bargain with. And as the Ninety-ninth Congress dawned, Majority Leader Jim Wright, his longtime rival, announced that he had enough commitments to have the Speakership sewn up, effectively thwarting the Chicagoan's ambition.

If Rostenkowski wanted to be a power in Washington, an inside strategy alone would no longer suffice. With the arrival of tax reform on the congressional agenda in 1985, he was presented with an intriguing opportunity to make policy. The progress of tax reform was a textbook case of Washington policymaking in the 1980s, combining doggedly entrepreneurial politicians and a keen desire on everyone's part to avoid blame.[30] The idea to simplify the system by reducing the number of tax brackets and to bring down the rates by eliminating loopholes had been the core of legislation introduced by Senator Bill Bradley and Representative Richard

29. On the Daley machine's avoidance of publicity, see Milton L. Rakove, *Don't Make No Waves, Don't Back No Losers: An Insider's Analysis of the Daley Machine* (Indiana University Press, 1975), especially chap. 4. On the connection of Chicago and congressional politics under Daley, see Leo M. Snowiss, "Congressional Recruitment and Representation," *American Political Science Review*, vol. 60 (September 1966), pp. 627–39.

30. See, especially, Jeffrey H. Birnbaum and Alan S. Murray, *Showdown at Gucci Gulch: Lawmakers, Lobbyists and the Unlikely Triumph of Tax Reform* (Random House, 1987).

Gephardt in 1982. In 1984, to defuse a potential Democratic presidential campaign issue, President Reagan announced that after the election Treasury Secretary Donald Regan would present recommendations on rewriting the tax code, which he did, coming up with a remarkable draft that wiped out many loopholes and raised corporate taxes to boot.

Despite executive support, however, in early 1985 no one gave tax reform much chance. Public opinion was split. Well-organized lobbies— many with a spokesperson of their own on either the House Ways and Means Committee or the Senate Finance Committee—were loath to lose their cherished deductions. And the proposal's so-called revenue-neutral goals seemed less important than reduction of the federal budget deficit. That tax reform ended up being dramatically endorsed and passed was a tribute to legislating under the spotlight. President Reagan's decision to push tax reform before Congress did ensure its initial visibility, but the issue was custom-made for media attention. Simplifying the tax structure and sealing the loopholes that wealthy lobbyists had put in place matched journalists' needs for a clear issue and a progressive, good-government solution.

Thereafter, tax reform became a good in itself, almost regardless of the details. Anyone opposed to it might well be held responsible in the event of its demise, so few politicians opposed the goal. Since the House initiates revenue legislation, the Ways and Means Committee had to be first to respond. From the outset House Democrats agreed with Reagan's overall goals and offered their support in principle. The response was primarily defensive. As Speaker O'Neill said, "I have to have a bill, the Democratic party has to have a bill, and Danny's got to put one together that will sell. If we don't, we'll be clobbered over the head by the President of the United States."[31] To avoid being clobbered by blame and to prevent the Republicans from establishing what many saw as an issue that might attract more voters to their party, Democrats had to come up with a high-profile initiative—if only to pass the buck to the Republican Senate.

Rostenkowski responded in part with an inside strategy, discouraging the introduction of bills until the Reagan administration decided what it wanted to do. But he also hired a new speechwriter and endorsed reform before the Economic Club of New York. The outside strategy became more important when he was chosen to give the Democratic response to President Reagan's prime-time speech in May 1985 that unveiled the plan.

---

31. Quoted in Steven V. Roberts, "A Most Important Man on Capitol Hill," *New York Times Magazine*, September 22, 1985, p. 48.

Gruff, gravel-voiced, and scarcely telegenic, Rostenkowski was a curious choice, but with the assistance of a media consultant, he matched the intimate style perfected by Reagan, closing with a homely invitation to "Write Rosty." The ward heeler was suddenly becoming a statesman. With some disbelief, Mary McGrory wrote in the *Washington Post,* "What have we here? Has a star been born? People are talking about that new television personality, Rep. Dan Rostenkowski," and she referred to him as "a man who at 8:15 Tuesday night was a hack and who, 15 minutes later, had become TV's political rookie of the year."[32]

Not only did the speech provide Rostenkowski a place in the spotlight, it also put the House Democratic hierarchy squarely behind the effort to simplify the tax structure and established the chair of Ways and Means as the authoritative source on tax reform for reporters and for his colleagues.[33] But the new outside strategy was intended less to mobilize public support than to shore up the inside strategy so the chair could get a bill out of committee. Having grabbed the position of authority, Rostenkowski then made sure that the bill would be considered in full committee rather than a subcommittee presided over by someone else. Next the committee heard a great many witnesses so that no group could claim it was ignored. The tactic also gave journalists something to cover in open hearings while negotiations went on behind the scenes. Finally, Rostenkowski asked House members to make no advance commitments on the bill in general or on any aspect of it. This ensured the flexibility necessary for the chair to come up with a package because, in the words of one Ways and Means member, legislators then had to respond to lobbyists, "Gee, I'd love to be with you on this one, but the chairman has prevented me from committing myself." This may not have deterred members from trying to protect pet loopholes or from making alliances among themselves, but it did prevent them from taking unchangeable public positions.

Because they saw Rostenkowski as the principal mover behind tax reform and because Ways and Means was using his plan as the basis for amendments, reporters could easily expose a modification that favored special interests. Even if the public was noncommittal or bemused, the obviousness of such a proposal and the possibility that pushing for it could be turned against them pressured members to support the chair. In partic-

---

32. Mary McGrory, "Has a Star Been Born?" *Washington Post,* May 30, 1985, p. A2.

33. Alongside the smoother and more open Bob Packwood, who chaired the Senate Finance Committee, Rostenkowski was still not the ideal television source. As one network correspondent commented, "Consider what the House does—it initiates all the tax bills, and this is all fine, but we've had one good tax story and Packwood was easier to cover than Rostenkowski."

ular, after Rostenkowski was overruled by the committee's adoption of an amendment proposed by Ronnie Flippo that expanded a tax break for banks, he delayed reconsideration to allow media pressure to build. "This one's gonna hang out there," he warned. "Just let them stew in it for a while." Jeffrey Birnbaum and Alan Murray described what happened next:

> Newspaper and trade publications did their part to help. They humiliated the committee by reporting the gloating words of the bank lobbyist: "We won! We won!" The embarrassment was compounded by a scathing article by tax reporter Anne Swardson in the *Washington Post* headlined: TAX REFORMERS TURN RECIDIVIST; BANK LOBBYISTS WON ANOTHER BREAK FROM WAYS AND MEANS. The piece featured pictures of members who voted for the offending amendment with their lame explanations as to why. The story was exactly the kind of public pulverizing the chairman was counting on to help turn his members around. "The last thing that any of these guys want," explained one aide, "is for it to be written that tax reform dies in the Ways and Means Committee because sleazebag politicians want to take care of First National City Bank so the average public gets screwed."[34]

With the spotlight turned on the dissenters, the chair became a behind-the-scenes bargainer, working out a new compromise with Flippo and later with members who worried about the loss of a deduction for state and local taxes.

Adroitly balancing strategies, Rostenkowski was able to goad a balky committee into reporting out a bill, and after numerous reversals, including a Republican rebellion, tax reform was passed. To be sure, such a publicized process had its pitfalls. When the press highlighted this issue, the important point became whether a member was for or against reforms, even though there were as many ways to achieve reform as there were reformers and though simplification was soon forgotten. But when forced to choose, members did not think they could oppose reform in principle, and they often voted in spite of the details, incorrectly hoping that matters would be cleared up on the floor or in the Senate or in the House-Senate conference. The results are mixed; whether the reformed system is fairer

---

34. Birnbaum and Murray, *Showdown at Gucci Gulch*, p. 127. Rostenkowski would later use a similar threat of "three-inch-high newspaper headlines" if the members bucked him on reducing the deduction for business entertainment.

or economically sounder or simpler than its predecessor seems open to debate.

But for Rostenkowski himself, tax reform had no such disadvantage. His victory made him a public figure to be reckoned with in Washington—something more than just another committee chair, especially when taxes became news again. As an indication and reinforcement of that power, Rostenkowski was one of the first Democrats to appear on television after George Bush's victory on election night 1988. When NBC anchor Tom Brokaw asked him about Bush's famous sound bite, "Read my lips: no new taxes," Rostenkowski, in his best gruffly good-humored style, crossed his arms and said, "Tom, I don't read lips." And when the *New York Times* ran an update on Capitol Hill prospects just days before Bush's inauguration, six members of Congress were profiled; only two hailed from the House—Wright and Rostenkowski.

## Legislating under the Spotlight

In the 1960s House, inside strategists were usually thought to hold the best cards. Such is no longer the case. Now when members want to shape policy and build their influence, the outside strategy is at least as attractive. Legislating through the media is a reasonable option to a House member who otherwise faces obstacles or inertia. For those looking for new ways to address the public interest and advance their careers, linking media strategies and legislative strategies can call attention to the larger issues and overcome seemingly entrenched interests. In fact, the success of the Ninety-ninth Congress with tax reform may remain the model of how to effect sweeping change in the face of interest-group politics.

But an outside strategy cannot stand alone. Television and newspapers may help set the agenda, but they do not clearly discriminate among the various potential solutions or reforms. When filtered through reporters' preferences for clear-cut issues, an outside strategy may pressure members to choose sides. How the policy is to be carried out can easily become less important than whether it is enacted in some form. The subtleties of Aspin's position on the MX missile in 1985 were lost amidst reporters' concerns about whether he was for or against it. Rostenkowski's and Reagan's successes with going public on tax reform may have resulted precisely from their lack of preoccupation with details; as long as the top rates were lowered and the number of tax brackets reduced, all was well. Yes-or-no, either-or appeals are custom-made for achieving publicity. Details of execution are not. So using the media to legislate may require impressive skill at the acrobatics of balancing strategies—even though the training, the tactics, and the expectations for the two diverge more often than they converge.

There is much to be said for making news in order to make laws. The strategy can establish that the general aims of the legislation are worth pursuing. It implicitly encourages members to clarify their positions and may well also push them to look beyond servicing the organized interest groups and toward extrinsic standards of public policy in the public interest.[35] But an outside strategy is no panacea; it can too readily slip into position taking that accomplishes only symbolic or even other ends.[36]

Moreover, the extent to which a media strategy actually involves the public in the legislative process is open to question. Many examples of successfully going public have occurred when the public has been divided or uncertain. The prominence of matters before Congress is a product more of what sells to the media than of what sells to public opinion. Journalists have little knowledge about their audiences, and their priorities often differ from popular concerns.[37] And so long as this is the case, the media will be imperfect guardians of representative democracy.

35. David E. Price, "Policy Making in Congressional Committees: The Impact of 'Environmental' Factors," *American Political Science Review*, vol. 72 (June 1978), pp. 548–74.

36. Recall David Mayhew's conclusion in *Congress: The Electoral Connection* (Yale University Press, 1974), p. 138, that laws display "the congressional penchant for the blunt, simple action" because the public judges members by positions rather than effects. He may have been right about tendencies toward broad-brush, quickly understood legislation, but one could easily point to legislating through the media, with their preference for clear-cut solutions, as much as Mayhew blamed truckling to the people.

37. Herbert J. Gans, *Deciding What's News: A Study of CBS Evening News, NBC Nightly News, Newsweek, and Time* (Pantheon, 1979), chap. 7; and Robert Darnton, "Writing News and Telling Stories," *Daedalus*, vol. 104 (Spring 1975), pp. 175–94.

# 8

# Media Power and Congressional Power

The House of Representatives has long witnessed the chaotic comings and goings of its 435 members—from offices to committee rooms to the floor and back again while lobbyists and constituents try to get in a word or two on the run. But increasingly relations with the news media seem to take up legislators' time and effort. Dressed in telegenic blue shirts and red neckties, they stand before television cameras in the swamp, the section of the Capitol lawn set aside for interviews. Inside the Capitol, too, floor debates are often aimed at the discreetly placed cameras that broadcast the proceedings to members' offices, the press galleries, and homes across the country. Staffers and interns dash from one gallery to the next with stacks of press releases to be distributed. Reporters crowd outside hearing rooms to receive a committee report or corner a witness. In short, much of the hubbub of Capitol Hill today is contributed by the press and their would-be subjects. Making laws is far from the only business of the House. It has been supplemented by making news.

Making news was not always so important. Reporters have been present on Capitol Hill for nearly two centuries, but rarely before has seeking publicity been such a significant part of every House member's job. For most of the twentieth century the way to get things done and to advance a career in Washington was to play an inside game, building relationships with colleagues, deferring to senior members, and bargaining, while slowly building up the legislative longevity necessary to achieve a position of power. Legislators paid little attention to reporters except those from the press back home, and they severely restricted the access of radio and television to the House. The House was governed by party leaders and committee chairs who preferred to stay out of the spotlight whenever possible.

Now all that has changed. The media are useful to members for publicity to help them get reelected, of course, but increasingly also in policymaking, wielding influence in Congress and in Washington, and pursuing their personal ambitions. Making news has frequently become integral to the legislative process. Reporters for all kinds of news outlets can now be present at any stage of the legislative process and can be instrumental in shaping the results. Sophisticated House press operations try to create national constituencies for issues on which members can serve as authoritative sources and build reputations. At the very least, legislators who wish to be considered influential experts have to ensure that their media image fits their chosen self-portrait, so few of them, inside or outside leadership circles, can pass up opportunities to be newsworthy. Making news, in short, has become a crucial component of making laws.

This reliance shows few signs of abating, even after the departure of Ronald Reagan, whose presidency has thus far been the high-water mark of going public. His successor, George Bush, has carefully crafted a media strategy, but it has shown him off as more a manager than a great communicator. However, Bush's recent choice of the Iwo Jima Memorial as the backdrop for introducing a constitutional amendment to ban flag burning shows that the adept use of sound bites and visual imagery that marked his presidential campaign could easily turn into a strategy of governing by campaigning. On Capitol Hill the Senate in 1986 finally followed the House's lead in broadcasting floor proceedings, further cementing the conjuncture of making laws and making news. And Tip O'Neill, the self-confessed backroom politician who brought the House into the television age, was succeeded first in 1987 by Jim Wright, whose aggressive, policy-oriented loner style was well-suited for the press, and in 1989 by Thomas Foley, perhaps "the first House Speaker whom most colleagues feel comfortable putting in front of television cameras" and whose tenure as majority leader had been marked by unprecedented attention to publicity.[1]

The conditions that made it not only possible but necessary to use the media to get legislative business accomplished also show few signs of abating. The expansion of congressional staffs in the 1970s will not be reversed; and each new Congress will see members naming more full-time press secretaries. Likewise, the number of Washington reporters should continue to grow steadily. News organizations may be tightening their belts, but the rise of newspaper chains, the abundance of stringers, and the cre-

---

1. Janet Hook, "The Turmoil and Transition: Stage Set for New Speaker," *Congressional Quarterly Weekly Report*, May 27, 1989, p. 1225.

ation of groups such as Conus that contract out television news services mean that virtually any news outlet can have a relatively inexpensive link to Washington. Such easy hookups allow members to add their comments to stories that are bouncing among various newsbeats in the capital. Above all, the news media help House members set the legislative agenda, define the alternatives, influence public moods, and affect outcomes at a time when the political process is confused and unpredictable.

Yet if legislators need reporters, reporters also need legislators to create the events or provide the observations that can become the basis of a story. Even though the needs of the two are rarely identical, they can work in a symbiosis. House members, even at high levels of power, cannot automatically make news. Instead, they must ensure that their information and stories meet journalistic standards of timeliness, pertinence, and interest. Reporters' dependence on authoritative sources to suggest news means that journalism tends to reflect the perspectives of the more powerful. But such power is not absolute, because while politicians control definitions of importance, journalists still decide what is interesting. So House members and reporters negotiate and renegotiate newsworthiness. The question should not then be what the news media have done *to* the House, or what the House has done *to* the news media, but what these two institutions have done *with* one another. What is the effect of this negotiation on policymaking and on representative democracy? The answers must be speculative, but they are well worth contemplating.

## Policymaking Processes and the Media

The power of the press often buttresses established power and procedures in the House. Hill traditions of pursuing expertise and influence dovetail with reporters' search for sources who are in a position to know. Reporters accord a reassuring coherence to the legislative process by focusing on "particularly and peculiarly congressional actions," stressing the gradual, orderly nature of the way bills are passed rather than the chaos or stasis that characterizes much of congressional life.[2]

2. Most news about Congress and its members is neutral. Negative accounts predominate in part because positive stories are almost nonexistent, but most stories cannot be confidently coded one way or the other. See Michael J. Robinson and Kevin R. Appel, "Network News Coverage of Congress," *Political Science Quarterly*, vol. 94 (Fall 1979), pp. 407–18; and Charles M. Tidmarch and John J. Pitney, Jr., "Covering Congress," *Polity*, vol. 17 (Spring 1985), pp. 463–83. Individual

But the priorities of journalists and politicians are not always so syn-chronized. Reporters have less leeway in whom to report about or when to report it than in the issues that will receive coverage. Some of the coverage of Congress is a by-product of the coverage of issues. Issues most likely to make news are easily described, have clearly characterized sides, affect a large part of the audience, and come with straightforward reform reme-dies. Journalists tend to pass up matters that are complex, unfamiliar, spe-cialized, or not apparently easily addressed.

If members want news coverage, they must choose clear-cut issues or try to present the complex as simple. But such choices invite distortion or omission of complicating factors. The alternative ways to achieve tax re-form in the Ninety-ninth Congress, for instance, were displaced by an either-or question: "Are you for tax reform or against it?" Likewise, the inadequacies of the patchwork system of unemployment compensation went unreported when journalists converged on the single problem of hundreds of thousands of unemployed in danger of being precipitously dropped from the rolls when the Federal Supplemental Compensation program expired.

Setting the agenda is only the first step in the journey of legislation; press attention affects later stages, too. Bargaining among members, once the hallmark of a legislative institution, becomes more difficult when reporters are watching—not so much because members act differently in public than in private but because reporters' dislike for noncommittal stances tends to discourage the fluidity and maneuverability necessary to resolve differences on the fine points and to enact legislation.

Legislators who wish to get something done must be both outside and inside players. Press coverage can enhance their reputations and direct colleagues' attention toward them as people to listen to. Inside strategies can lead to the influential post that can be used to gain the media's atten-tion. Using them together can be synergistic, accomplishing more than using either one on its own. But as Les Aspin's chastening experience in his first term as chair of the Armed Services Committee illustrates, chang-ing from one approach to another is not always easy to handle.

To the extent that the press spotlights problems and helps set the legis-lative agenda, an additional complication arises: the clock of Congress will resemble that of the news. The media have a limited attention span. They

members of Congress do get raked over the coals periodically for abuse-of-power stories, but such accounts tend to emphasize rotten apples in the barrel rather than problems with the barrel itself.

discover problems suddenly, but their interest rapidly wanes, whether or not the problems have been solved.[3] As entrepreneurial politicians take advantage of the brief window of opportunity to get something done, agenda items can rise and fall in importance with dizzying rapidity. In such a fast-forwarded context legislators feel pressured to respond and may grab the first alternative presented to them, often in spite of the details, while hoping that the other chamber will take care of the problem. Cooling-off periods in committee or in conference may be necessary, as with the anti–drug abuse bill in the One-hundredth Congress, when the legislative process overheats.

Yet for all these drawbacks, the conjunction of media strategies and legislative strategies can aid policymaking, particularly in surmounting entrenched interests and facilitating large-scale legislative initiatives. The news suggests problems or alternatives that Congress has bypassed. It helps inform and mobilize public opinion. At the very least it forces legislators to look beyond the interests of organized groups with the most immediate stakes and perhaps toward the larger public interest. When members would prefer to do nothing, publicity can increase the risks of inaction. In short, members in the spotlight are pressured to deal with problems in a way that corresponds to their readings of public opinion.

## Congress and Mass-Mediated Democracy

To evaluate more fully the implications of the media's role in the House, though, one must set forth standards for the roles of legislators and legislatures in representative democracy.[4] After all, the Constitution assigned the House in particular to represent the people. At its most basic, political representation means that officials are elected to act on behalf of

3. G. Ray Funkhouser, "The Issues of the Sixties: An Exploratory Study in the Dynamics of Public Opinion," *Public Opinion Quarterly*, vol. 37 (Spring 1973), pp. 62–75. A recent example of such a cycle is television's coverage of the AIDS epidemic; see David C. Colby, Timothy E. Cook, and Timothy B. Murray, "Social Movements and Sickness on the Air: Television News on AIDS and Agenda Control," paper presented at the 1987 annual meeting of the American Political Science Association.

4. It is impossible to pin down a definitive description of representation. My version has been influenced by Hanna Fenichel Pitkin's *The Concept of Representation* (University of California Press, 1967), while community building is best discussed in Nancy L. Schwartz, *The Blue Guitar: Political Representation and Community* (University of Chicago Press, 1988).

their constituents' interests. Legislators should be accountable and responsive to (though not fully bound by) their electors. Ideally, a dialogue between representative and constituency would lead to some sort of shared agreement on the best course of action. These views would then be aggregated in Congress through an institutional arrangement ensuring that all interests are taken into account in the process and the outcome.

At the local level the relationship of House member and constituency would initially seem to be working wonderfully. If, as in 1988, nearly 99 percent of the House incumbents standing for reelection are returned for another term, what could possibly be wrong? But as Hanna Pitkin has pointed out, a legislator's reelection "is not absolute proof that he is a good representative; it proves at most that the voters think so."[5] And when reasons for that approval are examined, optimism about the idealness of the relationship must be tempered. Incumbents win reelection more or less by default against invisible opposition. To be sure, even under these circumstances members are constrained by the realization that they might have to account for their actions.[6] To compile a record that can be easily explained back home, when they present themselves in person to as many constituents as possible, they end up anticipating their constituents' will and responding to it. Their accessibility can result in dialogue. But when legislators rely on explaining through the media rather than explaining in person, dialogue is replaced by one-way rhetoric.

The ascendancy of rhetoric might not be a problem if it were informative and balanced, but it is not. Even local news outlets rarely report House elections with the same effort and initiative they devote to statewide or presidential elections. This neglect works to the incumbents' advantage, because in effect they can shape the timing, content, and tone of their own coverage. All of this means that the voters lack enough information and tilt toward incumbents because they have no reason to be against them. Far from being watchdogs, the local media usually reinforce an incumbent's advantage by benign neglect.

What can be done? Cutting back on the incumbent's franking privilege or other perquisites of office is no answer: it can be valuable in a democracy to have legislators communicate with their constituents or travel home. And regulating perks does little to right the balance. Banning mass mailings within sixty days of an election simply moved them from November

5. Pitkin, *Concept of Representation*, p. 165.
6. The fullest accounts are in John W. Kingdon, *Congressmen's Voting Decisions* (Harper and Row, 1973), chap. 2; and Richard F. Fenno, Jr., *Home Style: House Members in Their Districts* (Little, Brown, 1978).

to September. Regulating the content of postal patron newsletters has created a Franking Commission that diligently counts the number of times a personal pronoun is used but that has little say over substance.

To ensure dialogue and choice, more information must be available. For all the criticism of television advertisements, their content is sometimes more substantive than that allowed by the horse-race mentality of election coverage, and voters may actually learn as much from them.[7] But though campaign managers have considered television the most crucial medium, they rarely buy television time.[8] Airing ads, even those lasting no more than thirty seconds, is so prohibitively expensive that by themselves they are responsible for spiraling campaign expenditures. Reforms must control the expense at its root, or else such proposals as publicly financing congressional elections or placing limits on fundraising (as by restricting the contributions of political action committees) would not improve the quality of information and the quality of voters' decisionmaking.

One answer: since television and radio are regulated by the government, they could be required to broadcast a certain number of messages from the major candidates of each district in the media market, much as stations are already obliged to carry a certain number of public service announcements. Naturally, incumbents are not keen on this idea; in a 1986 survey, 61 percent of the challengers endorsed the idea but only 30 percent of the incumbents.[9] Similar provisions could allow an equal number of campaign mailings sent at government expense by challengers opposing representatives who have sent out newsletters. Members may think twice about blanketing the district with self-serving propaganda if they know their challengers will receive equal treatment. Without some such reforms, elections will remain trials that are all defense and no prosecution.

Of course, providing candidates with free air time does not preclude them from using it to obscure or distort—witness the number of liberal Democrats who used television ads to portray themselves as fiscal conserv-

---

7. The most famous statement of this view is Thomas E. Patterson and Robert D. McClure, *The Unseeing Eye* (G. P. Putnam's, 1976). Other evidence is reviewed in Lynda Lee Kaid, "Political Advertising," in Dan D. Nimmo and Keith R. Sanders, eds., *Handbook of Political Communication* (Beverly Hills: Sage Publications, 1981), pp. 249–71.

8. Edie N. Goldenberg and Michael W. Traugott, *Campaigning for Congress* (Washington: CQ Press, 1984). Another study of House candidates in 1986 concluded that more than half of those surveyed spent less than $10,000 on advertising. Center for Responsive Politics, *Beyond the Thirty-Second Spot: Enhancing the Media's Role in Congressional Campaigns* (Washington, 1988).

9. Center for Responsive Politics, *Beyond the Thirty-Second Spot.*

atives in the Reaganite year of 1984.[10] And reforms aimed at television or at newsletters only indirectly affect newspapers. To answer these concerns, news about House members and House campaigns must be made easier to report. A barrier to providing enough information to the voters is the nature of district boundaries. The few districts that receive complete coverage of House elections correspond closely to television media markets or newspaper circulation areas. The less overlap, the less coverage and the less information about the candidates, especially the challenger. House districts, assembled to meet court standards of population equality, are gerrymandered to protect partisans or incumbents. Their boundaries do not match those of existing political communities or, more importantly, media markets.[11] In 1986 the Supreme Court ruled that political gerrymandering is a justiciable issue, so plans may now be tossed out for favoring particular political outcomes, including protection of incumbents.[12] If state legislatures considered media market boundaries in carving up districts, or if, perhaps more likely, courts took them into account when reviewing redistricting plans, there would be fewer election contests for each news organization to try to cover and probably more information about both incumbent and challenger.

Redrawing district lines would make House races easier to cover, but for reelection to be less routine, journalistic definitions of newsworthiness, balance, and completeness must change. If news organizations are not to give incumbents a boost for reelection, there must be stories other than those instigated by the members themselves. Instead of waiting for legislators to provide a peg for news, local outlets could easily come up with stories out of the public record such as analyses of what the members did in committee or on the floor and how they voted. During the campaign itself, editors and publishers should take care to identify both the incumbent and the challenger as serious candidates, perhaps even assigning different reporters to each one to ensure treatment that is as even-handed as possible. Until this is done, local news organizations, if only by overlook-

10. Richard A. Joslyn, "Liberal Campaign Rhetoric in 1984," in Jan Pons Vermeer, ed., *Campaigns in the News: Mass Media and Congressional Elections* (Westport, Conn.: Greenwood Press, 1987), pp. 31–49.

11. The low overlap of district lines with already existing political communities is less detrimental to information gathering by voters than a similarly low overlap with media markets. See Richard G. Niemi, Lynda W. Powell, and Patricia L. Bicknell, "The Effects of Congruity between Community and District on Salience of U.S. House Candidates," *Legislative Studies Quarterly*, vol. 11 (May 1986), pp. 187–201.

12. *Davis v. Bandemer*, 478 US. 109, 92 L Ed 2d 85 106 S Ct 2797.

ing the House campaigns, will end up being on the incumbent's side, and accountability will be poorly overseen.

At the national level, too, the increasing presence of the media may have some unfavorable effects for representative democracy. Outside strategies tend to converge on only some issues—those that fit the media's preferences. How closely are these issues connected to the people's concerns and preferences? Do media strategies help to open the legislative process to public scrutiny and encourage informed democracy or do they reinforce inequities of access and of power?

To answer these questions, perhaps it would be wise to ask to whom the media themselves are responsive. Though national journalists operate outside of Congress, they are inside the Washington beltway, routinely involved with elected officials, congressional staff, interest-group representatives, bureaucrats, and think-tank scholars. By facilitating communication within Washington, news organizations tend to represent the views of organized groups or otherwise already prominent actors, not only to each other but to the rest of the nation. The debates that Washington reporters discuss are those among organized political and economic groups, and if there is no debate, they do not rush in to fill the void.[13]

Often, the media's role in the political process is akin to recirculating air in a building with no windows. The unexpected becomes so routinized that news itself is almost predictable. Freshness is only occasionally brought in by unanticipated dramatic events: the death of a basketball star from cocaine poisoning, an accident at a Soviet nuclear power plant, hospital waste washing up on New Jersey beaches, a massacre of schoolchildren by a gunman carrying an AK-47. Such disruptions of routine provide an opportunity for sources outside governmental and corporate hierarchies to be heard. But the sources are usually insufficiently organized, and by the time they are ready the spotlight is back to the existing agenda and the usual authoritative sources.[14]

13. The classic case remains Vietnam before the 1968 Tet offensive, but more recent aspects of foreign policy, such as policy on funding the Nicaraguan contras, have been affected by the failure of the news to go beyond apparent consensus. See Daniel C. Hallin, The "Uncensored War": The Media and Vietnam (Oxford University Press, 1986); and W. Lance Bennett, "Marginalizing the Majority: Conditioning Public Opinion to Accept Managerial Democracy," in Michael Margolis and Gary Mauser, eds., Manipulating Public Opinion (Homewood, Ill.: Dorsey Press, forthcoming).

14. Harvey Molotch and Marilyn Lester, "Accidental News: The Great Oil Spill as Local Occurrence and National Event," American Journal of Sociology, vol. 81 (September 1975), pp. 235–60.

"Washington news gathering, in other words, is an interaction among elites," Stephen Hess has written. "One elite reports on another elite."[15] An advertisement in the *New York Times* business section even encouraged this interaction:

> If the news were about you, you'd read it, wouldn't you?
> So Washington reads Washington Talk in the New York Times.
> It's where corporate messages will be seen and read by government leaders.
> Reserve the Washington Talk ad corner for your important corporate ad. Just call (212) 556-1446.
> The New York Times.[16]

Elites partly adopt and incorporate the concerns of other elites, an interaction only somewhat mitigated by the connections that each has with the people. But if representatives can become detached from constituents, journalists have even fewer direct connections with their readers or viewers, except for fellow reporters, superiors, and sources. Far from giving the public just what it wants, they prefer to avoid information about their mass audiences. Anticipating the latter's needs and reactions adds a potentially paralyzing complication, not to mention a threat to journalists' control of choosing and presenting news. They may ask people outside positions of power for opinions in person-in-the-street interviews or polls, but they choose the subject, which usually reflects issues that are hot in Washington. The result may be top-down policymaking: instead of bringing public opinion to official Washington, the news disseminates the views of Washington across the country.

None of this is the fault of reporters in general or of politicians in general. The Hill reporters I have met are exceedingly conscientious about standards of objectivity and excellence. And even though House press secretaries may present one-sided accounts, their reports are seldom fabrications or distortions of their bosses' records. But these people work within news organizations or political institutions that define what is worth attending to and what may be neglected, and reward workers accordingly. As Warren Breed noted, "Newsmen define their job as producing a certain quantity of what is called 'news' every 24 hours. . . . They are not re-

15. Stephen Hess, *The Washington Reporters* (Brookings, 1981), p. 118.
16. *New York Times*, October 4, 1988, p. D29.

warded for analyzing the social structure, but for getting news."[17] Or in the words of Todd Gitlin, "Political news is like crime news; it's about what went wrong today, not what goes wrong every day."[18]

As House members and their staffs decide what course to pursue and increasingly incorporate a definition of news as something that happened since yesterday, they become directed toward problems that are quickly fixed and away from chronic conditions that find a news peg only with difficulty. Political debate under the spotlight is directed to more technical, less politicized questions of governance instead of essential social concerns that the news rarely directly addresses and that thus remain rarely discussed.

Turning to the news media to help the process of governance is a reasonable option that House members and their staffs may profitably adopt. But merely linking media and legislative strategies, although it could well be a precondition for democratic decisionmaking, is insufficient. Legislating in the spotlight can move politicians away from the influence of organized groups, encourage them to take account of the public interest, and allow them to build coalitions on complex issues. The paradox of the 1980s, however, has been that such results have often occurred without the full-scale public mobilization that marked Reagan's 1981 campaign to cut taxes and spending. Just as theater critics can shut down a play even if the public likes it, so the involvement of the media can turn legislators toward or away from particular issues and particular options whether or not public opinion is on one side or the other.

If representative democracy is to work well, there must be more participation not merely by news organizations on behalf of the people but by the people themselves in shaping the options and decisions of government. Bringing the public back into politics, of course, entails many possible steps not connected with either Congress or the media. Reforms in House election campaigns to cut down the inherent advantage of the incumbent could help, as would more general reforms, such as easing voter registration requirements. But the democratization of political news to include perspectives besides those provided by Washington is also necessary. It has been suggested that "multiperspectival" news is needed—news that would include opinions of the public as well as those of officials, news about programs as they actually operate rather than as they are intended to work,

17. Warren Breed, "Social Control in the Newsroom: A Functional Analysis," *Social Forces*, vol. 33 (May 1955), p. 331.

18. Todd Gitlin, *The Whole World Is Watching: Mass Media in the Making and Unmaking of the New Left* (University of California Press, 1980), p. 271.

and news that reflects a much greater variety of sources.[19] None of this need necessarily change how Washington reporters go about their work; but it does require that officials' views be supplemented by others so that news organizations do not become unwitting adjuncts to the already powerful.

Of course, this very willingness on the part of the media to negotiate a relationship favorable to politicians enables House members to use publicity and to craft media strategies in pursuit of legislative goals. By taking advantage of news routines that emphasize a scripted process with authoritative sources, by working to manage journalists' access both formally and informally, by building a professionalized press operation with a full-time press secretary, House members today are adroitly pursuing and using the opportunities presented to them. Media strategies in the House have become valuable, not merely to take positions or gratify egos; they are now crucial ways to attain, maintain, and exert power in Washington.

19. Herbert J. Gans, *Deciding What's News: A Study of CBS Evening News, NBC Nightly News, Newsweek, and Time* (Pantheon, 1979), pp. 313–14.

# Appendix A
# Methodology

THIS STUDY has three major empirical components: the analysis of House members' visibility in television network evening news and in the *New York Times*; a series of semistructured interviews conducted in the fall of 1984 with forty press secretaries to House members; and a three-page questionnaire sent in November 1984 to all press secretaries of Democratic members of the Ninety-eighth Congress. This appendix briefly describes these three studies, the questions asked, the measures used in the quantitative analysis, and the logic of the specification of the models, in addition to providing the quantitative evidence cited in chapter 4.

## Measuring Media Visibility

The Vanderbilt University Television News Archive has been videotaping broadcasts of television evening news programs since 1968 and publishing abstracts of and indexes to them that are the bases of the analysis in chapter 3. The measure for media visibility is straightforward. First, a count was made for the number of times each member of Congress was mentioned or quoted on news broadcasts during each year from 1969 to 1986 inclusive. Such an index, while basic, gives valuable information on who is covered most frequently. Mentions were summed across the three networks, given the evidence that they tend to overlap greatly in their choice of subjects, even if they do differ stylistically.[1] A similar count was

---

1. For some examples, see James B. Lemert, "Content Duplication by the Networks in Competing Evening Newscasts," *Journalism Quarterly*, vol. 51 (Summer 1974), pp. 238–244; and C. Richard Hofstetter, *Bias in the News: Network Television Coverage of the 1972 Election Campaign* (Ohio State University Press, 1976).

made from the *New York Times Index* for the years from 1969 to 1984 inclusive. The choice of the *Times* instead of another newspaper of record, the *Washington Post*, was occasioned by the greater comparability of the *Times Index* to the Vanderbilt index. Unlike these two, the *Post's* index lists members only if the story is about them. It does not list them if they are mentioned in the course of another story. Since levels of visibility are highly correlated across national newspapers, these results, while more reliable, are not likely to be dramatically different from results that would be obtained from another national newspaper.[2]

## The Semistructured Interviews

In fall 1984, as part of an exploratory effort to establish how House press operations proceed and to delineate more precise hypotheses, I began semistructured interviews with press secretaries of House members. The sample of forty interviews, while designed to be representative of the full House membership, was not chosen randomly. Instead the interviews were collected by networking to ensure honest and open responses. I began by interviewing the presidents of the two associations of House press secretaries, the Association of House Democratic Press Assistants and the Republican House Communication Association. These people referred me to others, and I went from there, building a sample representative of distributions along lines of region, seniority, party, and the expected marginality of the district as of spring 1984. The characteristics of the sample are reported in table A-1.

Interviews were conducted on Capitol Hill during September and October 1984, whenever possible in the congressional office itself.[3] They lasted between thirty minutes and two hours, sometimes including observation of the secretaries' work. All interviews were held under openly "not-for-attribution" conditions; that is, I could quote the press secretaries as long as I took pains to hide their identities and those of their bosses. In line with the exploratory nature of the research, I followed a semistructured format that allowed me to ask particular questions while permitting the press secretary to digress into potentially important areas. At the close of the interview, I would check over the questions in figure A-1 to ensure that

2. See Eric P. Veblen, "Liberalism and National Newspaper Coverage of Members of Congress," *Polity*, vol. 14 (Fall 1981), pp. 153–59.

3. My guide was Lewis Anthony Dexter, *Elite and Specialized Interviewing* (Northwestern University Press, 1970), especially chaps. 1–2.

TABLE A-1. Characteristics of Interview Sample of House Press Secretaries

| Characteristic | Interview sample[a] | | Total House[b] | |
|---|---|---|---|---|
| | Percent | Number | Percent | Number |
| Member region[c] | | | | |
| South and border | 27.5 | 11 | 34.2 | 148 |
| New England and Mid-Atlantic | 27.5 | 11 | 22.2 | 96 |
| Midwest and Plains | 25.0 | 10 | 24.0 | 104 |
| Far West and Rockies | 20.0 | 8 | 19.6 | 85 |
| | | | | |
| Member seniority[d] | | | | |
| 1982 | 15.0 | 6 | 19.6 | 85 |
| 1980 | 10.0 | 4 | 14.5 | 63 |
| 1978 | 20.0 | 8 | 15.2 | 66 |
| 1976 | 15.0 | 6 | 11.1 | 48 |
| 1974 | 15.0 | 6 | 10.9 | 47 |
| 1970–72 | 7.5 | 3 | 10.6 | 46 |
| 1966–68 | 7.5 | 3 | 6.5 | 28 |
| 1962–64 | 5.0 | 2 | 6.2 | 27 |
| Before 1962 | 5.0 | 2 | 5.3 | 23 |
| | | | | |
| Anticipated electoral marginality, 1984[e] | | | | |
| Solid | 65.0 | 26 | 64.0 | 277 |
| Likely | 13.9 | 6 | 21.0 | 91 |
| Leaning | 12.5 | 5 | 7.6 | 33 |
| Toss-up | 0 | 0 | 2.3 | 10 |
| Not running for reelection | 7.5 | 3 | 5.5 | 24 |
| | | | | |
| Party | | | | |
| Democrat | 55.0 | 22 | 61.4 | 266 |
| Republican | 45.0 | 18 | 38.6 | 167 |

SOURCE: Author's calculations.
a. Interviews with forty House secretaries.
b. House of Representatives included 433 members because of 2 vacancies.
c. According to the definitions in Norman J. Ornstein, Thomas E. Mann, and Michael J. Malbin, *Vital Statistics in Congress, 1987–88* (Washington: CQ Press, 1987).
d. Those elected in by-elections are included in the previous year of election.
e. Charles Cook, *National Political Review,* vol. 1 (April 27, 1984), pp. 3–6.

all listed matters had been covered. Such a format does not permit easy quantification of results but provides a rich basis for generalizations that can then be more rigorously tested with the survey to follow.

# The Survey of Democratic Members' Offices

In one of those moments of good luck that a researcher sometimes encounters, Lynn Drake, press secretary to Representative Gerry Sikorski and

FIGURE A-1. List of Questions Asked Press Secretaries during Interviews

1. What is the major focus of your job?
2. What do you spend the most time doing? Is there anyone else to handle press relations (in D.C., in the district)? How much time per year do you spend in the district?
3. Who do you deal with? (Probe for national vs. local, print vs. electronic.)
4. What ways can your boss get into the news? Are those usually successful?
5. Do the national media help in getting the job done?
6. What is the impact of televising floor proceedings? How would your job be different if they were not televised?
7. What is the major problem you face in getting the news out? Is it difficult to get your message across?

president of the Association of House Democratic Press Assistants (AHDPA), notified me that she was thinking of assembling a brief questionnaire for her colleagues that she would use for her master's thesis in journalism and political science. I asked if we could collaborate on a somewhat longer questionnaire, and we assembled it shortly after the November 1984 election. Using the semistructured interviews as a pretest, we asked the press secretaries about the work they performed, the value of various media outlets and strategies, and the long-term goals of their operations. The full questionnaire is reprinted in figure A-2.

The questionnaire was sent out under the aegis of the AHDPA (with a cover letter by Drake) in November 1984 to all Ninety-eighth Congress Democratic House offices. A second wave of questionnaires was sent to those offices that had not sent a response by December. The response rate was a reasonably strong 46 percent ($N = 124$), an acceptable percentage, given that a few offices still lack a designated press aide. The sponsorship of the AHDPA ensured that we could match the responses to particular members. Of the 124 questionnaires returned, only 5 came back anonymously. The rest reasonably represent the full Democratic House membership, as table A-2 shows. Fortunately, the areas for which the questionnaire was less representative balanced off the errors of the semistructured interviews, so together these present a decent picture of the House in 1984. Because press strategies are guarded with considerable care, the sponsorship of the AHDPA should have contributed to greater honesty. The answers, at least at face value, appear candid and complete.

Ideally I would also have had quantitative data from Republicans. However, a comparable study of members of the Republican counterpart of the AHDPA, the House Republican Communications Association, was not possible, since the HRCA had already distributed and collected a questionnaire in the late summer of 1984, the data from which were not made public. Fortunately for the purposes here, the interviews with press secre-

TABLE A-2. Characteristics of Sample of Democratic House Press Secretaries[a]

| | Sample | | Total House Democrats | |
|---|---|---|---|---|
| Characteristic | Percent | Number | Percent | Number |
| Region | | | | |
| South and border | 44.9 | 53 | 39.7 | 106 |
| New England and Mid-Atlantic | 19.5 | 23 | 22.1 | 59 |
| Midwest and Plains | 18.6 | 22 | 21.0 | 56 |
| Far West and Rockies | 16.9 | 20 | 17.2 | 46 |
| | | | | |
| Seniority | | | | |
| 1982 | 31.4 | 37 | 23.2 | 62 |
| 1980 | 6.8 | 8 | 9.0 | 24 |
| 1978 | 15.3 | 18 | 13.1 | 35 |
| 1976 | 13.6 | 16 | 12.4 | 33 |
| 1974 | 14.4 | 17 | 13.9 | 37 |
| 1970–72 | 7.6 | 9 | 8.2 | 22 |
| 1966–68 | 3.4 | 4 | 6.0 | 16 |
| 1962–64 | 3.4 | 4 | 7.1 | 19 |
| before 1962 | 4.2 | 5 | 7.1 | 19 |

SOURCE: Author's calculations.

a. Questionnaire replies equaled 118 because of 5 anonymous returns and 1 return from a nonvoting delegate. There were 267 House Democrats because of 1 vacancy.

taries to twenty-two Democrats and eighteen Republicans had showed little interparty variation. Both Democrats and Republicans favored local instead of national media; both favored print more than television; and of the fifteen who made some spontaneous reference to the usefulness of the media in the legislative process, seven worked for Republicans and eight for Democrats. Finally, another survey of press secretaries in 1981–82 on local press operations concludes that "the data fail to provide any evidence that Republicans would have more active news media operations than Democrats."[4] While one must approach the data with caution, there is no reason to expect that my results would be different had Republicans been included.

Data were collected on the characteristics of the members and their districts. Members' seniority was measured by the consecutive years of service. The impact of seniority is generally presumed to be curvilinear—greater differences are expected between members in their first and second terms than between those in, say, their tenth and eleventh terms. So I logarithmically transformed the raw value of seniority to reflect its dimin-

4. Robert E. Dewhirst, "Patterns of Interaction between Members of the U.S. House of Representatives and Their Home District News Media," Ph.D. dissertation, University of Nebraska, 1983, p. 65.

FIGURE A-2. Questionnaire for Democratic Press Secretaries,
November–December 1984

Name _____

Member _____ State _____ District _____

Age _____ Sex _____ Marital Status _____

Length of time in current position _____

Home: Same district as member _____ Same state but different district _____ Different
state (which state) _____

Education: High School _____ Some college _____ College degree _____
Some graduate work _____ Master's _____ Doctorate _____

Major in college _____

Experience prior to Capitol Hill? (Check all applicable)
Broadcasting _____ Print _____ Public Relations/Advertising _____
Other _____

Have you worked for another member? _____ In a press function? _____

How many hours, on the average, do you work per week? _____ hours

Do you plan on remaining in your present position, or are you considering a move to the private
sector or another member? Plan on staying _____ Considering
a move _____

What percentage of time you do spend on nonpress functions per month? _____percent

Does anyone else in your office handle press functions? Yes _____ No _____

Is there anyone in the district office who handles press functions? Yes _____ No _____

How much time in a year do you spend in the district? _____

Have you taken a leave in the last year to work on your member's campaign?
Yes _____ No _____

Did you work on your member's campaign prior to coming to the Hill?
Yes _____ No _____

Has your campaign hired a political/media consultant? Yes _____ No _____

Are you required to provide the bulk of speechwriting? Yes _____ No _____

How many times per *month* do you:
Put out a press release? _____ times per month
Call a press conference, either in the district or in Washington?
_____ times per month
Send a radio actuality? _____ times per month
Contact the national press? _____ times per month

How many times per *year* do you:
Send out postal patron newsletter? _____ times per year
Send out targeted mailings? _____ times per year

How often are you the official spokesperson for your boss in press calls?
Always _____ Often _____ Occasionally _____ Seldom _____ Never _____

Do you have direct access to the member or do you work through the AA?
Direct _____ Through AA _____

How often do the LAs handle press calls without your consultation? Always _____
Often _____ Occasionally _____ Seldom _____ Never _____

Ideological agreement with other staffers:
Compared with other staffers in the office, I am: Much more liberal _____ Somewhat more
liberal _____ About the same _____ Somewhat more conservative _____ Much
more conservative _____

## FIGURE A-2 *(continued)*

Ideological agreement with member:
Compared to my boss, I am: Much more liberal _____
Somewhat more liberal _____ About the same _____ Somewhat more conservative _____ Much more conservative _____

Please rate how *valuable* each is in getting your job done (on a scale of 1 to 10 with 1 being very low and 10 being very high).

| | | | | | | | | | |
|---|---|---|---|---|---|---|---|---|---|
Radio actualities | 1 2 3 4 5 6 7 8 9 10
Newsletters | 1 2 3 4 5 6 7 8 9 10
Press releases | 1 2 3 4 5 6 7 8 9 10
Recording studio | 1 2 3 4 5 6 7 8 9 10
Targeted mail | 1 2 3 4 5 6 7 8 9 10
Weekly columns | 1 2 3 4 5 6 7 8 9 10
Local television news | 1 2 3 4 5 6 7 8 9 10
Network television news | 1 2 3 4 5 6 7 8 9 10
Local dailies | 1 2 3 4 5 6 7 8 9 10
Local weeklies | 1 2 3 4 5 6 7 8 9 10
*New York Times* | 1 2 3 4 5 6 7 8 9 10
*Washington Post* | 1 2 3 4 5 6 7 8 9 10
Televised floor proceedings | 1 2 3 4 5 6 7 8 9 10

Here is a list of statements about the press secretary's job. Please circle your response: You agree strongly, agree somewhat, neither agree nor disagree, disagree somewhat or disagree strongly.

I would rather get in the front page of my hometown daily any day than in the *New York Times* or in the *Washington Post*: (1) agree strongly, (2) agree somewhat, (3) neither agree nor disagree, (4) disagree somewhat, or (5) disagree strongly.

The local media are fairer to my boss than the national media: (1) agree strongly, (2) agree somewhat, (3) neither agree nor disagree, (4) disagree somewhat, or (5) disagree strongly.

If I had to pick one medium to sell a story, I would pick television any day: (1) agree strongly, (2) agree somewhat, (3) neither agree nor disagree, (4) disagree somewhat, or (5) disagree strongly.

What a press secretary does is not that different from public relations; the difference is that the member is the product: (1) agree strongly, (2) agree somewhat, (3) neither agree nor disagree, (4) disagree somewhat, or (5) disagree strongly.

How important is each of the following long-term goals in your job? Please rate their importance on a scale of 1 to 10 with 1 being very low and 10 being very high:

1. Building name recognition of the member in the district _____
2. Creating a national constituency for an issue _____
3. Enabling the member to run for higher office _____
4. Serving as liaison to different constituent groups _____
5. Making the member a national spokesperson on an issue _____

Any additional comments:

_____
_____
_____
_____

Your cooperation has been greatly appreciated. Please send this questionnaire to Lynn Drake, 414 Cannon Building. Thank you.

ishing impact. The competitiveness of the media market was measured by Campbell, Alford, and Henry's index, which estimates the overlap of the population of the congressional district with that of the local television market or markets.[5] Information on the counties contained in the 211 media markets came from the *Broadcasting/Cablecasting Yearbook 1982*. The Campbell-Alford-Henry measure begins with the product of the number of constituents within a media market divided by the overall population of the district, times the number of constituents within a particular media market divided by the overall population in the entire market. For districts covering more than one media market these figures were summed. This measure is skewed toward the lower end of the scale, since there are few districts that are as much as 50 percent congruent with the television markets. For this reason, and since one would expect diminishing impact at higher levels (the difference between 90 percent overlap and 60 percent overlap is presumably less influential than a difference between 35 percent overlap and 5 percent overlap), the media market variable is also a logarithmic transformation of the raw index. An alternative measure was constructed from the total circulation of those daily newspapers distributed principally in the district that would be expected to pay primary attention to the local representative. Only newspapers without significant circulation outside the district (ones that did not have a circulation of more than 20,000 daily copies in another district) were included to avoid exaggerating the circulation of papers that were widely distributed but happened to be geographically based in one district.[6]

Other data measured members' activities. As a measure of position taking, I counted the number of bills cosponsored in the Ninety-eighth Congress according to the Library of Congress's SCORPIO index. Cosponsoring legislation can be done to pursue a variety of goals, but the ease with which it can be done at low expenditure of resources makes this a good measure.[7] I measured the member's conservatism by the rankings of the American Conservative Union, which are similar to the ratings of the liberal Americans for Democratic Action but do not penalize the member for missed votes. Finally, from Smith and Deering's categorization based on

5. James E. Campbell, John R. Alford, and Keith Henry, "Television Markets and Congressional Elections," *Legislative Studies Quarterly*, vol. 9 (November 1984), pp. 665–678.

6. The source of these data was Martha V. Gottron, ed., *Congressional Districts in the 1980s* (Washington: CQ Press, 1983).

7. See James E. Campbell, "Cosponsoring Legislation in the U.S. Congress," *Legislative Studies Quarterly*, vol. 7 (August 1982), pp. 415–22.

interviews with newly elected representatives to the Ninety-seventh Congress, I counted the number of policy-oriented committees. These committees were Banking, Education and Labor, Energy and Commerce, Foreign Affairs, Government Operations, and Judiciary.[8]

The measures taken from the survey are generally straightforward. Some directions of coding were changed, as in the measure to estimate how much time the press assistant spent on media-related matters. In the rankings of the long-term goals of the office's media strategy and of the usefulness of various media outlets and strategies, I examined the intercorrelations to see if variables could be combined to form a more complete, richer scale. Among the long-range goals the variables of the importance of building a national constituency for an issue and of making the member a spokesperson on an issue were so highly intercorrelated ($r = .65$) that I averaged them to measure the underlying concept.

The significant intercorrelations for the usefulness of outlets were so plentiful that I ran an oblique factor analysis that permits correlation between dimensions underlying the data. The resultant factor solution for the thirteen variables found five factors with an eigenvalue of $1.0$ or greater.[9] These factors measure the rankings of the national media (loading most heavily: the *Washington Post*, the *New York Times*, and the network news); print outlets with little editing (loading most heavily: press releases, weekly papers, weekly columns); electronic member-controlled releases (loading most heavily: radio actualities, House recording studio); in-House print media (loading most heavily: newsletters, targeted mail); and local media (loading most heavily: local dailies and local television news). This factor analysis provided a rationale to combine the measures for the *Post*, the *Times*, and network news into a single average for the perceived utility of national news. However, the measures for national newspapers were uncertain for some members who could consider either the *Post* or the *Times* a local paper. To extricate the local and national aspects of the *Post* and the *Times*, and since the two measures were highly correlated ($r = .73$), I replaced the *Post* ratings with the *Times* ratings when members came from states within the *Post*'s local circulation area (Maryland and Virginia) and did the reverse for members from the *Times*'s local circulation area (Connecticut, New Jersey, and New York). In another case I con-

8. Steven S. Smith and Christopher J. Deering, "Changing Motives for Committee Preferences of New Members of the U.S. House," *Legislative Studies Quarterly*, vol. 8 (May 1983), pp. 271–81.

9. The factor solutions are available from the author upon request.

structed a subtractive interactive measure comparing in-House media to local outlets. This measure subtracted the average rating of local television and local dailies from the average ranking of targeted mail and newsletters.

The regression equations were obtained by ordinary least squares methods. If any of the variables was missing for a given case, that case was omitted from the analysis.

## Specification of the Models

The choice of the variables for the equations analyzed in chapter 4 tended to err on the generous side, assuming that the omission of a potentially pertinent variable could undercut the reliability of the results.[10] Nevertheless, the variables chosen differ from one equation to the next.

In attempting to predict the value of national news outlets, I first have noted that members differ in their access to the media, whether national or local, which presumably shaped their offices' responses. Those characteristics that would make a member more newsworthy, such as liberalism and seniority, should increase the perceived value of national media, while competition from other media, occasioned by a close overlap of television markets with the House district, should decrease.

Second, members' media strategies can connect with the activities they pursue elsewhere in Congress. Members who take positions (measured again by the number of bills cosponsored in the Ninety-eighth Congress) or sit on policy-oriented committees that are traditionally inclined toward individualistic approaches to policymaking should find national media more valuable, as would younger members who are presumed to be more media-conscious.

Third, the attraction of publicity in the national media may be enhanced by strategic considerations in the media operations and the goals that are sought. Allocating more of the press secretary's time to press matters or hiring a campaign consultant should indicate a more sophisticated operation that would include pursuing publicity in the national media. Among the five long-term goals rated by the press secretaries, making the member a national spokesperson on an issue and building a national constituency on an issue, along with progressive ambition, should increase the perceived importance of national media. Finally, to examine Michael

10. See James A. Davis, *The Logic of Causal Order* (Beverly Hills: Sage Publications, 1985).

Robinson's argument that the national media are tougher, those who consider the local media fairer should be less inclined to value the nationals.

The importance of the linked goals of building a national constituency for an issue on which the member will become a spokesperson was predicted by several variables. Certain members are better placed to become spokespersons for an issue as well. Insofar as seniority enables members to devote increasing attention to Washington concerns, tenure in office should make these goals more important, but greater age should make them less so if younger members hail from a generation of legislators less inclined to go along and get along. Availability of access to the local media, such as when the district and media market overlap well, should distract press secretaries from working on national issues.

To study the offices' orientation to television, I chose their rating of local television news, which is more empirically separable from the perceived utility of local print media, than is the case with national counterparts. In the case of in-House media, I constructed a variable comparing the average ranking given to newsletters and to targeted mail against the average ranking given to local television news and local dailies, since these choices are negatively related. In each of these cases, I used the same variables to predict the value that press secretaries place on local television news and on in-House media. But I hypothesized that the effects would sometimes be different. The range of opportunities available to the press secretary, best measured by the overlap of the television market with the district and by the local circulation of daily district newspapers, should shape the attractiveness of each approach. If seniority leads to routinized relations with constituencies, it should discourage the time-consuming pursuit of television coverage and encourage the time-saving use of in-House media. The reported percentage of time that the aide spent working with the press should likewise enhance the value of television coverage and decrease the value of in-House media. Members' desire to become spokespersons for an issue and the extent of their ambition would be expected to enhance the value of local television coverage, which has a potential for outreach beyond the district, but to diminish the worth of more parochial in-House media. Finally, if they consider local media fairer than national media, their press operations should be more inclined to submit themselves to the editing processes of television and less prone to rely on self-generated communications.

At other times the effects on the ratings of local television and of in-House media may be similar. Position taking could impel members toward both the twenty-second bites of television and the self-advertising possibilities of newsletters and targeted mail. Younger representatives should be more accustomed to the requirements of local television and in-House media. And the goal of constituency liaison should enhance either of these ways to reach a large audience.

The quantitative results are shown in tables A-3–A-6. The estimates shown are the unstandardized regression coefficients. A coefficient should be about twice as large as its standard error for the estimate to be statistically significant at the .05 level that is appropriate for a sample of this size. Said differently, the probability is then less than 5 percent that the results could be caused by chance alone.

TABLE A-3. Determinants of the Value of Local Television News and of In-House Media Relative to Local Media

| | Local TV news | | In-House media | |
|---|---|---|---|---|
| Variable | Coefficient | Standard error | Coefficient | Standard error |
| Media market | 2.329 | .740 | −1.705 | .821 |
| Member's seniority | −.288 | .315 | −.044 | .346 |
| Circulation of local papers | −.004 | .005 | .005 | .005 |
| Age of representative | −.016 | .026 | −.035 | .028 |
| Bills cosponsored | .004 | .001 | −.001 | .002 |
| Percent of aide's time spent on press | .014 | .010 | −.038 | .011 |
| Campaign consultant (1 = yes) | .844 | .453 | −.673 | .501 |
| Goal of speaking for issue | .245 | .105 | −.290 | .116 |
| Ambition | −.065 | .084 | .094 | .093 |
| Goal of constituent group liaison | .182 | .084 | −.109 | .092 |
| Assessment of local media as fairer | .712 | .259 | −.414 | .291 |
| Constant | −2.594 | 2.457 | 8.102 | 2.884 |
| Multiple R | .602 | . . . | .556 | . . . |
| Adjusted $R^2$ | .286 | . . . | .227 | . . . |

SOURCE: Calculated by the author from the Democratic press secretary questionnaires, November–December 1984.

a.  Estimates are the unstandardized regression coefficients. A coefficient should be about twice as large as its standard error for the estimate to be statistically significant at the .05 level that is appropriate for a sample of this size. In other words, the probability is then less than 5 percent that the results I have obtained could be caused by randomness or by chance alone.

TABLE A-4. Determinants of the Value of National News Outlets
(Regression Estimates)

| Determinant | Coefficient | Standard error |
|---|---|---|
| Member's seniority | .544 | .313 |
| Media market | − .452 | .749 |
| Conservatism (ACA rating) | − .025 | .013 |
| Bills cosponsored | − .002 | .002 |
| Number of policy committees | .777 | .385 |
| Age of representative | .033 | .026 |
| Percent of aide's time spent on press | .013 | .010 |
| Campaign consultant (1 = yes) | − .601 | .463 |
| Goal of speaking for issue | .445 | .105 |
| Ambition | .093 | .086 |
| Assessment of local media as fairer | .075 | .188 |
| Constant | .405 | 2.420 |
| Adjusted $R^2$ | .351 | . . . |
| Number 103 | . . . | . . . |

SOURCE: Calculated by the author from the Democratic press secretary questionnaire, November–December 1984.

TABLE A-5. Determinants of Ranking of the Goal of Building
a National Constituency for an Issue

| Determinant | Coefficient | Standard error |
|---|---|---|
| Member's seniority | .863 | .281 |
| Media market | − 1.593 | .587 |
| Age of representative | .012 | .025 |
| Ambition | .347 | .076 |
| Constant | 5.628 | 1.776 |
| Adjusted $R^2$ | .239 | . . . |
| Number 111 | . . . | . . . |

SOURCE: Calculated by the author from the Democratic press secretary questionnaire, November–December 1984.

TABLE A-6. Determinants of Ranking of the Goal of Enabling
the Member to Run for Higher Office

| Determinant | Coefficient | Standard error |
|---|---|---|
| Member's seniority | .415 | .356 |
| Media market | 1.125 | .739 |
| Age of representative | − .147 | .028 |
| Constant | 8.784 | 2.094 |
| Adjusted $R^2$ | .220 | . . . |
| Number 112 | . . . | . . . |

SOURCE: Calculated by the author from the Democratic press secretary questionnaire, November–December 1984.

# Appendix B
# House Members and
# Network Evening News

TABLE B-1. Ranking of House Members Most Often Mentioned on
Network Evening News, 1969–86[a]

| Year and rank | | Name | Times mentioned | Position[b] |
|---|---|---|---|---|
| 1969 | 1. | G. Ford (R-Mich.) | 87 | Pl |
| | 2. | A. Powell (D-N.Y.) | 54 | . . . |
| | 3. | M. Rivers (D-S.C.) | 34 | Cl |
| | 4. | W. Mills (D-Ark.) | 30 | Cl |
| | 5. | W. Patman (D-Tex.) | 23 | Cl |
| | 6. | J. McCormack (D-Mass.) | 17 | Pl |
| | 7. | R. Morton (R-Md.) | 15 | Pl |
| | 8. | E. Celler (D-N.Y.) | 14 | Cl |
| | 9. | R. McCarthy (D-N.Y.) | 13 | . . . |
| | 9. | W. Moorhead (D-Pa.) | 13 | Subcl |
| | 11. | O. Pike (D-N.Y.) | 10 | Select subcl |
| | 12. | H. Boggs (D-La.) | 9 | Pl |
| | 12. | K. Hechler (D-W.Va.) | 9 | Subcl |
| | 12. | R. Taft, Jr. (R-Ohio) | 9 | Pl |
| | 12. | C. Vanik (D-Ohio) | 9 | . . . |
| | | | | |
| 1970 | 1. | J. McCormack (D-Mass.) | 46 | Pl, S |
| | 2. | G. Ford (R-Mich.) | 36 | Pl |
| | 3. | M. Rivers (D-S.C.) | 20 | Cl |
| | 4. | R. Morton (R-Md.) | 16 | Pl |
| | 5. | R. Roudebush (R-Ind.) | 15 | Ran |
| | 6. | C. Albert (D-Okla.) | 14 | Pl |
| | 6. | W. Brock (R-Tenn.) | 14 | Ran |
| | 6. | R. Taft, Jr. (R-Ohio) | 14 | Pl, Ran |

TABLE B-1 *(continued)*

| Year and rank | | Name | Times mentioned | Position[b] |
|---|---|---|---|---|
| | 6. | J. Tunney (D-Calif.) | 14 | Ran |
| | 10. | G. Bush (R-Tex.) | 13 | Ran |
| | 10. | E. Celler (D-N.Y.) | 13 | Cl |
| | 10. | W. Cramer (R-Fla.) | 13 | Ran |
| | 10. | R. Ottinger (D-N.Y.) | 13 | Ran |
| | 14. | F. E. Hébert (D-La.) | 12 | Cl |
| | 15. | A. Powell (D-N.Y.) | 11 | . . . |
| 1971 | 1. | W. Mills (D-Ark.) | 80 | Cl |
| | 2. | P. McCloskey (R-Calif.) | 63 | Pc |
| | 3. | H. Boggs (D-La.) | 31 | Pl |
| | 4. | C. Albert (D-Okla.) | 27 | Pl |
| | 5. | R. Steele (R-Conn.) | 23 | . . . |
| | 6. | G. Ford (R-Mich.) | 20 | Pl |
| | 7. | W. Patman (D-Tex.) | 12 | Cl |
| | 8. | S. Chisholm (D-N.Y.) | 11 | Pc |
| | 8. | H. Reuss (D-Wis.) | 11 | Subcl |
| | 8. | H. Staggers (D-W.Va.) | 11 | Cl |
| | 11. | B. Abzug (D-N.Y.) | 10 | . . . |
| | 11. | F. E. Hébert (D-La.) | 10 | Cl |
| | 13. | J. Ashbrook (D-Ohio) | 9 | Pc |
| | 13. | C. Diggs (D-Mich.) | 9 | Caucus |
| | 13. | J. Dowdy (D-Tex.) | 9 | S |
| 1972 | 1. | W. Mills (D-Ark.) | 56 | Cl, Pc |
| | 2. | W. Patman (D-Tex.) | 32 | Cl |
| | 3. | H. Boggs (D-La.) | 26 | Pl |
| | 4. | B. Abzug (D-N.Y.) | 24 | . . . |
| | 4. | G. Ford (R-Mich.) | 24 | Pl |
| | 6. | J. Schmitz (R-Calif.) | 21 | Pc |
| | 7. | E. Edwards (D-La.) | 20 | Ran |
| | 8. | J. Rooney (D-N.Y.) | 17 | Subcl, S |
| | 9. | F. E. Hébert (D-La.) | 15 | Cl |
| | 10. | N. Begich (D-Alaska) | 13 | . . . |
| | 11. | C. Albert (D-Okla.) | 12 | Pl |
| | 12. | Fl. Thompson (R-Ga.) | 10 | Ran |
| | 13. | E. Celler (D-N.Y.) | 9 | Cl |
| | 14. | W. Ryan (D-N.Y.) | 7 | . . . |
| | 14. | L. Stokes (D-Ohio) | 7 | . . . |
| 1973 | 1. | C. Albert (D-Okla.) | 63 | Pl |
| | 2. | J. Anderson (R-Ill.) | 19 | Pl |
| | 3. | T. O'Neill (D-Mass.) | 18 | Pl |
| | 4. | P. Rodino (D-N.J.) | 16 | Cl, Judic |
| | 5. | W. Mills (D-Ark.) | 15 | Cl |
| | 6. | B. Podell (D-N.Y.) | 11 | S |
| | 7. | W. Patman (D-Tex.) | 10 | Cl |
| | 7. | J. Waldie (D-Calif.) | 10 | Judic |

TABLE B-1 *(continued)*

| Year and rank | | Name | Times mentioned | Position[b] |
|---|---|---|---|---|
| | 9. | K. Hechler (D-W.Va.) | 8 | Subcl |
| | 10. | B. Abzug (D-N.Y.) | 7 | . . . |
| | 10. | J. Brooks (D-Tex.) | 7 | Subcl, Judic |
| | 10. | E. Holtzman (D-N.Y.) | 7 | Judic |
| | 10. | W. Mailliard (R-Calif.) | 7 | Cl |
| | 10. | H. Reuss (D-Wis.) | 7 | Subcl |
| | 10. | J. Rhodes (R-Ariz.) | 7 | Pl |
| 1974 | 1. | P. Rodino (D-N.J.) | 209 | Cl, Judic |
| | 2. | W. Mills (D-Ark.) | 125 | Cl, S |
| | 3. | J. Rhodes (R-Ariz.) | 89 | Pl |
| | 4. | E. Hutchinson (R-Mich.) | 77 | Cl, Judic |
| | 5. | T. Railsback (R-Ill.) | 75 | Judic |
| | 6. | R. McClory (R-Ill.) | 71 | Judic |
| | 7. | C. Albert (D-Okla.) | 70 | Pl |
| | 8. | C. Wiggins (R-Calif.) | 61 | Judic |
| | 9. | J. Waldie (D-Calif.) | 47 | Judic, Ran |
| | 10. | L. Hogan (R-Md.) | 40 | Judic, Ran |
| | 11. | C. Sandman (R-N.J.) | 34 | Judic |
| | 12. | E. Mezvinsky (D-Iowa) | 33 | Judic |
| | 13. | D. Dennis (R-Ind.) | 30 | Judic |
| | 14. | W. Cohen (R-Maine) | 29 | Judic |
| | 15. | Three others (R. Drinan, D. Edwards, W. Flowers) | 28 | . . . |
| 1975 | 1. | A. Ullman (D-Oreg.) | 94 | Cl |
| | 2. | C. Albert (D-Okla.) | 58 | Pl |
| | 3. | O. Pike (D-N.Y.) | 56 | Select Cl |
| | 4. | J. Rhodes (R-Ariz.) | 46 | Pl |
| | 5. | M. Udall (D-Ariz.) | 36 | Pc |
| | 6. | B. Abzug (D-N.Y.) | 23 | . . . |
| | 7. | L. Nedzi (D-Mich.) | 22 | Subcl, Select Cl |
| | 7. | T. O'Neill (D-Mass.) | 22 | Pl |
| | 9. | W. Hays (D-Ohio) | 19 | Cl, Pl |
| | 10. | R. Dellums (D-Calif.) | 18 | . . . |
| | 10. | W. Patman (D-Tex.) | 18 | Cl |
| | 12. | J. Moss (D-Calif.) | 13 | Subcl |
| | 13. | P. Burton (D-Calif.) | 12 | Caucus |
| | 13. | M. Harrington (D-Mass.) | 12 | . . . |
| | 13. | F. E. Hébert (D-La.) | 12 | Cl |
| | 13. | P. McCloskey (R-Calif.) | 12 | Past Pc |
| | 13. | G. Mahon (D-Tex.) | 12 | Cl |
| 1976 | 1. | W. Hays (D-Ohio) | 93 | Cl, Pl, S |
| | 2. | C. Albert (D-Okla.) | 45 | Pl |
| | 3. | T. O'Neill (D-Mass.) | 44 | Pl |
| | 4. | A. Howe (D-Utah) | 34 | S |

TABLE B-1 *(continued)*

| Year and rank | Name | Times mentioned | Position[b] |
|---|---|---|---|
| 5. | A. Young (D-Ga.) | 29 | Appt |
| 6. | J. Flynt (D-Ga.) | 23 | Cl |
| 7. | R. Sikes (D-Fla.) | 22 | Subcl, S |
| 8. | O. Pike (D-N.Y.) | 21 | Select Cl |
| 9. | J. Moss (D-Calif.) | 20 | Subcl |
| 10. | B. Abzug (D-N.Y.) | 19 | Ran |
| 11. | J. Rhodes (R-Ariz.) | 19 | Pl |
| 12. | P. Rodino (D-N.J.) | 17 | Cl |
| 12. | J. Wright (D-Tex.) | 17 | Pl |
| 14. | B. Adams (D-Wash.) | 14 | Appt |
| 15. | B. Bergland (D-Minn.) | 10 | Appt |
| 15. | J. Young (D-Tex.) | 10 | S |
| 1977 1. | T. O'Neill (D-Mass.) | 98 | Pl |
| 2. | A. Ullman (D-Oreg.) | 35 | Cl |
| 3. | M. Udall (D-Ariz.) | 27 | Cl, Past Pc |
| 4. | J. Flynt (D-Ga.) | 23 | Cl |
| 4. | J. Rhodes (R-Ariz.) | 23 | Pl |
| 6. | P. Mitchell (D-Md.) | 20 | Caucus |
| 7. | T. Ashley (D-Ohio) | 18 | Task force chair |
| 7. | J. Wright (D-Tex.) | 18 | Pl |
| 9. | J. Dingell (D-Mich.) | 15 | Subcl |
| 9. | E. Koch (D-N.Y.) | 15 | Ran |
| 11. | J. Brooks (D-Tex.) | 12 | Subcl |
| 11. | L. Stokes (D-Ohio) | 12 | Select Cl |
| 13. | H. Hyde (R-Ill.) | 10 | . . . |
| 13. | J. Murphy (D-N.Y.) | 10 | Cl |
| 15. | J. Moss (D-Calif.) | 9 | Subcl |
| 15. | C. Pepper (D-Fla.) | 9 | Select Cl |
| 15. | P. Rodino (D-N.J.) | 9 | Cl |
| 1978 1. | T. O'Neill (D-Mass.) | 67 | Pl |
| 2. | J. Eilberg (D-Pa.) | 40 | S |
| 3. | D. Flood (D-Pa.) | 27 | Subcl, S |
| 4. | A. Ullman (D-Oreg.) | 25 | Cl |
| 5. | L. Stokes (D-Ohio) | 24 | Select Cl |
| 6. | J. Wright (D-Tex.) | 22 | Pl |
| 7. | C. Diggs (D-Mich.) | 15 | Cl, S |
| 8. | D. Fraser (D-Minn.) | 14 | Subcl, Ran |
| 9. | J. McFall (D-Calif.) | 12 | Pl, S |
| 10. | J. Anderson (R-Ill.) | 11 | Pl |
| 10. | P. Mitchell (D-Md.) | 11 | Caucus |
| 12. | J. Rhodes (R-Ariz.) | 10 | Pl |
| 12. | C. Wilson (D-Calif.) | 10 | S |
| 14. | Six others | 9 | . . . |
| | (H. Gonzalez, J. Kemp, T. Moffett, J. Moss, R. Preyer, E. Roybal) | | |

TABLE B-1 *(continued)*

| Year and rank | Name | Times mentioned | Position[b] |
|---|---|---|---|
| 1979 1. | T. O'Neill (D-Mass.) | 79 | Pl |
| 2. | P. Crane (R-Ill.) | 33 | Pc |
| 3. | J. Anderson (R-Ill.) | 31 | Pl, Pc |
| 4. | D. Flood (D-Pa.) | 21 | Subcl, S |
| 5. | G. Hansen (R-Idaho) | 19 | . . . |
| 6. | C. Diggs (D-Mich.) | 18 | Cl, S |
| 7. | R. Nolan (D-Minn.) | 15 | . . . |
| 7. | M. Udall (D-Ariz.) | 15 | Past Pc, Cl |
| 9. | J. Rhodes (R-Ariz.) | 14 | Pl |
| 10. | R. Bauman (R-Md.) | 12 | . . . |
| 10. | A. Gore, Jr. (D-Tenn.) | 12 | . . . |
| 10. | B. Rosenthal (D-N.Y.) | 12 | Subcl |
| 10. | A. Ullman (D-Oreg.) | 12 | Cl |
| 14. | J. Dingell (D-Mich.) | 11 | Subcl |
| 14. | J. Wright (D-Tex.) | 11 | Pl |
| 1980 1. | T. O'Neill (D-Mass.) | 79 | Pl |
| 2. | J. Murphy (D-N.Y.) | 44 | Cl, S |
| 3. | M. Myers (D-Pa.) | 37 | S |
| 4. | J. Kemp (R-N.Y.) | 35 | . . . |
| 5. | R. Kelly (R-Fla.) | 33 | S |
| 6. | J. Jenrette (D-S.C.) | 32 | S |
| 6. | F. Thompson (D-N.J.) | 32 | Cl, S |
| 8. | R. Bauman (R-Md.) | 24 | S |
| 9. | D. Stockman (D-Mich.) | 20 | Appt |
| 10. | M. Udall (D-Ariz.) | 18 | Past Pc, Cl |
| 10. | J. Wright (D-Tex.) | 18 | Pl |
| 12. | A. Ullman (D-Oreg.) | 17 | Cl |
| 13. | J. Rhodes (R-Ariz.) | 13 | Pl |
| 14. | R. Giaimo (D-Conn.) | 12 | Cl |
| 14. | B. Green (R-N.Y.) | 12 | . . . |
| 1981 1. | T. O'Neill (D-Mass.) | 184 | Pl |
| 2. | R. Michel (R-Ill.) | 73 | Pl |
| 3. | D. Rostenkowski (D-Ill.) | 57 | Cl |
| 4. | J. Jones (R-Okla.) | 49 | Cl |
| 5. | J. Wright (D-Tex.) | 49 | Pl |
| 6. | P. Gramm (D-Tex.) | 38 | . . . |
| 7. | C. Pepper (D-Fla.) | 26 | Select Cl |
| 8. | J. Kemp (R-N.Y.) | 22 | . . . |
| 9. | B. Conable (R-N.Y.) | 20 | Cl |
| 10. | D. Latta (R-Ohio) | 17 | Cl |
| 11. | C. Long (D-Md.) | 13 | Subcl |
| 11. | J. Florio (D-N.J.) | 13 | Subcl, Ran |
| 11. | K. Hance (D-Tex.) | 13 | . . . |
| 14. | S. Montgomery (D-Miss.) | 12 | Cl |
| 14. | M. Udall (D-Ariz.) | 12 | Past Pc, Cl |

TABLE B-1 *(continued)*

| Year and rank | | Name | Times mentioned | Position[b] |
|---|---|---|---|---|
| 1982 | 1. | T. O'Neill (D-Mass.) | 146 | Pl |
| | 2. | R. Michel (R-Ill.) | 75 | Pl |
| | 3. | J. Wright (D-Tex.) | 49 | Pl |
| | 4. | J. Jones (D-Okla.) | 32 | Cl |
| | 5. | J. Kemp (R-N.Y.) | 25 | Pl |
| | 5. | D. Rostenkowski (D-Ill.) | 25 | Cl |
| | 7. | M. Fenwick (R-N.J.) | 21 | Ran |
| | 8. | C. Pepper (D-Fla.) | 20 | Select Cl |
| | 9. | H. Reuss (D-Wis.) | 18 | Cl |
| | 10. | S. Conte (R-Mass.) | 16 | Cl |
| | 11. | P. McCloskey (R-Calif.) | 14 | Past Pc, Ran |
| | 12. | J. Addabbo (D-N.Y.) | 13 | Subcl |
| | 12. | A. Gore, Jr. (D-Tenn.) | 13 | . . . |
| | 13. | Six others | 10 | . . . |
| | | (R. Bolling, B. Conable, P. Gramm, T. Lott, P. Mitchell, F. Richmond) | | |
| 1983 | 1. | T. O'Neill (D-Mass.) | 159 | Pl |
| | 2. | J. Dingell (D-Mich.) | 31 | Cl |
| | 3. | R. Michel (R-Ill.) | 29 | Pl |
| | 4. | E. Markey (D-Mass.) | 24 | . . . |
| | 5. | J. Scheuer (D-N.Y.) | 23 | Subcl |
| | 6. | C. Long (D-Md.) | 22 | Subcl |
| | 7. | G. Studds (D-Mass.) | 21 | S |
| | 8. | D. Albosta (D-Mich.) | 19 | Subcl |
| | 8. | R. Dellums (D-Calif.) | 19 | Cl |
| | 10. | J. Wright (D-Tex.) | 18 | Pl |
| | 11. | H. Hyde (R-Ill.) | 17 | . . . |
| | 12. | M. Barnes (D-Md.) | 15 | Subcl |
| | 12. | C. Wilson (D-Tex.) | 15 | S |
| | 13. | D. Crane (R-Ill.) | 14 | S |
| | 14. | A. Gore, Jr. (D-Tenn.) | 13 | . . . |
| | 14. | S. Solarz (D-N.Y.) | 13 | Subcl |
| 1984 | 1. | T. O'Neill (D-Mass.) | 168 | Pl |
| | 2. | J. Wright (D-Tex.) | 29 | Pl |
| | 3. | R. Michel (R-Ill.) | 26 | Pl |
| | 4. | J. Kemp (R-N.Y.) | 19 | Pl |
| | 5. | M. Barnes (D-Md.) | 18 | Subcl |
| | 6. | T. Coelho (D-Calif.) | 17 | Pl |
| | 7. | G. Hansen (R-Idaho) | 17 | S |
| | 8. | D. Edwards (D-Calif.) | 14 | Subcl |
| | 9. | A. Gore, Jr. (D-Tenn.) | 13 | Ran |
| | 9. | P. Simon (D-Ill.) | 13 | Ran |
| | 9. | H. Waxman (D-Calif.) | 13 | Subcl |
| | 12. | T. Wirth (D-Colo.) | 11 | Subcl |
| | 13. | N. Gingrich (R-Ga.) | 10 | Caucus |

TABLE B-1 *(continued)*

| Year and rank | Name | Times mentioned | Position[b] |
|---|---|---|---|
| 13. | P. Gramm (R-Tex.) | 10 | Ran |
| 13. | P. Schroeder (D-Colo.) | 10 | Caucus |
| 13. | M. Udall (D-Ariz.) | 10 | Past Pc, Cl |
| 1985   1. | T. O'Neill (D-Mass.) | 104 | Pl |
| 2. | R. Michel (R-Ill.) | 43 | Pl |
| 3. | D. Rostenkowski (D-Ill.) | 33 | Cl |
| 4. | J. Wright (D-Tex.) | 28 | Pl |
| 5. | W. Gray (D-Pa.) | 23 | Cl |
| 6. | J. Kemp (R-N.Y.) | 17 | Pl |
| 6. | H. Waxman (D-Calif.) | 17 | Subcl |
| 8. | R. Gephardt (D-Mo.) | 13 | Pl |
| 8. | S. Solarz (D-N.Y.) | 13 | Subcl |
| 8. | J. Dingell (D-Mich.) | 13 | Cl |
| 11. | C. Pepper (D-Fla.) | 11 | Cl |
| 12. | T. Lott (R-Miss.) | 10 | Pl |
| 12. | G. Molinari (R-N.Y.) | 10 | . . . |
| 12. | P. Schroeder (D-Colo.) | 10 | Caucus |
| 15. | Three others (B. Alexander, R. Cheney, H. Hyde) | 8 | . . . |
| 1986   1. | T. O'Neill (D-Mass.) | 78 | Pl |
| 2. | D. Rostenkowski (D-Ill.) | 45 | Cl |
| 3. | J. Wright (D-Tex.) | 43 | Pl |
| 4. | S. Solarz (D-N.Y.) | 42 | Subcl |
| 5. | M. Barnes (D-Md.) | 34 | Subcl, Ran |
| 6. | R. Michel (R-Ill.) | 33 | Pl |
| 7. | W. Gray (D-Pa.) | 25 | Cl |
| 8. | J. Kemp (R-N.Y.) | 21 | Pl |
| 9. | B. Mikulski (D-Md.) | 20 | Ran |
| 9. | C. Rangel (D-N.Y.) | 20 | Select Cl |
| 11. | L. Aspin (D-Wis.) | 17 | Cl |
| 12. | R. Cheney (R-Wyo.) | 15 | Pl, Select Cl |
| 13. | T. Foley (D-Wash.) | 14 | Pl |
| 13. | L. Hamilton (D-Ind.) | 14 | Select Cl |
| 15. | T. Daschle (D-S.D.) | 13 | Ran |
| 15. | J. Dingell (D-Mich.) | 13 | Cl |

SOURCE: Author's compilation from *Vanderbilt Television News Abstracts and Indices.*

a. Excludes major candidates for president and those seats for which a special election was held to fill a vacancy during that year.

b. Appt = presidential appointee at expiration of term. Caucus = leader of caucus such as Congressional Black Caucus, Conservative Opportunity Society, or Congresswomen's Caucus. Cl = committee leader (chair or ranking minority member). Judic = member of the Judiciary committee during debates over impeachment of Richard Nixon. Pc = presidential candidate. Pl = party leader. Ran = candidate for office other than that of president or vice president. S = scandal. Subcl = subcommittee leader (chair or ranking minority member).

# Appendix C
# Press Secretary's Job Description

Objective: To report to the public, through the news media and various projects, the goals, positions, activities, and accomplishments of the representative; to inform constituents of services available through their representative; and to increase the representative's national profile when possible.

### General Responsibilities

Respond to all inquiries and requests from members of the press, by telephone or in person.

Consult with representative periodically to determine press priorities and development.

Seek out opportunities to increase representative's exposure.

Establish and maintain regular contact and strong working relationship with reporters, editors, and producers to facilitate achieving the objective above.

Full responsibility for all aspects of press and public relations activities.

### Print and Broadcast Media Activities

Research, write, produce, and distribute all news releases.

Research, write, record, and distribute all radio news actualities.

Seek opportunities for representative's opinion (op-ed) articles and letters to the editor; help edit staff-written articles; solicit placement in major daily newspapers, magazines, journals, and district newspapers.

Arrange news conferences.

Consult with representative on topics for weekly newspaper column; type, produce, and distribute column.

Periodically responsible for researching and writing "Dear Congressman X" columns for use in place of weekly column when representative is unable to write one.

Research, write, produce, and distribute bimonthly video "X Report" for cable television stations in district; secure visual aids and guests when required; prepare cue cards and teleprompter material; rehearse representative. Maintain dialogue with local station managers regarding use and content of program; coordinate return of tapes from stations. Publicize and promote program through other media.

### Mailings

Design, research, write, produce, and distribute quarterly postal patron newsletter.

Research, write, produce, and distribute triannual *Letter from Washington*.

Design, write, produce, and distribute annual opinion poll; tabulate and publicize results.

Design and write cover copy for annual consumer catalog; determine areas to receive catalogs and manage distribution.

Design, write, produce, and distribute notices of representative's public meetings.

Design, research, write, produce, and distribute regular targeted mailings to specific areas of the district.

### Public Relations Activities

Design and produce promotional posters for representative's seminars and academy day.

Design, research, write, and produce public meeting programs.

Maintain and update photo files. Hire photographer to update stock file photos when necessary. Supply photos to press.

Update and order office location cards as necessary.

## Miscellaneous and Clerical Duties

Plan annual press schedule and budget. Plan production schedules for each project.

Consult regularly with legislative staff, district staff, and caseworkers to keep abreast of new developments.

Prepare weekly column for insertion as extension of remarks in *Congressional Record*.

Maintain an up-to-date knowledge of franking regulations and postal patron mailing procedures.

Monitor coverage of representative. Clip hometown newspaper daily; receive and organize clippings from district staff and route to representative. Circulate clippings among staff.

Organize and maintain central clip file.

Manage newspaper subscriptions.

Forward photographs to constituents.

Draft and type correspondence relating to press and mailings.

Maintain and update press and citizen mailing lists; update *Letter from Washington* mailing list; update postal patron tallies regularly.

Organize and maintain newsletter, news release, Washington report files; organize and maintain general press files.

Oversee stock of news release letterhead stationery, cassette tapes, video tapes, public meeting program stationery, and other press-related materials and replenish when necessary.

Be available for special press and public relations projects as they arise.

# Index

Drake, Lynn, 181–82
Drummond, William J., 38n
Duncan, John, 145
Dunkum, Betty, 110n

Easterbrook, Gregg, 4
Eddy, John, 108n
Edelman, Murray, 119n
Edgar, Bob, 158
Edsall, Thomas Byrne, 2n
Edwards, Mickey, 54
Ehrenhalt, Alan, 131n, 147n, 157n
Ellerbee, Linda, 42–43
Elliot, James, 16
Epstein, Edward Jay, 8n, 61n
Erbring, Lutz, 121n
Erikson, Robert S., 81n
Eubank, Robert B., 112n
Evans, Katherine Winton, 123n, 127n, 156n
Evans, Susan H., 11n, 108n, 110n, 117n

Fair, Matthew, 116n
Fascell, Dante, 53
Federal Supplemental Compensation pro-
gram (FSC), case study of agenda setting,
119, 132–46
Fenno, Richard F., Jr., 11n, 33n, 81n, 172n
Fiedler, Bobbi, 53
Fishman, Mark, 8n, 33n, 50, 54n
Fleisher, Richard, 115n
Flippo, Ronnie, 164
Flood, Dan, 67
Floor proceedings, historical reporting, 17–
19; one-minute speeches and special or-
ders, 29n, 54, 93; television coverage, 1,
25–30, 38, 97, 167
Florio, Jim, 126
Foley, Michael, 25n
Foley, Thomas, 101, 131, 142, 168
Foote, Joe S., 58n, 59n, 60n
Ford, Harold, 135, 136, 144, 145
Foxe, Fanne, 66, 67
Frank, Barney, 57, 116, 159
Frankel, Max, 46
Franking Commission. See Commission on
Congressional Mailing Standards
Franking privilege, 91–92, 172–73
Frantzich, Stephen E., 92n
*Freeman's Journal*, 16

Fuerbringer, Jonathan, 143n
Full Employment Action Council (FEAC),
137–38, 140, 145
Fuller, Buckminster, 80
Funkhouser, G. Ray, 127n, 171n

Gais, Thomas L., 123n
Gans, Herbert J., 8n, 10n, 30, 46n, 90n,
166n, 178n
Garay, Ronald, 24n, 27n, 28n, 30n
Garfield, James, 23
General Accounting Office, 125
Gephardt, Richard, 64n, 100, 101, 142, 143,
161–62
Gerry, Elbridge, 15, 29
Giaimo, Robert, 26n
Gieber, Walter, 8n
Gingrich, Newt, 29n, 56, 64, 99–100, 130
Ginsburg, Douglas, 39n
Gitlin, Todd, 12n, 177
Glenn, John, 111
Gobright, L. A., 20n, 21n
Goldenberg, Edie N., 11n, 94n, 107n, 108n,
121n, 173n
Gottron, Martha V., 186n
Government-funded communication: frank-
ing privilege, 91–92, 172–73; House re-
cording studio, 92–93, 97–98; in-House
media, 91, 97–99
Graber, Doris A., 96n, 110n, 111n
Granat, Diane, 93n, 100n, 158n
Grandy, Fred, 106n
Gray, William, 53, 64, 101
Greeley, Horace, 18
Greenhouse, Linda, 160n
Grossman, Michael Baruch, 7n, 33n
Gunderson, Steve, 101n
Gurevitch, Michael, 9n, 71n
Gusfield, Joseph R., 123n

Hackett, George, 91n
Halberstam, David, 24n
Hall, Richard L., 68n, 82n, 153n
Halleck, Charles, 130
Hallin, Daniel C., 61n, 175n
Hamilton, Lee, 50
Hansen, George, 64
Harding, Warren, 23
Hart, Gary, 111